Cowboys, Ranching & Cattle Trails

A New Mexico Federal Writers' Project Book

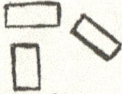

Block Ranch
EL CAPITAN Livestock Co.
CAPITAN. N. M.

Circle X Ranch
George W Coe
Fort Stanton. N.M.

Bell Ranch. Red
River Valley Company
Eastern N. M.

Lea Cattle Co.
Roswell. N.M.

Diamond A Ranch. Bloom Land
& Cattle Co. Roswell. N.M.

Bridle Bit. Merchant Ranch
CAPITAN N.M.

Circle Ranch   Pat F
Garrett. Las Cruces N.M.

Double   Heart,
Pat Coghlan. Tularosa N.M.

Bar W Ranch
Carrizozo N.M.

Bow & Arrow. Mescalero
Apache Indians. Mescalero N.M.

Cowboys, Ranching & Cattle Trails

A NEW MEXICO FEDERAL WRITERS' PROJECT BOOK

COMPILED AND EDITED BY

Ann Lacy and Anne Valley-Fox

SUNSTONE
PRESS

SANTA FE

Sunstone books may be purchased for educational, business, or sales promotional use.
For information please write: Special Markets Department, Sunstone Press,
P.O. Box 2321, Santa Fe, New Mexico 87504-2321.

Book and Cover design › Vicki Ahl
Body typeface › Palatino Linotype
Printed on acid-free paper
∞

Library of Congress Cataloging-in-Publication Data

Lacy, Ann, 1945-
  Cowboys, ranching & cattle trails : a New Mexico Federal Writers' Project book / compiled and
edited by Ann Lacy and Anne Valley-Fox.
    pages cm
  ISBN 978-0-86534-945-2 (softcover : alkaline paper)
  1. New Mexico--History--20th century--Anecdotes. 2. Cowboys--New Mexico--History--20th
century--Anecdotes. 3. Ranch life--New Mexico--History--20th century--Anecdotes. 4. Cattle trails-
-New Mexico--History--20th century--Anecdotes. 5. New Mexico--Social life and customs--20th
century--Anecdotes. 6. New Mexico--History, Local--Anecdotes. 7. New Mexico--Biography-
-Anecdotes. I. Valley-Fox, Anne.
  II. Federal Writers' Project. New Mexico. III. Title. IV. Title: Cowboys, ranching and cattle trails.
  F801.L234 2013
  978.9'053--dc23
                                            2013008505

WWW.SUNSTONEPRESS.COM
SUNSTONE PRESS / POST OFFICE BOX 2321 / SANTA FE, NM 87504-2321 /USA
(505) 988-4418 / ORDERS ONLY (800) 243-5644 / FAX (505) 988-1025

To the writers of the
New Mexico Federal Writers' Project
who left us with so many good stories.

———

CONTENTS

COWBOYS

RANCHING

SHEEP

CATTLE TRAILS

COWBOY LORE

COWBOY TERMS

Acknowledgments

We wish to thank the archivists at the New Mexico State Records Center and Archives for their interest and assistance in our research.

We are grateful to the Museum of New Mexico Palace of the Governors Photo Archives and the Fray Angélico Chávez History Library, Santa Fe, New Mexico, for providing access to their fine collections.

Special appreciation to Elise Rymer and Project Crossroads for supporting the five volumes in our New Mexico Federal Writers' Project series.

Editors' Preface

Landscape plays a dominant role in the history and cultures of a people. For centuries, New Mexico was a place where peoples hunted game over broad distances and grew crops in the contrasting lands of dry desert, riverine valleys, grasslands, plains and mountains. After the Europeans arrived in the sixteenth century with domesticated animals, land use began to shift towards life on the range. The stories in *Cowboys, Ranching & Cattle Trails* illustrate this changing relationship to land and its resources.

When Francisco Vásquez de Coronado and his *conquistadores* entered New Mexico in 1540 they encountered a farming culture in which Pueblos grew corn, beans, calabashes and other crops. The Spaniards introduced new crops as well as sheep, cattle and horses. The following spring, when they gave up hope of finding gold and returned to Mexico, most of the livestock disappeared with them or wandered off.

Domesticated animals were reintroduced to New Mexico in 1598, when Juan de Oñate arrived with 846 goats, 198 cart oxen, 2,517 sheep, 316 horses, 41 mules, 53 hogs, 500 calves, 799 cows, steers and bulls. The cultivation of livestock took hold. Sheep herds proliferated; Franciscan friars and the Pueblos began to produce woolen cloth.

When the Pueblos revolted against Spanish rule in 1680 and drove the invaders out, they kept some of the herds and flocks. Cattle roamed freely over the ranges. In 1692, when Spanish conquistadores reentered the area, a few wealthy landowners dominated the landscape with vast herds of sheep. The *partido* system—a sort of sharecropping arrangement in which the sheepherder, paid in sheep, could establish his own herd over time—controlled the area's economy. Later, when New Mexico became part of the Territorial United States, merchants flooded into the region by way of the Santa Fe Trail to buy up wool for shipment east.

But a major change in the livestock economy was occurring. In 1866, Charles Goodnight and Oliver Loving drove their first herd of longhorn cattle across west Texas and up the Pecos River to Fort Sumner in search of grasses and markets for their cattle. Their outfits supplied beef to the U.S. Army as well as to Navajos held captive at Fort Sumner; they also drove herds to railheads, such as Magdalena and Dodge City, for shipment east.

More cattlemen streamed into New Mexico from Texas on the heels of the Civil War. The more ambitious among them established vast spreads (sometimes on original Spanish land grants) with hundreds of cowboys employed to ride herd, work roundups and drive cattle to railheads and markets. By 1875, a year before the Lincoln County War broke out between rival ranchmen, John Chisum's Jinglebob Ranch in Chaves County supported 80,000 head of cattle.

The 1880s was a dynamic decade for ranchers and sheepmen in New Mexico. Those years saw the establishment of a regional railroad system, which facilitated shipping of livestock. It also encompassed a devastating spate of blizzards and drought, resulting in widespread loss of livestock. In 1881 an increase in cattle prices caused many ranchers to sell out to large ranching syndicates; the same year saw the introduction of barbed wire fences on the Southern Plains.

By the 1890s, cattle ranching overshadowed the sheep industry. But sheep remained an essential part of life on the range. Around the time that New Mexico Federal Writers' Project writer Lorin W. Brown filed his eloquent interview with the sheepherder Basílico Garduño, there were still 2,337,000 sheep in New Mexico. Sheepmen, like ranchers, played an essential role in the iconic western landscape.

As some of the stories in this collection remind us, the Mexican *vaquero* taught the Texas cowboy much of what he needed to know to survive in the new land. Of the cowboy in New Mexico, Brown wrote, "His everyday life was full of expressions descriptive of events, tasks, and physical features of the country itself, so commonly used in the original Spanish as to have become a part of his native tongue without his being aware of it."

During the 1890s the open range was increasingly fenced in with miles and miles of drift fences to keep the herds within boundaries. Huge range spreads began to shrink. The present era of fenced-in cattle ranching had begun.

Cowboys, Ranching & Cattle Trails features oral histories by and about the many enterprising men, women, and children who inhabited Territorial New Mexico. Whether living on remote ranches, herding sheep or driving cattle along the trails, they exhibited initiative, endurance and downright toughness—qualities that readers may recognize as aspects of a collective western imagination.

Cowboys, ranchers and sheepherders in this volume tell their stories in their own words; these stories were transcribed, translated and sometimes elaborated by the able writers of the New Mexico Federal Writers' Project. As editors, we have tried to remain faithful to each writer's style and intent, making grammatical changes to the original documents only where deemed necessary for readability. Although the manuscripts in this collection do not tell the whole story—most notably, the voices of Native Americans were omitted, and women informants are rare—they do give us a picture of a vibrant era in New Mexico history.

We are grateful to the writers of the New Mexico Federal Writers' Project who made this collection of stories possible. In *Cowboys, Ranching & Cattle Trails*, as in the four previous volumes in this series, the field writers' spirited documentation provides us with an authentic, lively and truly splendid record of life in Territorial New Mexico.

About the New Mexico Federal Writers' Project

The Great Depression that came on the heels of the stock market crash of 1929 threw the country's financial institutions into chaos and put many people across the nation out of work. In 1933, in response to this national crisis, President Franklin Delano Roosevelt inaugurated his New Deal administration, a comprehensive program designed to stimulate the country's economy while lending a hand to the unemployed.

The Federal Writers' Project was one of a number of white-collar relief projects of the Works Progress Administration (later called the Work Projects Administration) that put Americans back to work. In addition to the Federal Writers' Project, New Deal administration projects included the Federal Art Project, the Federal Music Project, the Federal Theater Project and the Historical Records Survey.

The New Mexico Federal Writers' Project (NMFWP) was officially launched on August 2, 1935, under the direction of poet and writer Ina Sizer Cassidy. Between October, 1935, and August, 1939, a cadre of field writers recorded stories, collected articles, conducted interviews and transposed documents for the public record. During its tenure, the New Mexico program also produced *Calendar of Events,* written by project writers and illustrated by Federal New Mexico Art Project artists, as well as *Over the Turquoise Trail* and *The Turquoise Trail,* two anthologies of New Mexican poems, stories, and folklore and *New Mexico: A Guide to the Colorful State.*

Although each of the forty-eight states across the nation launched their own Federal Writers' Project, New Mexico was seen as geographically and culturally unique. Henry G. Alsberg, the national director of the Federal Writers' Project, urged New Mexico project writers to emphasize the state's visual, scenic and human interest subjects: "Try to make the readers see the white midsummer haze, the dust that rises in unpaved New Mexican streets, the slithery red earth roads of winter, the purple shadows of later afternoon."

New Mexico field writers apparently felt a similar enthusiasm, as they created thousands of documents to preserve the state's vivid lore, scenic locale and colorful past for future generations. Their subjects ranged from the colonial New Mexico days of the 1600s clear to the early 1900s—

from horse-drawn cart to car. Their many lively selections included firsthand oral accounts and remembrances by settlers and residents who lived to tell the story of New Mexico's Territorial days.

Project writers in New Mexico mined their trove of sources well. They collected tales from a host of characters—explorers, outlaws, ranchers, cowboys, sheepherders, homesteaders, miners, prospectors, farmers, merchants, lawmen, diarists, journalists, poets, artists, anthropologists and folklorists—who animate New Mexico history.

The efforts of NMFWP field writers left us a rich compilation of documents stored in various collections in New Mexico, including the New Mexico State Records Center and Archives in Santa Fe as well as museum and university collections. The Library of Congress in Washington, DC also holds copies of many of the manuscripts. Now, nearly eight decades after FDR launched the New Deal, the New Mexico Federal Writers' Project Book series makes these readings available in print for the public's edification and enjoyment.

Foreword by Sharon Niederman

Our vision of the cowboy-rancher is our culture's dream of who we are. In our communal imagination, we see a strong man astride a tireless horse, making his way through the open landscape of the American West. Sheltered by the sky, he travels at his own pace and he makes his own decisions. Endowed only with his wits and his Winchester, he overcomes any obstacle he encounters and continues his long journey. He is self-sufficient, capable, trustworthy and unstoppable. He is alone but not lonely; the master of his soul; generous but unsentimental; proud but humble; and he asks nothing from anyone. Above all, he is free.

And we are in love with him. Regardless of our gender or ethnicity, and regardless of where our faith in this legendary character has led us, we continue to be entranced with this myth of American manhood. He is the single colossal figure with the guts and stamina to contend with the land that tests every nerve and muscle. It's his grit and ingenuity that inspires the "git 'er done" philosophy that triumphs over obstacles large and small.

The New Mexico Federal Writers' Project legacy gives us insight into our national mythology. Field writers gathered these accounts over eighty years ago; their assignment provided much-needed employment for writers on the heels of the Great Depression; furthermore, the work they did was an investment that grows in value with each passing year. These documentarians recorded the living memories of Wild West pioneers as they recalled the days of the open range. Their unadorned accounts, many only fragments, communicate the history of the West as direct experience. The oral histories, newspaper articles, census accounts, and book reprints are authentic stories of hardship, coping, hard work, luck, and wiles. From them we learn how places got their names, how to cook for a crew on a chuck wagon, and how to tend sheep.

The language of these tales is remarkable for its terse and direct poetic qualities, its relationship to the land, and its humor. We read of "second-story biscuits" and hear Pecos Valley pioneer Sallie Chisum's father tell her: "Cheer up, Sallie, the worst is yet to come." It is a language of urgency that does not have a moment to waste. It communicates instantly and directly. Like those who speak it, it says precisely what it means, then moves on.

These are not romanticized accounts. The land dictated the lives of trailblazers like Chisum, Goodnight and Loving. They encountered every possible obstacle, from quicksand to alkaline water to the steep banks of the Pecos River. They show us cowboys singing to the cattle at night to keep them calm, and they tell us how to survive a stampede.

The mandate of their generation was to settle the frontier, and hardship and danger were to be endured without whining. Paul Bunyan-esque feats of strength, like wrestling a horse to the ground and holding him there until help came, were required. A keen power of observation could make the difference between life and death.

Several of the accounts in this book may irk readers with their demeaning attitudes toward Native Americans, condemning them as outlaws and thieves. Unfortunately, the WPA writers represented here omitted the perspective of indigenous people. At the time they worked, such perspectives were not considered valid or valuable; furthermore, Manifest Destiny was the cultural dictate for those whose accounts are preserved in these pages. They feared those who were defending their land and their way of life and so made them into the "other," whose lives were therefore judged as less valuable than their own. Violence against them appeared justified. This is not to excuse the pioneers' limited outlook, only to note that point of view has expanded to become more inclusive.

These accounts inform us how the pioneers lived subject to the ravages and mercies of the land. There was no turning back from drought, flood, and blizzard. These are the stories of unsung heroes, those who built towns we inhabit and industries that feed and clothe us. Here we have stories of common folk shared in their common tongue. It's a hard life most of us would rather read about than endure.

However, as we have moved off the land into a virtual world where many of us spend more hours before a computer screen than communicating with one another or communing with the landscape, we wonder where we are headed. We question our choices and we are anxious about the future. The cowboy remains our icon because, even in the embrace of the dominant society, he holds his own.

The values instilled by the land refined and polished the tough character necessary to cope and survive in harsh circumstances. We still like to think of ourselves as authentic, bold, trustworthy, inspired, innovative, and up to any challenge. That is why the values of the cowboy-rancher will continue to be embraced as quintessential American values.

Cowboys, Ranching & Cattle Trails is the final volume in the series of Depression-era Federal Writers' Project compilations of writings rediscovered, compiled and edited by Ann Lacy and Anne Valley-Fox. The accounts in this volume celebrate the qualities of cowboys and ranchers, both man and woman, and they give them the dignity they are due.

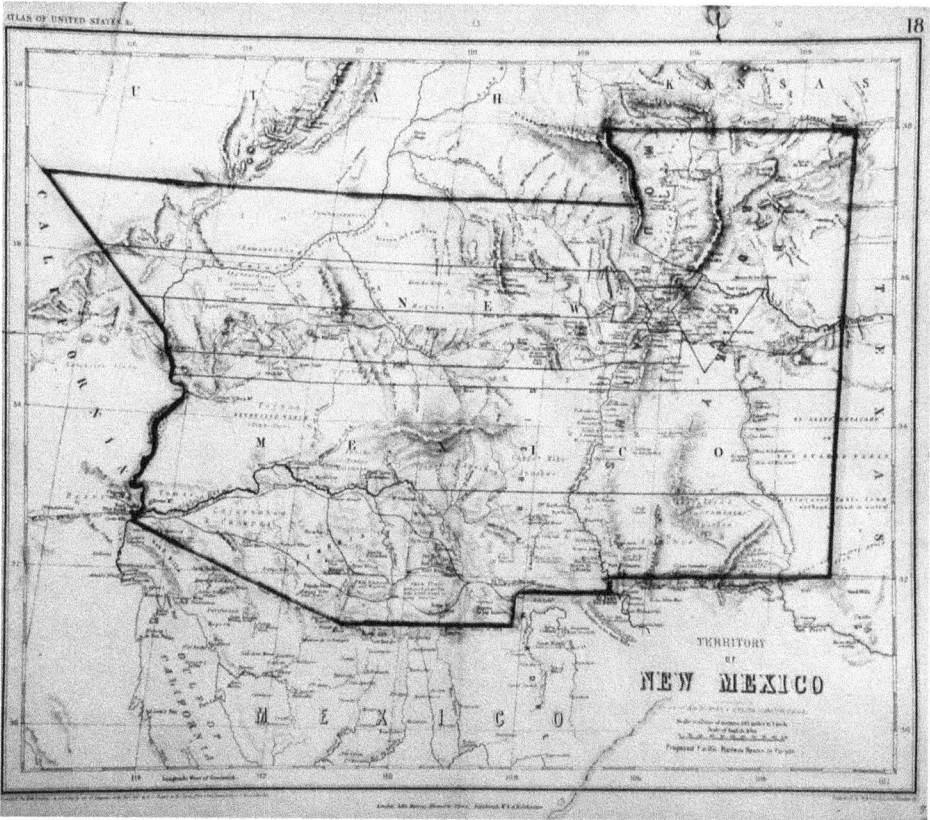

Territory of New Mexico, ca. 1857 by A. D. Rogers (artist), A. Keith Johnston (artist). Courtesy Fray Angélico Chávez History Library, NMHM, Map Collection, (78.9)

COWBOYS

"One Saturday, a cowboy from the Slaughter Ranch nearby, after securing a few drinks at Milligan's Saloon, was proceeding to shoot up the town when a deputy sheriff from Socorro (then the county seat) rode into the Frisco Plaza."

—From "Introduction" (Excerpt) by Allen A. Carter

The Spanish Vaquero and His Influence on the Language of the Range and Roundup

by Lorin W. Brown

The cowboy or Mexican *vaquero* of the Spanish ranches of New Mexico, first under Spanish and later Mexican regimes, used a language descriptive of his everyday activities and gear, which was adopted by his American brother after the American Occupation (1846).

In essential characteristics the *vaquero* was not greatly different from his American or English speaking prototype, but he did leave him a lingo, which, though Americanized, filled the need of a burgeoning industry, and is readily traceable to its source.

Those who have seen rodeos use the word with no thought of its origin. This exhibition of skill is staged indoors before sophisticated audiences in metropolitan centers as well as in the cowboys' own habitat. The very word rodeo, pronounced in the language of its origin (ro-da-o), is descriptive of the greatest activity in the annual round of successive activities on a western ranch. *El Rodeo* is the round-up, the annual gathering by hard riding cowboys of all of the cattle belonging to the home ranch as well as cattle from a neighboring ranch that have strayed out of bounds. Cattle grazing in the farthest corners of the range of a particular ranch are diligently sought out and hazed, by ones and twos at first, to join similar groups "choused out" of thickets and hidden corners; thus is concentrated a gradually increasing herd of cattle, all driven toward a predetermined center, preferable a large open plain. The cowboys of the neighboring ranches are employed in the same task, the day for the rodeo having been previously determined by all owners cooperating.

Converging herds driven by as many bands of cowboys from the various ranches meet on this open plain, where feats of horsemanship and the handling of cows, steers, and calves are exhibited in the discharge of routine duties. No fancy costumes here; only the well worn work clothes are seen. This is strictly business. The cutting out and roping of recalcitrant "cow brutes," and the branding and marking of calves, amid sweat and dust, are matters to be dispatched with the utmost efficiency. Pride of performance and a job well done, coupled with a desire to discharge an onerous duty in workmanlike fashion, make for precision and expertness which win money at public exhibitions.

All life on a cattle ranch centered around the ranch house, the bunkhouse, and the home corral. The word ranch comes from the Spanish *rancho* as does corrals, the latter having been adopted into English with no change in spelling.

The *vaquero* used leather pants to protect him in the brush and from the inclemencies of the weather; these he called *chaparejos* or *chaparreras*. The American cowboy adopted this very utilitarian item of wearing apparel, added adornments, and called them "chaps," pronounced shaps. In the rest of his apparel, the American cowpoke did not differ materially from his Mexican contemporary, but the English nomenclature was observed throughout, i.e., boots, spurs, hat, etc.

With reference to the cow pony and his equipment there were more of the Spanish terms adopted or Anglicized. The pony himself might be a "paint" (from the Spanish *pinto*) because of his spotted coat. The hemp or horsehair band which secured the saddle to the pony's back was called a cinch from the Spanish *cincho*. The hackamore, an effectual bitless curb for an unruly horse, came from *jáquima* (há-kē-ma). The "taps," leather cups affixed to the stirrups for warding off brush and thorns, were called *tapaderos* by their originators. *Látigos*, straps affixed to the saddle for securing the lariat in front and carrying a poncho or slicker behind, went by the same name in English; and *conchas* was the descriptive name for the (usually) silver, shell-shaped adornments attached to the saddle and bridle and with the same motif carried out in some cases to the adorning of spur straps, chaps, and hatband.

The hempen or rawhide loop which the cowboy used so skillfully, called lasso or lariat, derived from the Spanish *lazo* for slipknot and *la reata* or *reata* alone, meaning to tie or secure, to attach for leading. From *caballo* the word for horse, there are several derivations: *caballero*, the man on horseback, the gentleman, a title of respect equivalent to Sir; *caballada*, corrupted into "cavy" and "cavvy yard," is the band of horses from which the cowboys took their remounts, changing a tired horse for another of their own "string." The *caballada* was in charge of the *caballocerango*, usually a mere boy, an apprentice cowboy; some authorities say that the horse-wrangler is a corruption of this Spanish term. *Remuda*, another term adopted whole, denoted also the band of saddle horses held readily accessible for a quick change of mounts.

The cowboy's strenuous life did not deter him from strenuous recreation. He used the words *baile* and *fandango* easily, mixed them with his English as he danced and flirted with the blackeyed *señoritas*. If he were drunk and disorderly or became involved in a fight, he might find himself in the "hoosegow" (Spanish, *juzgado*; pron. hoos-gah-do), as the local jail was called. In that case, if he did not break jail, he sent for a "lobbygow" and had a "palaver" with him. "Lobbygow" seems rather remote from its origin, which is *el abogado* (lawyer). "Palaver" comes directly from *palabras* (words), meaning to discuss or talk over something. Once out of jail, the cowboy rode back to his home ranch singing; perhaps the song was "Get Along Little Dogies." The "little dogies" (not doggies) was an adaptation of *dogal*, the Spanish for calf. His way home might take him across an *arroyo*, and across a *mesa*, pausing on his way to tail a cow up out of a sink hole filled with viscous "dobe" (mud). His everyday life was full of expressions descriptive of events, tasks, and physical features of the country itself, so commonly used in the original Spanish as to have become a part of his native tongue without his being aware of it.

Group of Mexican cowboys in Southern New Mexico near Deming, Unattributed, ca. 1890–1900, NMHM/DCA #013502

Introduction (Excerpt)

by Allen A. Carter

Just to the northwest of Aragon, and south of Tularosa Mountain, old Fort Tularosa was established in 1871 as the outgrowth of numberless depredations in this area by the Apache Indians. The never-ending list of Indian atrocities, which were almost daily occurrences, finally induced the Government to select this site for a post on the Tularosa River. This post grew to be an important station, and, in a limited way, the soldiers were able to keep the trail open although not altogether safe for travellers and stage coaches.

In this same year, 1871, the second of the Indian reservations established for Apaches was located in this immediate neighborhood on the Tularosa River, but it failed to solve the problem of furnishing these Southern Apaches with a permanent home, for they absolutely refused to remain on the reservation and it was finally abandoned. Any resident of Aragon can direct the tourist to the exact sites of both this old fort and the proposed reservation.

The present town of Reserve, in the 1880s, was a tiny Mexican settlement known as "Frisco," with an Upper Plaza, Middle Plaza, and Lower Plaza. It was then the happy romping ground for certain outfits of cattlemen and cowpunchers who spent their Saturday evenings and Sundays raising cain generally and taking pot shots at both the populace and the scattered buildings.

One Saturday a cowboy from the Slaughter Ranch nearby, after securing a few drinks at Milligan's Saloon, was proceeding to shoot up the town when a deputy sheriff from Socorro (then the county seat) rode into the Frisco Plaza. The name of the cowboy was McCarty and the deputy was none other than Elfego Baca, the hero of "Law & Order, Ltd." (written by Kyle S. Crichton in 1928), still alive in Albuquerque.

Baca asked the Justice of the Peace and other residents of Frisco (Reserve) why they allowed this cowboy to jeopardize their lives and property in such a manner. He was told that if they arrested or harmed McCarty his friends would come and do a lot of harm to the settlement. As a special deputy sheriff, Baca then took it upon himself to disarm and arrest McCarty. Slaughter's cowboys, by some means, heard about this arrest. Headed by their foreman, one Perham, they rode into town and demanded his release. By some chance Perham's horse fell and killed its rider, and Baca's curt order to the cowboys to depart was almost more of a stunner than Perham's unusual accident.

A courier rushed out to the ranch house of Mr. J. H. Cook nearby and called out that the Mexicans had gone on the warpath at Frisco, Baca being a Spanish-American and therefore branded as a Mexican in those days in this region.

By the time the Cook outfit reached Frisco the Slaughter boys were likewise riding in, words were bandied about, and to save his own hide Baca was forced to abandon his prisoner and make for a small adobe house nearby for protection. A cowboy named Jim Herne, a Texan with a bounty already on his head, advanced to catch Baca and Baca's answer was two shots, either of which would have been fatal. Herne's friends bore the body away and the battle was on.

Two men were killed before Mr. Cook and a deputy sheriff named Ross arranged with the cowmen for Baca to be taken in custody to Socorro for trial for murder. In the meantime Baca had held off the crowd for a period of over thirty hours while barracked behind the walls of the "dobe."

One story has it that such an arrangement was made so that the cowmen could hold up the sheriff on the trip to Socorro and hang Baca to a tree. However, it seems that both the Slaughter and the Cook outfits understood that the other was to do this, and due to some conflict in the plan, neither one intercepted the sheriff and Baca was taken to Socorro, where he was tried for murder but was acquitted.

These stories all vary, of course, one version being told by Mr. Chricton in his "Law & Order, Ltd." And another one being told by Mr. J. H. Cook in his "Fifty Years on the Old Frontier." The course of the narrative is a little doubtful, although a person may try to check up faithfully on all items entering into its history, but these incidents bring out the interest, humor, life, and strangeness of this Southwestern New Mexico, and are characteristic of the romantic color of the area.

The W. S. Cemetery

by H. P. Collier

Have you ever seen a cemetery where every occupant therein was killed, murdered without being given a chance to defend himself? On a pinon, cedar-covered mesa six miles north of Glenwood, Catron County, New Mexico, on State Highway No. 260 and one mile north of the dilapidated town of Alma near the headquarters of the old W. S. Ranch (founded by Wilson and Stephens) is located this unique cemetery. The names mentioned here later are those who helped make history in this section of the country, then, Socorro, now, Catron County. Lyons worked for the S U Ranch (Stephens and Upcher) about 35 miles north of Alma where he had gone for the ranch mail (Alma was the nearest post-office). On his return, he was murdered by Victorio's Apache Indians and laid to rest in the W. S. cemetery. The six soldiers ambushed on Dry Creek Hill (now Soldiers' Hill) by Victorio's Apaches led by their fighting captain, Nana, were also buried at the W. S. Charlie Moore, called "Old Charlie," a W. S. cowboy whose savings and salary went into mining property some of which (Mogollon and Morenci, Arizona) later became very valuable, was murdered by Penny of the saloon firm of Penny and Shelton at Cooney in 1888 and buried at the W. S. Luke Flanagan of Ireland, farm boss of the W. S. and a close personal friend of Capt. French, manager of the W. S. ranch properties in Socorro and Colfax Counties and who later wrote the book, "Some Recollections of a Western Ranchman," was killed by a cowardly assassin named Saunders at Mogollon, Nov. 9, 1899. Luke was buried at the W. S.

Billy the Kid Story

by Edith L. Crawford

My father, Major William Brady, was fifty-six years old when he was killed by Billy the Kid and his gang in Lincoln, New Mexico, April 1, 1878. Father, Billy Mathews, his chief deputy, George Heinman, George Peppin and Jack Long were on their way to the courthouse to open a term of court. Father and George Heinman had stopped to tell Timoteo Analla, Ignacio Torres and Navor Chávez, they were members of the grand jury, that he was going to open court and adjourn it as he had a letter from the Judge saying he was afraid to come to Lincoln and hold court at that time. Billy Mathews, Jack Long and George Peppin had walked on down the road ahead of them. After talking to the three jurors a few minutes, Father and Heinman started on down to the Court house, which was later used as the Catholic Church. Just as they arrived in front of where the Penfield home now stands, Billy the Kid and his gang opened fire on them. Father fell mortally wounded, he was shot sixteen times in the back. George Heinman ran for his life and escaped without a scratch. Billy Mathews, Jack Long and George Peppin were in front of Mrs. Lupe Sisneros' house and they ran in there and watched the shooting from a window. Father's body lay in the street for an hour after he was killed and while he was laying there Billy the Kid and gang went out to where his body lay and were going to take his guns, when Billy Mathews saw them from the home of Mrs. Sisneros. He opened fire on them and ran them away. Billy the Kid and his gang were firing on Father from a high adobe wall which was built around the old tower which is now El Torreon. Everybody was afraid to go near Father's body for quite awhile. Mrs. Saturnino Baca finally went out to where he lay and in a few minutes several more people came out. They got a hack and took his body to the courthouse and later to our home, which was six and one half miles below Lincoln on the Río Bonito. Father was buried on the flat out in front of our house where his body still rests.

My father was sheriff at the time the papers were issued to attach the McSween and Tunstall cattle. He sent Billy Mathews, his chief deputy, to get the cattle and bring them in to Lincoln. On the way back some of the Murphy Dolan gang shot Tunstall, and the Lincoln County War was on.

When father heard of the killing of Tunstall he sent another deputy, Pablo Pino, to help bring the cattle in to Lincoln. They did not keep the cattle very long as Billy the Kid and his gang recovered the cattle and drove them back to the Pajarito Mountains and turned them loose. Most of them were stolen during the Lincoln County War. Billy the Kid and his gang were hiding in the mountains, just back of the McSween home in Lincoln and while there they sent a note to Vicente Romero to meet them in the Chaves flat, which is about three quarters of a mile southeast of Hondo, New Mexico. It was planned so that the Murphy-Dolan gang would get hold of this information.

The Murphy-Dolan gang immediately planned to waylay Billy the Kid and his gang on the Chaves flats. Billy and his gang were watching from their hiding place in the mountains and when they saw the Murphy-Dolan gang leave Lincoln they came into town and took possession of it. As soon as the Murphy-Dolan gang realized this was a trap they rushed back to Lincoln to find Billy and his gang in possession of the town. The town people were very much frightened for they knew there would be a battle between the two factions. Billy the Kid's gang finally made a stand in the McSween home. The Murphy-Dolan gang surrounded the house. The town people were so alarmed that they sent for the soldiers from Fort Stanton, New Mexico, to come down and make peace between the two factions but their presence did no good.

The Murphy-Dolan faction made plans to set the McSween house on fire. They sent a negro man by the name of George Dixon out to get all the coal oil he could find. When he returned with the oil they had some boxes piled up against the porch and they poured the oil on them and struck a match to them but Billy the Kid's gang were watching them and had some wet blankets that they threw on the fire and put it out. The Murphy-Dolan gang got some red shirts and soaked them in the coal oil, set them on fire and threw them at the house. Finally they got a spot to burning where the people in the McSween house could not get to it. The house began to burn and the smoke was so thick that they could not see on the outside so Bob Beckwith slipped up to the front porch and when McSween opened the door and started out Beckwith shot him dead in his tracks, and shot several others at the front door.

While this was going on at the front door of the house, Higinio

Salazar started out the back door on the run; as he reached the yard he was hit by three bullets in the left shoulder and fell to the ground and made out like he was dead. Several of the Murphy-Dolan gang went up to him and wanted to shoot him between the eyes but a man by the name of John Kinney said, "No, he is dead and his face looks pretty good so leave him alone," so they did, but on leaving several of the men picked up some old adobes that were in the yard and threw them on his body. He survived all of this and lived to be a very old man.

I remember one night Billy the Kid and his gang came to Lincoln and let all the prisoners out of jail. Jess Evans, Frank Baker, Tom Hale, Tom O'Fallard, Catrino Romero and Lucas Gallegos were the prisoners. The jail was a dugout, twenty-four by twenty-eight feet and about ten feet deep; on top of the ground were logs chinked up with mud, with a dirt roof and one door. They had a ladder that they put down in this dugout to put the prisoners in jail and when they were all inside they pulled the ladder up and hid it. When Billy and his gang came to town and found some of their pals in jail they hunted up the jailer (I don't remember his name) got the key and ladder and let all the prisoners out. Another time Charlie Crawford, Marion Turner and Lucio Montoya were hid in the mountains just back of the Ellis house and barn. They shot Ben Ellis through the neck and killed two horses and one mule in the barn. When Billy's gang went after them and began shooting at them Lucio Montoya took to a corn patch and ran into Mrs. Lupe Sisneros' house and she hid him in the flour barrel. When the Kid's gang went up to her house and asked her if Montoya was there she replied that she had not seen him. After dark he got out of the flour barrel and made his getaway. A fellow by the name of Frank Freeman went into Sam Wortley's hotel in Lincoln. There were two negro soldiers sitting at the table. Freeman walked over to them and ordered them to get out. They told him they were waiting for their supper, that they had ordered it and they intended to pay for it and did not see why they couldn't stay and eat. Freeman pulled his six shooter and killed them both where they sat. He got on his horse, rode six and one half miles to our house below Lincoln. Father saw him coming and stepped outside the door. When Freeman came up he had two boxes of cartridges in his hand, he asked Father for his cartridge belt. Father handed it to him and he filled it full of cartridges and turned to leave. He said to Father as he was leaving, "You will be looking for me tomorrow, I just killed two negro soldiers in Sam Wortley's hotel in Lincoln." He got on his horse and rode away. Ten days later Father captured him and turned him over to the officers at Fort Stanton, New Mexico.

Father worked for Murphy and Dolan when they had cattle and owned most of the Carrizozo flats. That was before he was sheriff and before the Lincoln County War.

I had many fights after the Lincoln County War. I used to fight with Higinio Salazar every time we met because he was one of Billy the Kid's gang. I always had a hatred of all of them because they killed my father. My father was born in Covan, Ireland in 1825.

Source of Information: Robert Brady, Hondo, New Mexico, aged 71 years.

Estancia Spring, New Mexico, J. R. Riddle, ca. 1886, NMHM/DCA #076109

A Day on the Round Up

by W. M. Emery

The day of the picturesque, daring cowboy is over. The round-up wagon has given place to the motor truck and railroad trains. Cattle are kept within fenced pastures, where a handful of men can gather them in a day, put them into trucks and in a few hours have them on the train on their way to market. The romance and adventures of the old cattle trails are gone.

The cattle are still branded. Oh, yes, it is a law in most Western States that this must be done, and the brands must be recorded with the State Sanitary Board. But even the method of branding is modernized. Where once the cattle were rounded up on the prairie, with several men "holding up" the herd, and more riding through them, roping a calf, dragging it to the branding fire, calling the brand to be burned on its hide to the men running the branding iron. After the brand was on and the ears marked the calf was turned loose to go back to the mother, who usually had followed and stood as near as possible watching the ordeal. Now the calves are run into a crowding pen, then through a chute where the brand is burned on and the ears marked.

Yes, this is a very civilized and humane way to brand, but the real fun and thrill of the old brandings are gone. The men have lost their skill in handling a rope, riding a horse or reading brands. And there are few horses that are expert cutting horses or rope horses. Horses that can dodge that duck through a herd of cattle and stay with one certain animal until it is out of the herd, or that know just when to brace their feet and hold the rope taut after the animal has been roped.

These things and more the old cowboys did. Their courage, skill and daring is only known to the majority of people through stories, motion pictures and songs; but the few old cowmen who are still with us will sit by the hour and tell the stories of their adventures and that of some comrade, and in so doing live again through the scenes and events of the past.

Such a story is often told of Bud Sumpter, whose home was on the Dry Cimarron River, about twelve miles from Folsom. Bud was known from the Canadian river in New Mexico to the Arkansas in Colorado. He was wagon boss for some of the largest cow outfits in this part of the State, and was known as one of the strongest men on the range. It was due to his physical strength and his presence of mind that his life was saved in this incident.

The cattle had been rounded up and were being held on the prairie at the head of Long Canyon, a few miles south of the Colorado-New Mexico line. Bud was riding a big brown horse, a fine cutting horse, when Wilcox, one of the owners of the herd, drove up in a buckboard, and stopped as near the herd as he dared, to watch the men work and see that none of his cattle were cut into the wrong herd.

The cattle were afraid of the strange object and the team of horses which were parked so near to them, and would hardly leave the herd. This caused lots of unnecessary riding and running, with the tempers of the cowboys rising every minute. Bud was chasing a big steer from the herd when his horse nearly collided with the team and buckboard. The horse, in making a quick turn to avoid the collision, fell. As he came up Bud realized that his foot was caught in the stirrup and he was in danger of being dragged to death. He caught the horse's hind foot in both arms, throwing the horse back on the ground. He held the horse down in this manner until he was out free by Jabe Burton (who still lives near Trinchera, Colorado) one of his fellow cowboys.

It would really not do to put into print what Bud told Wilcox after he regained his feet, but the fact remains that Wilcox was not found guilty again of watching a round-up in a buckboard, or getting in the way of the cowboys when they were at work.

Sources of Information: Jabe Burton, Trinchera, Colorado; Bud Sumpter.

Block Ranch
EL Capitan Livestock Co.
Capitan. N. M.

Circle X Ranch
George W Coe
Fort Stanton. N.M.

Bell Ranch, Red
River Valley Company
Eastern N, M.

Lea Cattle Co.
Roswell. N, M,

Diamond A Ranch. Bloom Land
r Cattle Co. Roswell. N. M.

Bridle Bit, merchant Ranch
Capitan N. M.

Circle Ranch Pat F
Garrett. Las cruces N M

Double Heart,
Pat Cochinn, Tularosa N M,

Bar W Ranch
Carrizozo N M

Bow + Arrow, mescniero
Apache Indians, Mescalero N M

Rough sketches compiled by Pauline Briscoe,
Excerpted from "Grazing" by B. W. Kenney, NMFWP, WPA #109a, NMSRCA

Cow Camp Entertainments
by W. M. Emery

After a long hard day in the saddle the cowboys would gather around the camp fire, where they would enjoy the only form of amusement that they could indulge in for weeks at a time. Every man was required to take part in the fun in some manner. If it was telling stories then each one had to tell his tale; if it was playing tricks on each other everyone took part; and if they were singing—for singing was a favorite pastime to them all—every man had to favor the crowd with a song.

There were some good singers with every outfit—and there were some not so good—but most of them were willing to do their part. Such old favorites as "Black Jack Davy," "Bury Me Not On The Lone Prairie," "The Old Chisholm Trail," and others were sung in the camps.

One evening when the boys of the IOI outfit were on the round-up, every man had done his bit toward the evening's entertainment with the exception of one man by name of Hollister. He was called upon to sing for the bunch.

"Aw, I cain't sing," he pleaded. "Let me off when it comes to that. I jest cain't carry a tune in a basket."

But the boys refused to "let him off." They used every form of argument they could think of, but to no avail, until one of the boys decided to try a little bribery.

"I'll give you a plug of tobacco if you will sing," he offered.

The offer was immediately accepted and the singing—if such a noise could come under that heading—began. Song after song floated out on the still night air. The words varied, but the tune remained the same. Over and over, hour after hour, until the cowboys were wishing there was some way of shutting him up, the man continued to sing in a monotonous, sing-song voice.

It was nearly midnight when someone in the crowd offered two plugs of tobacco if the singer would only quit, and let them get some sleep. This offer, like the other, was graciously accepted, and the camp quieted down for the night.

Needless to say that it was the last time Hollister was prevailed upon to sing for that outfit.

Source of Information: Albert Easley, Kenton, Oklahoma.

"Tall Tales": Strawberry Roan's Rival
by W. M. Emery

"Talk about pitchin' hosses, well, you ought'er have been with me one time when I was a workin' down here on the lower Cimarron with the Cross-ells.

"The hoss wrangler had brought in the remuda and put them in the rope corral. We all went to catch our mounts for the day.

"In my string was a poor reprobate whose ribs stuck out so far that they made him look like he had been dead a year, and you could hang your hat on his hip bones. He stood with his head between his knees like he didn't have energy enough to take a bite of corn if it was put between his teeth.

"Well, it was his turn to be rode that day, and I took down my rope and dropped it over his head. I was a wondering if I'd ever make it back to camp that night.

"'Old Bones' never moved when I threw my blanket and saddle over his back, and cinched him up. But when I stepped into the stirrup and swung my leg across him the fun began.

"Old Bones came to life in a flash, and of all the pitchin' I ever seen a hoss do, that old bag of bones did it. I stayed with him for the first few jumps, then I was catapulted into the air so high that—well, believe it or not, boys—when I got back to earth again that old fool hoss was hog fat."

Source of Information: This story was told by Mr. Grude Crow, an old time cowboy on the Dry Cimarron.

The Stampede

by W. M. Emery

The cattle had been pooled together for the long drive to Lamar, Colorado, the nearest shipping point. The Mizer and Whitaker outfit had been the first to arrive at the designated meeting place, not far from Springfield, Colorado; then Gordon came in with his car load, closely followed by young Jones, who was in charge of the Cristy herd. The last to arrive was the Brookhart outfit, with Arthur driving the cattle and Mary, her mother and brother, Henry, in the covered wagon. Henry was to cook on the drive, with his mother and sister as his assistants.

The Brookhart ranch was on the Dry Cimarron, near the New Mexico–Oklahoma line, and they had had a two days drive before meeting the other herds. Mrs. Brookhart, Mary and Arthur were on their way to Missouri, where they would visit with relatives for a short time.

Mary would have much preferred riding after the cattle than poking along in a covered wagon and assisting with the camp chores. Nearly all of her life she had helped Arthur with the cattle, and she could ride and rope with the best of them. But since she was going east for a visit, and also most of the men on the drive were practically strangers to her, she had kept her place in the wagon.

When the Brookharts arrived, all outfits were ready to continue on up the trail. Gordon, a big, domineering fellow, had assumed the responsibility of hard boss, even though he had less cattle than anyone in the herd. Young Jones was a "tenderfoot" from the east, who had come to Colorado for his health, and was working for the Cristy ranch. Mr. Cristy has sent him on this trip as he himself was unable to go. Jones was a willing worker, and tried at all times to do his part or even more, but Gordon had apparently taken a dislike to the "tenderfoot" and never missed a chance to double his work, or reprimand him for some minor mistake. The largest number of cattle belonged to Mizer and Whitaker, with Mr. Mizer in charge. According to the custom of trail driving, Mr. Mizer, as owner of the most cattle, should also have been the herd boss. But he would not dispute Gordon's claim as long as everything was going alright.

The first night out, camp was made near Butte Creek. When the guards were picked for the night herd, it was found that they were one man short. Gordon immediately ordered Jones to stand first guard—from 8:00 to 11:00—with Arthur, although he would have to stand his regular guard from 2:00 to 5:00 in the morning.

Mary offered to stand guard in place of Jones. She was used to the work, and she and Arthur—like all the others in the party—knew that Jones had been imposed upon from the start and he was not strong enough to do so much work, even though he had never complained.

Every man in the outfit gave his consent to Mary's taking her place as guard, but Gordon.

"What does a girl know about cattle?" he demanded, "Send her back to the wagon where she belongs. Jones, get out there. No girl is going to ride with this outfit as long as I'm boss."

For once, his orders were ignored and Mary made preparations for taking her place on guard. "Dandy," a young race horse belonging to Arthur, was saddled for her. They sent Jones back to the wagon to get his rest, as they knew there was no need for three to watch the cattle.

Arthur was riding a half broke horse, and this was its first experience driving cattle. After the cattle were quieted, Arthur dismounted to rest awhile, as he had ridden hard all day and was tired. Mary circled the herd alone. With the exception of three head, all the cattle were lying down, but on every round the three head had to be turned back to the herd.

The night was clear but dark, the only light coming from the distant stars sparkling in the black velvet dome overhead. The soft padding of her horse's hoofs, the occasional click of hoof against stone, the distant crunching of grass by the saddle horses staked near the wagon, waiting their turn at guard, and the far away cry of a lone coyote, were the only sounds to break the peaceful quietness which lay over the herd.

The night slowly crept on. By the changing stars, Mary knew that it would not be very long before the second guard would come out, and they would be free to go to their well earned rest.

Suddenly, and without warning, the entire herd jumped to their feet as one cow, and dashed away in the darkness. There was no time to speculate on the reason for such action; however, it was later believed that a rattlesnake or skunk had frightened them. Mary spurred her horse toward the lead. She had never seen a stampede, but she had read about them, and she decided to follow the instructions given in the stories, praying that her horse would be able to keep all four feet under him, and miss all prairie dog holes in the darkness, for woe be to the rider and horse that was unfortunate enough to fall under the sharp, flying hoofs of a stampeding herd.

On and on Mary sped with the herd, always drawing closer and closer to the lead animals, and turning them from their direct course. The other animals blindly followed their leaders and soon were beginning to mill in an ever tightening circle.

When the stampede had started Arthur had jumped for his pony, but the frightened animal had pulled away, and was too excited to let Arthur get on him. By the time he was quieted and Arthur had reached Mary, the herd was milling nicely, with every animal there. When the rest of the men, who had been aroused by the commotion, had reached them, the cattle were again as quiet as though nothing had happened.

Everyone praised Mary for handling the situation with such skill and courage. Only Gordon, who again began to roar about a girl standing guard, "It's no place for a girl. What did she know about handling cattle? What right did they have in sending Jones back to the wagon?"

Arthur whirled on him and demanded, "If you think you can hold a herd and stop a stampede any better than that girl did, we'll all go to camp and let you hold the herd the rest of the night."

Gordon shut up; he was not looking for work, he was trying to dodge it. From that time on he lost his prestige in the crowd. Mr. Mizer took charge of the herd, and Gordon was taunted and ridiculed all the rest of the trip.

It was a week before the cattle reached their destination, and then they were forced to wait two days, about five miles from Lamar, before they could obtain cars for shipment. During all this time Mary stood her regular guard.

After she and her mother and Arthur returned from their trip to Missouri, Mary helped trail several herds to both Lamar and Syracuse, Kansas, but she never again saw a stampede.

Source of Information: Mrs. Mary Baker, Clayton, New Mexico.

Pioneer: "Hunting on First Street"

by Kenneth Fordyce

Occasionally people wonder if the stunts that they see in western movies are things which ever really happened.

When First Street was the main street in Raton, New Mexico, and cowboys wore six-shooters, the boys from the range would come into town and get too happy after imbibing in the liquors served at the local bars.

A Frenchman operated a restaurant on First Street between Cook and Park Avenues. He had the good fortune to get some prairie chickens which he intended to serve to his customers. As an advertising feature he hung some of them on the sign in front of his restaurant, and prepared the rest for his table.

Two cowboys, in from the rangeland, looking for a good time, and having found a little more than their share, came up First Street arm in arm, and none too steady.

On the ranch, when they saw prairie chickens, they always shot some to take home for dinner, so they opened fire and continued to blaze away until every chicken was shot to the sidewalk.

First Street in Raton was deserted, the Frenchman was beside himself with rage, and the officers were on their way to the scene. Peace and order was restored when the two cowboys were led away to the new jail which had just been completed.

Source of Information: C. B. Thacker, Raton.

Pioneer: "No Labor Trouble" and "Rest"

by Kenneth Fordyce

"No Labor Trouble"

Today with our seven and eight hour days, we hear of labor trouble very frequently. Back in the early days, when the cattle were turned loose to roam over the range and cowboys worked at the job of rounding them up, labor trouble, on account of hours, might have been explainable.

The cow puncher's day started at four in the morning usually, and he was in the saddle until five or six in the afternoon. This day was long enough but there were yet three shifts to be taken care of during the night—the cattle must be guarded at night. The cow hand who had the first shift ate his supper and returned to the herd at once and remained on duty until eleven at night. This completed his day of approximately nineteen hours. He was then free until four the next morning.

"Rest"

The cow hand of the early days was such a rugged individual that when he did tire during his long day, he could step down off of his horse, lie down and nap for five or ten minutes in the shadow cast by his mount, and then be fit and ready to take up his duties again.

Source of Information: C. B. Thacker, Raton.

Cowboy campsite, New Mexico, Unattributed, ca. 1890, NMHM/DCA #005127

Pioneer: "Overnight in the Open"

by Kenneth Fordyce

Among the men who worked at the cattle business in Northern New Mexico in those days when fences were unknown and the cattle went where the grass was longest, it was thought no great hardship to make long trips on horse back. Distances were great in this new southwestern country and places to stop and get a room for the night were not thought of yet. Immediately back of a man's saddle, there was a roll—a blanket—and when night-fall overtook him some distance from a better bed, he would unroll his blanket, hobble his horse, and roll up (or bed down) on the softest spot nearby. The cowmen were use to it and did not seem to mind. They did it often, it was not just a rare occurrence resorted to in time of necessity.

"Burned Out" by Apaches

by Joyce Hunter

At dawn one foggy morning in 1867 near the location of the present city of Carlsbad, the Casey family was stirring after a night of well deserved sleep. The boys with the herd were camped some distance from the family camp site. This camp was on a grassy spot near a spring where the oxen, saddle horses and a small bunch of sheep could graze without wandering off. This arrangement had been made against the wishes of Mrs. Casey who insisted that as they were approaching Indian country extra precautions should be taken and both wagons placed together. Her husband laughed at her fears and decided the chuck wagon should stay with the herd further up the river.

At daybreak Mrs. Casey arose to see to the safety of the stock. Just as she neared the sheep, pets which she had raised "by hand" from lambs, a yell broke out upon the quiet morning air. She called a warning to her husband who sprang from his bed roll, pulling on his boots and shouting, "If they charge make for—Great God, here they are now. Put the children in the wagon and make them keep their heads in."—but they didn't.

The Apaches materialized out of the fog and stampeded the oxen and horses. The sheep started to follow. Mrs. Casey standing on the wagon tongue cried at the top of her lungs, "Lambie, lambie, lambie," her call to her pets at feeding time. Food appealing more strongly than fear, the sheep stampeded toward instead of away from her and were the only livestock saved from the Indians except one yoke of oxen, the quietest and most peaceful of the lot. The rest of the stock disappeared with the Apaches in full pursuit.

Meanwhile, the main herd was also in stampede. The men, thinking the Apaches were ready to attack, in their excitement threw their guns in the wagon bed and the bed rolls on top of them. While they were dragging the chuck wagon to the spring some of the Indians returned to the camp fire, stole the beans, coffee and bacon and ran off with all the pots and pans. One cowboy, hoping to save his special mount, loosed the hobbles, slapped him on the rump and started him off in the opposite direction. Other Apaches were on the watch, they circled the horse, headed him upstream and took him off with the others. Weeks later the party reached its destination on the upper Pecos. Instead of a well-to-do family they were practically "burned out" by the Indians.

Source of Information: Mrs. Lillie Klassner, San Patricio, N. Mex., who at the time of the story was Lillie Casey, a girl of 14 and one of the children who didn't keep their heads in.

Uncle Jimmie: Cowboys' Cruel Prank

by Joyce Hunter

Indians are usually accused of unspeakable cruelty. It was not Indians but cowboys of a rival cattle company who were guilty of the torture related in the following tale, a tale of the seventies or early eighties when feeling ran high between cattlemen and their employees followed their lead. It may be that these men did not intend to inflict the suffering they did, believing that it would not be long before the rival group would come by and release their comrade. However, here is the tale as it was told to me many years ago.

It was not often that a cowboy from any outfit was found out on the prairie alone. Mostly they traveled in pairs or more. This time Jim (later known as "Uncle Jimmie") seeing some cattle in the distance loped over to look at them and left his partner to go on north driving the few head they had previously rounded up. He rode to the head of the Cottonwood where there was a spring of water and a large cottonwood tree from which it got its name. The tree was still standing at the time this tale was told me. Here a number of cattle were gathered around the water and in rounding them up and cutting out his brand, Jim forgot his usual caution.

Suddenly he heard a whoop and looking up saw several men of the rival outfit riding over the hill toward him. It was useless to try to escape and the others leaped upon him with joy. At first Jim was not much worried as he thought the worst they would do would be to tease him a bit and maybe rope him to show their skill. Just about the time he was beginning to feel relief, one of the newcomers had an idea that took hold of the imaginations of the rest immediately.

"Let's tie him up in the tree and let his outfit find him there and cut him down."

That seemed a good idea so Jim was hoisted up into a crotch of the big cottonwood and tied there so that he could scarcely move.

"Let him holler for help now," jeered the boys, "he'll soon get tired."

It was near sundown so after watering their horses they rode off leaving Jim's horse at the spring, for horse stealing was a worse offense than murder at that time.

All night Jim hoped the horse would leave for the ranch for then he knew he would be looked for, but the next morning there the horse was contentedly munching the grass around the spring. By this time Jim was becoming thirsty and his craving grew hour by hour as the sun became hotter and hotter and the shade given by the cottonwood leaves was so sparse as to be inadequate to keep the sun from him. His eyes searched the hills but no help was to be seen.

The sight and sound of the water from the spring running along its bed was an added torture as the hours past so that by the time night fell there was no lessening of his suffering.

The second day was never distinct in his remembrance as he was so crazed with thirst that nothing else mattered.

It was not until the morning of the third day that help came. Comment had been made when he did not appear the first day but as his horse had not returned no great anxiety was felt. The next day, however, the search began in earnest and at last on the early morning of the third day his horse was seen wandering in the vicinity of the spring.

Jim was found, cut down and given water, little by little, until he was able to talk. Then to their horror they realized that nothing could be learned from him, he merely babbled of water and juicy apples. Many weeks passed before he became at all rational and could give any sort of a clear account of what had happened at the spring.

The torture of Tantalus suffered by Uncle Jimmie could not have been greater if, as it was at first supposed, they had been inflicted by the savage Apaches, but when it was finally learned that the Indians were innocent and supposedly civilized white cowboys were the guilty parties the rage of Jim's companions was without bounds and reprisals against the torturers were demanded. By that time it was too late to take vengeance on them for the criminals had left the country as they knew that while murder might be condoned, torture so great that it caused a man to lose his mind would not be taken lightly.

Although Uncle Jimmie lived to be an old man, to the day of his death his mind was never the same as it had been and he could never talk about his experience in the cottonwood tree without trembling and weeping.

Some Tales from the Past: Rustlers and Romance

by B. W. K.

It was the second day of the cattlemen's convention. The streets of Roswell resounded with the click of high-heeled boots and the jingle of spurs. In the hotel lobby a bunch of old-timers lolled in the chairs, and all evening I had been trying to get old Jess Wilson started on a story. Three trips to the bar didn't help much. It was only when I forked over a sweet-smelling two-bit cigar that he finally loosened up.

"Cattle rustlers?" he repeated, in answer to my question. "Well, I've horned into 'em several times, son. Once I took three of the dad-burned jaspers all by my lonesome."

I settled back in the big rocker, waited while he puffed to get the cigar going.

"Don't recollect the year it was," he resumed. "But I was much younger them days. Had a job with the old Circle Dot outfit, down below Alamogordo in the Sacramento hills. We'd been loosin' stock right along, but it was kinda mysterious-like. And mystery generally burns a feller up. It got under all our hides. Us boys got to be a bunch of mangy hornets. We'd eye each other like as if we suspected each other.

"Well anyway, we hunted and scoured the country south for miles, figurin' of course that the stuff was bein' shoved over the border into Mexico. No sign—no tracks—You'd think the critters had wings and flew off the ranch. The biggest puzzle was how they got through the four-wire fences without wires bein' cut or pulled down.

"I had to make a trip to El Paso for the boss, but when I got back I decided to examine every damn post on the place. Figured maybe a couple posts were loose so's they could be lifted to raise the wires. The boys kidded me plenty. Said they'd furnish me with a peach limb like some fellers use when they go to dig a well. They got to callin' me Posthole Johnny. But I kept right on. At night I'd mark my last post an' next day take up where I'd left off. Maybe you don't think there's a lot of posts all the way round a ten thousand acre ranch. Why, that's enough posts to give a sawmill the headache.

"An' then—One day I came across somethin'. Yes sir, there was a post with two rows o' staples nailed into it. Between the staples the wires had been cut in two. The varmits had cut the wires down along the post where it wouldn't show up hardly a-tall. Then they'd staple the cut ends together on the post, like nothin' had been fooled. We'd been looking for patched wire, not for a neat job o' double staplin'.

"I started looking for tracks. Damn my hide if there was 'ary a thing round there but sheep tracks. The ground was all chopped up with 'em. Tim Mosley had a raft o' sheep on an adjoining place, so at first I figured he'd been lettin' the sheep run on our grass. But that was out, 'cause there was no call for cuttin' the wires. Sheep could get under the low wire with hardly loosin' a hair. No, Tim hadn't cut the wires to let his sheep in. It set me to thinkin', though. There was too many tracks in that one spot to satisfy my curiosity. I began to put two and two together.

"'Sheep tracks,' I says, 'will *cover up* cow tracks!'"

"Beyond our fence the tracks spread all over creation. But I began cuttin' sign an' 'fore long I saw where our stock had been taken. Dark was comin' on. I didn't have time an' didn't want to ride all the way back to get some of the boys, 'specially when they'd been kiddin' the daylights out o' me. So I rode alone. Now and then the tracks was plain as everything, in places where the ground was kind of soft. But it soon got rocky an' the marks disappeared. I knew by now where they was heading for—Devil's Canon. There was a pass through the canon like you was goin' north. It wound up in a sort of old crater which was pretty well filled with grass most of the time.

"That's what fooled us fellers all while we'd been huntin'. Here was our stuff bein' taken north, 'stead of south toward the border. Them slickers drove due north like they was goin' somewhere else; but it was plain now that they would reach the old crater an' after that they could loop around through Dead horse Canon, an' bring the trail back south again. Pretty good it was. A swell idea.

"All the while my pony was stickin' to the trail like a magnet, ramblin' as fast as he could in the rough goin'. It was dark now an' quiet as all get out. No sound 'cept a couple crickets that was tunin' up for the night. All to once I hears a faint 'baaw' of a two year-old. It was a long ways off. Pancho heard it too, but that pony had more sense than two ordinary men. I'd almost swear he knew I was after rustlers an' he just couldn't wait to find 'em. Pretty soon I knew we was gettin' close. There was a certain feelin' that's hard to explain. Besides, Pancho's ears were twitchin' an' he was sniffin' — now and then I'd get a whiff of smoke. Campfire! When it got plenty strong I left Pancho in a clump of alder an' took a sneak forward to see what I could see.

"The trail narrowed down where it dropped into the big crater basin. Down there was a bunch o' cattle. You could hear 'em millin' round an' makin' the usual grazin' noises. Didn't take long to size things up. Beyond where I lay there was a ledge that ran around toward the far side of the big crater. This cap rock dropped down straight like a wall probably a dozen feet to the bottom. And down there was a smolderin' campfire. While I was watchin', a feller got up an' threw fresh wood on the fire.

"In them days I wasn't 'fraid of nothin' with hair, horns, or shootin' irons. It's a wonder I didn't tackle that rustler right off the bat. But I didn't. For once I used my head. Somethin' made me go slow — somethin' kinda funny — the sudden yowling of a bobcat somewhere ahead of me. A long powerful howl it was. It nearly made me swaller my chew-tabac. First off I thought maybe it was a signal of some kind. But no, the varmit down by the campfire jumped and ran for his rifle. He began cussin' an' beafin' like he'd been hit by a bee or somethin'. I knew then it were no signal. It was a bobcat for sure an' I knew this bozo was scared stiff. That put him down in my mind as maybe some city crook, out of El Paso, hired to help snake the stuff across the Rio Grande.

"He was rarin' to shoot, that was certain. He was ready to plug his own shadow if it moved — showin' he was a nervous type and all that. But I saw a chance to have some fun.

"Maybe you remember some years ago when this radium stuff first came on the market? Remember how they put it on clocks an' made radium watches an' such truck? Well, among other things they made little glass balls with a bit of radium stuff inside so's you could hang 'em on the electric light cord and see it in the dark. I saw some in El Paso on that trip and bought a couple. You see, in them days I happened to be sweet on Eileen Mahoney. She was one o' them black-eyed Irish girls that make a cowpoke talk tongue-tied in his sleep. I hadn't asked her the big question yet, but—

"Well, anyhow, I had them radium things made up into ear-drops for Eileen. At a jewelry shop in El Paso they fixed 'em up so's they made swell-lookin' earrins. In the dark she'd have ear-drops that glowed like lightnin' bugs! Maybe you're wonderin' where all this gits in with cattle rustlers. But you'll see.

"That night while I was watchin' this poor scared cow thief, I remembered them ear-drops. They are still in my shirt pocket in the little box. I carried 'em with me in case I got a chance to ride over to Eileen's house. But I took the two pendants out an' looked at 'em. They flowed like a million bucks. An' that's just what I wanted. Like a snail I began to crawl out an' around on the rocky ledge till I got past the feller down by the campfire. Had to be careful not to knock pebbles loose. He'd mistake me for a wildcat an' make a sieve out of my carcass with that rifle. So I was real careful and kept goin' till I found a crevice in the rock wall. In this crack I fastened the ear-drops. Spaced 'em just about as far apart as the eyes of a big cat. Say! they did look natural—kinda skeery—glowin' there in the dark. From a distance you'd swear some animal was lookin' at you.

"I crept back till I was almost right above that jasper. Pretty soon I picks up a small rock and tosses it over there toward them glowing eyes. The rock fell an' made a clatterin' noise. It could a-been a cat scramblin'. Anyway, that rustler spun around at the sound an' he spied them big eyes first thing.

"Bang! Bang! Bang!

"He let a flock of shots fly before he knew what he was doin'. An' cuss-say, he could do it nice an' fancy. I was a-chucklin' to myself, an' after a minute I threw another pebble. Again he let loose with the rifle. A couple more *cracks*, an' then the hammer clicked on a dead shell or else the magazine was empty. He started to reload, but I didn't wait any longer. Like a puma I jumped an' landed right smack at his feet. Scared? Why he was simply paralyzed!

"'Paw for the stars, you son of a gun,'" I says to him, and in a minute I had him hog-tied. I asked him a lot of questions. But all he'd say was, 'Go to hell.'

"Just for that I tied a meal sack over his mouth. Didn't gag him. Fixed it so's he couldn't start yellin' in case his compadres came along. Then I dragged him into the shadows, pitched another log on the fire an' set down to wait. Sure enough, an hour or so later I heard the clatter of rocks on the trail an' two other buzzards came ridin' into camp. In a jiffy I had 'em covered. An' were they surprised!

"I made one of 'em tie the other's hands with a rope from their bed roll. Then I roped the third one myself, and hustled back to the Circle Dot to tell the boys. Everybody was asleep, but they sure piled out o' their bunks with a whoop an' went a-peltin to bring in the rustlers an' the stolen stock.

"I had one more job to do. I rode over an' nabbed Tim Mosley to make the night's job complete. Tim was in with them, an' his sheep was a part of the whole scheme.

"The next day, bein' a Sunday, I dropped around for Eileen. We both rode back over the trail and found them pendants, still hangin' on the wall where I'd put 'em . . ."

Old Jess paused and nodded toward a pretty woman who had just come downstairs and stood waiting beside the hotel desk.

"There she is. *That's* Eileen—waitin' for me to take her to a pitcher show. Golly—them ear-drops sure worked a miracle. She's been the missus ever since!"

Source of Information: American Guide Series, *Over the Turquoise Trail*, Compiled by The Workers' Federal Writers' Project of the Works Progress Administration.

Cowboy Hardships

by Mrs. Belle Kilgore

I was teaching near Ranger Lake (Long. 103 Lat. 331½), Lea County, New Mexico during the first part of 1917 and boarded with Mr. Boss Beal's family. It was a severe cold winter, and the cattle men were having a great deal of work to do to keep the cattle from drifting into the hills south and west. The cattle were weak and the grass was short, so it was necessary to keep them where they could be fed.

"Of course, now since there are so many fences," he said, ". . . smaller pastures, we do not have the trouble that we had in the country twenty or thirty years ago." Ranger Lake had been headquarters for a ranch operated by the Beal Brothers.

"The first drift fence that was built by the XIT syndicate company was operated by the company that built the Texas Capitol building in 1886. This fence was built west from the State Line Fence and built to keep the cattle from drifting into the southwest of New Mexico. Every year thousands of range cattle from Colorado, Kansas and northern parts of Texas and New Mexico would go as far south as they could. These herds were great by the time they reached the cap rock between here and Roswell."

Joe Cook and Jim Rogers were cowboys from one of the headquarters of the LFD, which was located south of Littlefield, Texas. These boys were sent out to New Mexico with others to turn their cattle towards the southeast course into Texas. But they could not handle their herd, with the straggling cattle that came and there was no way to turn them against the north and east winds, and the driving snows and rains. Tim took a bad cold and Joe had to take care of him and so on the cattle drifted. Joe and Tim housed up in a small shack that had been built by some trappers near Portales Springs. At night Joe sat by Tim expecting every breath to be the last, fearing to leave him for fear he would come back and find Tim dead. So for several days they stayed in the cabin without food and medicine.

Tim said, "Joe, you are starving, and I am dying, so you go and see if you can find something to eat, and get help." Joe refused at first, but Tim when in his rational moments begged so hard that at last Joe consented to go for help. The day was cloudy, but the snow was not so thick in the air as it had been for the last three days. Joe placed all the fuel he could find in the cabin near an old stove and put water where Tim could get it.

"So long, old chap," said Joe, "I'll be back with somethin' to chaw," and leaving his partner whom he did not expect to find alive again, he headed due east; as he rode the snow came thicker and the wind blew harder, but on he went as fast as his hungry horse could travel. When night came on he stopped in a clump of bushes and he had no idea where he was, he had lost all sense of direction. He tethered his horse on the windward side of the bushes and huddled up in the center of the thicket. He passed the night nearly froze and in his dreams he could see Tim's white face, and dream of good things to eat and warm fires. He was awakened by the whinnying of his horse, at early dawn. The horse was throwing his head around and looking in the direction of the northeast. "What is it, Blue?" asked Joe. "Well, if you know where we're going, you know more than I do." The horse started in the northeast direction and seemed to be anxious to go. They traveled perhaps about five or six miles, when Joe noticed tracks in the snow, horse tracks and cattle tracks, as if they were being driven. In a short time he knew by the increased number of tracks that some cowboys must be not far away. At last, he saw a smoke in the distance. The horse which was nearly past traveling headed that way, but staggered. Joe dismounted and led the horse, staggering as he went, but he was set on reaching that camp fire. He began to halloo and he sighted some cowboys, who had heard his calls. The boys came loping towards him.

"Hie, there, Joe Cook, you Ol-sun-uv-a-gun, we've been huntin' for you and Tim for a week. Where did you hide yooself? Bi, gosh, boys, he's dead," and Will Green ran up to him and picked him up. "He's starved and froze to death." They carried him to the fire and put him down on some saddle blankets, "Get him some whiskey, boys," and they poured all the whiskey that they could get down him. "Get some of that hot coffee, and git him somethin' to eat." And the boys worked on him until he was fed and warm. He told them that Tim was awful sick, "He's pro'bly dead by now," and dropped his head in his hands and sobbed. "Now, Joe, tell us where we can find Tim and we'll bring him back sound and you git some sleep you'self." Two cowboys went for a doctor, and several of the boys took food and blankets to bring in Tim. When they got there Tim was unconscious. They revived him soon and gave him hot food and the next morning, they put him on a horse and rode twelve miles, each one of them holding him. They did not expect him to be alive when they reached the camp, but he did not seem any worse, and soon the doctor from the ranch had him and Joe doped out and they were put in a chuck wagon and taken back to headquarters.

Through the two weeks of severe weather, the cowboys could do nothing but take care of the cattle and horses at the headquarters. When the storm broke, Joe and Tim were about recovered and they went on the roundup below Portales Springs. A rider from below Tatum came up and told them that the drift fence had been cut and thousands of cattle had fallen off the caprock and cowboys could make good money skinning the frozen cows. Cowboys and men from all over the country went down and as hides were bringing better money than steers, the wholesale skinning began. The brands were some of them well known and some of them were traced back up in Colorado and Kansas and Oklahoma. But to the skinner belonged the hide, though he had to have a bill of sale to the hide. This caused considerable trouble for some brands were not located. Well, that was a spring when all the boys had a little money even if the cowman did lose.

Old State Line Fence: From
Evening News-Journal, Clovis, New Mexico

by Mrs. Belle Kilgore

Fifty-two years ago the Capitol Reservation Land company of Chicago, which built the present Texas state capitol in return for 3,050,000 acres of land in the western tier of counties in the Texas Panhandle, enclosed its big domain in the first barbed-wire fence in this part of the country.

That same fence, 260 miles of it extending along the New Mexico–Texas border is still standing. And not only is it still standing, but it is just as tight today as when it was stretched in 1885! In a few places it is covered by drifting sand, and the "nesters" have stolen several miles of it. But miles and miles of it are still used to turn cattle.

Anybody who is interested in this old "state line fence," as it is called, may find plenty of it about 17 miles north of Texico-Farwell near the Pleasant hill community. It's a five-strand fence, with heavy twisted wire "stays" between the posts to add strength.

The cedar posts are 30 feet apart, and only occasionally does one find a post that has been put there in recent years to replace an old one. Most of the original posts are still as solid as the day they were put in.

Wire Made Differently

The wire can readily be distinguished from barbed wire used nowadays. It is heavier, in the first place, but the most noticeable feature is the unusual length of the barbs. Time has turned this wire dark but corrosion has caused such damage that the fence looks good for another half century.

J. Everett Haley in his famous book, *The XIT Ranch of Texas*, writes:

"By the fall of 1886, the Syndicate (as the Capitol Reservation Land company was called) had contracted and put up 781½ miles of fence. The west line fence with all its "jogs" was 260 miles long. It began at the northwest corner of the state and ran south 150 miles without a turn. The east line was 275 miles long, and line riders watched 575 miles of outside fence. Estimates place the material in this fence at over 300 carloads. It cost $181,000."

Had 1,500 Miles of Fence

"All syndicate land was enclosed late in 1886, except about 35,000 acres, which were not fenced immediately because of the hope of exchanging for state land lying inside of the enclosed Syndicate land. By the late nineties cross fences cut the XIT into 94 pastures, making a total of about 1,500 miles of fence. This wire in single strand would have stretched for over 6,000 miles.

"Besides the wire, over 100,000 posts, five carloads of wire stay, and one car of staples were required. So many gates were necessary in the corrals and along the fences, that the first manager just ordered a carload of gate hinges. Line riders rode these fences periodically, some of the divisions kept 'fence wagons' running all the time, and regular 'fencers' kept the lines in repair."

First Fence in Big Area

Haley says that Bill Metcalf, an old buffalo hunter and frontiersman, contracted to build the northern fence of the syndicate, and that J. M. Shannon, then a Scotch sheepherder but now one of the richest men in Texas, built those in the south. He does not record, however, who built the state line fence. Geo. F. McLean, an early settler in Curry county whose land adjoins this fence 18 miles north of Texico, says he was told that "a man named Ellsworth" erected it.

Before 1885, there wasn't a single sign of a fence in the western part of the Texas Panhandle, much less in Eastern New Mexico. Even after the XIT lands were fenced, there wasn't a strand of barbed wire between the Texas line and the Rio Grande river in central New Mexico—and probably a lot farther than that. There was more cattle on the New Mexico side of the line, however, than the XIT and other big outfits operated under fence on the other side.

Cattle Business Booming

The cattle business was in its heyday in Eastern New Mexico in the 1890s, although there was only a handful of men to work them. The animals ranged unrestricted from the Texas border to the Capitan mountains and the Pecos river.

Late in the 90s, a few drift fences were built to keep the cattle from travelling too far south in the winter, but the government was continually forcing the ranchers to take these fences down because they were on the public lands. All of these drift fences were tied onto the state line fence on the east.

Beginning Of The End

Fences built by the XIT spelled the beginning of the end of the open range in this section. The great influx of settlers didn't come until over 20 years later, but those barbs, which so many old-timer cowmen doubted would hold the wild cattle of those days, scratched deeply into the pages of the Southwest, as well as into the hide of many a "critter."

The Staked Plains' Stories (Excerpts)
Evening News-Journal, Clovis, New Mexico, June 1, 1936

by Mrs. Belle Kilgore

"The Locoed Immigrant Colony"

He said, "I expect I have witnessed the most unique tragedy ever pulled off on the great staked plains.

"I was holding down a job with the DZ outfit and it was back when hundreds of Texans were droughted out in Texas and a colony of immigrants passed by on the old immigrant and cattle trail going west every few days.

(This old trail began at Fort Concho, Texas, went to Fort Sumner, New Mexico and then on to Arizona. It crossed the staked plains coming from the east to the west and ran across the plains for some 300 miles lengthways with the Pecos river to the south.)

"I remember one afternoon one of the colony asked me about the grass and water ahead and I told them of a rainwater hole ahead several miles in a hard pan basin. It was in one of those fine loco valleys with loco big enough to mow.

"I thought then that I should have warned them not to let their stock have access to the loco; but I didn't.

"Well, what do you think? The second day after that a fellow came into my camp on a run and said, 'Get the boys together or there will be hell to pay over yonder.'

"I said, 'What is the matter?'

"He replied, 'Why that whole damn immigrant family is drunk on loco and rambling around on the prairie. You know why, without being told. You know in Texas the people are wild about their wild greens such as polk and lambsquarter. They thought this loco was lambsquarter and you can see the results.'

"We rushed off down there and commenced rounding them in. Some of them had become outlaws. We roped and tied them down and left them until we could get the milder ones."

Someone asked the question, "How long were they sobering up?"

"Oh," he said, "I think the second day we had all of them rounded up and the teams hitched up and our boss sent me along as one of the escorts to pilot them to the west side of the Pecos where it was too dry for loco."

Then someone asked, "Did you have any more trouble with them?"

"Yes," he replied "when passing the Tierra Blanco we went through another one of those loco valleys. It was hard to ride herd on them and keep them from breaking out."

We asked him if he was sure the immigrants were from Texas and he replied they might have been from Arkansas.

Then one of the boys wound up by asking Giles if he was through and saying: "We were telling facts, but can't help but think that you have taken advantage of us by having the last shot. We are not going to call you a liar, but believe you have handled the truth in a very careless manner."

Mocking Bird Springs

"It was in 1887, that I made my first trip to the Llano Estacado with several other Texas men. I liked the country, for the land was a sea of green grass and looked as if would be easy to farm. I spent the year working for the XIT and other big ranches. In the late fall I went back to east Texas and made preparations to come west and take up some of the land that would soon be open for settlement.

"In the spring of 1888 I made the second trip, and was accompanied by a boy who stopped at the ranch now known as the Spur headquarters, just below the caprock east of Crosbyton, Texas.

"I had secured two small barrels and filled them with water every time I came to a watering place. For two days I had a pleasant journey. The days were warm and the wind was calm. The nights were cool and the stars were the brightest that I had ever seen. At night I really enjoyed the howl of the coyote, the noises of the badger and other night animals. I saw no one. There were prairie chickens and antelopes, along with prairie dogs and ground squirrels.

"On the morning of the third day a sandstorm rolled up. It was clear and bright when I broke camp that morning, but I could see a red haze in the west and by ten o'clock I could not see how to drive and the horses could not face the wind. So I stopped on the bald prairie, tied my horses on the windbreak side of the wagon and crawled under my 'tarp' and tried to sleep. The sand was so heavy that I could not see twenty feet from the wagon. All day and night for two days and nights it did not cease. I could not feed the horses anything but corn, for it would blow anything away if it was loose. I dared not make a fire. I finally had to quit smoking my pipe for I was afraid that I would set my bedding afire. I ate cold food and drank cold water. The water in the barrels was giving out. On the morning of the third day the wind had nearly ceased, so I started to travel. I had lost all sense of direction except that I was going in a westerly direction. I do not know how far I traveled that day for there was nothing but dry grass on the prairie. At night I camped, watered the horses very meagerly, built a fire and made coffee, smoked and went to sleep early, for during the previous days and nights I could not rest or sleep for I wondered if I would ever see my family again, or if I would ever be able to find my way to ranch headquarters. Next morning I found out that the water had nearly all leaked out of the barrel, but I harnessed my horses and traveled until the horses gave out. It was very hot and the sun blazed down on the earth without any breeze. I camped that afternoon and waited until the moon rose, and then started west.

"The next day there was no water, no food, for me or the horses. I could not see anything for another sandstorm came up but soon passed on, and about two o'clock, I suppose, I rested the team, no grass, no feed, no water. I found a dry biscuit in my grub box, and drained a cup of water from the barrel. I sat down on the opposite side of the wagon from my horses for I could not look at them.

"Sitting there on my heels, my back against the wagon wheel with the cup of water between my feet, I drowsily nibbled the crust of bread.

"Suddenly I heard a 'tweet, tweet' and thought that I must be dreaming. Again came that note a little nearer, 'Tweet, tweet,' and I saw a speck in the sky flying directly toward me.

"The bird flew straight toward the wagon and lighted on the cup of water, drank several sips, twitched its tail and wings, saying 'tweet, tweet' as if it were saying 'thanks, thanks' and then with a final goodbye it rose into the air singing and flying due west, it seemed to me. I watched it as far as I could see it and it sang as it flew its song of gratefulness. Old and hardened as I am, it makes the tears come into my eyes when I think of that mocking bird, being wafted away from its home during the days of sand storm.

"'Well, boys,' I said to my tired, hungry and thirsty horses, 'we are going to follow that bird.' So I hitched them up and started in the direction that the bird flew. I came across a trail leading in that direction and followed it as fast as the horses could travel. I saw a mirage, in front of me, and I dared not take my eyes off it; I think the horses saw it too. We had traveled about six miles, and then as we went on the mirage changed into a reality, for we could see the tops of trees and then a bank or cliff covered with trees and shrubs. Soon we came to the edge of a canyon and on the other side were the green trees, with water trickling out of the bank underneath them; it flowed into a rock-lined lake. I unfastened the traces and got my cup, saying to the horses, 'Old boys I'll go down and test the water, and if it is good you shall have all you want to drink.' I had heard that in some parts of the west the water was alkali and would kill the stock. I went to the edge of the pool and dipped my cup in the running stream which was as clear as crystal. How delicious it was, how cool and satisfying! I knew it was pure for there was no alkali deposit anywhere near, and the grass and flowers were growing everywhere. I hastened to bring the horses down and let them drink some, not all they wanted, but turned them loose on the grass.

"As I stood contemplating the scene, giving thanks in my heart, a song burst from the trees, and soon flying and singing just over my head came the bird of the early afternoon. He sang and whirled and then settled on a tree very near me, sang as only a mocking bird can sing, with joyous abandonment, and then flew back to the tree. 'He has a mate there and she is covering her eggs,' I said to myself. Words fail me when I try to tell how I felt, for I thought of my family and how near death I had been, when I was saved by a famished bird.

"I spent the night there and all through the night I could hear the song of the bird. Next morning I walked toward the grove of trees from whence came the song and there hidden in the leaves sure enough was a nest, and the mate was sitting on the nest, while the mocking bird was singing in a tree nearby. He flew straight up and sang, then flew over me singing as he went.

"I called the place 'Mocking Bird Spring,' and as I traveled next morning, I could think of nothing else. I took a northwesterly trail and followed on the east side of the canyon as far as I could, then the ground grew so rough that I had to turn toward the east, when I came into a worn trail and was soon met by some cowboys, who told me that I was about a hundred miles from the headquarters. I went with them to the ranch where they were working. This place is anywhere between the caprock of Texas and the Pecos River, for when I at last got back to the Yellow House headquarters, the boys could not tell me just what place I had been for they did not know how far south or west I had gone.

"In my dreams I see that place, I hear that bird, and taste that life-giving water," and Mr. Groves would sit silent for some minutes before he would tell more of his early days on the Llano Estacado.

Sources of Information: Jack Potter; The *Evening News Journal*, Clovis, New Mexico; B. O. Groves, Lubbock, Texas. Mr. Groves lives about sixteen miles northwest of Lubbock and has lived there since 1891, for he said it was two years before he moved his family. He was still living last year, although he was very feeble. He told me this story and it has more pathos and drama in it than anything I have ever heard on the plains or in the west. My telling it of course has detracted from it because I cannot tell it as he told it, and the personality is lost by having to repeat it. But where are Mocking Bird Springs? There are several springs very much like the place he describes, but some of them seem too far west or too far north to have been the place he camped.

Branding cattle at Box S Ranch, New Mexico, Ben Wittick, ca. 1880–90, NMHM/DCA #015620

Mavericks

by Reyes Martinez

Many years ago, before the advent of the threshing machine into Taos County, some people were engaged in the business of raising large herds of horses. It was a fairly good paying business and, in later years when oxen went out of use, quite profitable. From these herds the farmers of the locality were supplied with draft teams and saddle horses. There was, also, a good demand in the fall of the year for "Las Lleguas" (the mares), as the horses, collectively as a herd, were called, for threshing wheat and oats; the owner charging ten per cent of the threshed grain as his fee. The horses were grazed most of the year on the public domain and were rounded up once or twice a year for the purpose of branding the colts, or bringing them to the villages to use them for threshing grain. When threshers came into use, they gradually replaced the horses for the purpose. This caused quite a lessening of interest in the horse-raising business. The owners turned their herds loose on the prairies west of the Rio Grande, and at first rounded them up once a year for the purpose of branding the colts and bringing over to the village some of the best specimens, to sell or break to the harness or the saddle, finally losing all interest in them and leaving the herds to roam the prairies at will, unmolested. This caused, in the few years following, an increase of unbranded horses, or "mavericks," that became so wild that near approach to them was almost an impossibility. They seemed to have developed such a keen sense of watchfulness, that rarely, if ever, were they caught unawares.

Previous to this time, when the owners tended their herds, no one not an owner of the herd was allowed to take in and brand a maverick, as he had no recognized legal way of claiming ownership to it. In the latter years, when the herds were permanently released by the owners, anyone who could catch one or more mavericks established ownership to them by placing his brand on them. To catch them required swift and untiring saddle horses. Never less than five or six persons "went to the mavericks." The herds, upon the approach of the men, always ran from the prairies to the wooded sections for cover. The men would then strive to drive them into the open again, so as to lasso them on the run with their lariats; and many a rider was knocked off his horse by the low limb or branch of a tree which allowed not enough space below it for both rider and horse to pass.

Once into the open, a merry chase started. Clouds of dust marked the course of the chase. Some of the riders would try to flank the herd on both sides, while the others brought up the rear. Over the uneven prairies, marked by shallow arroyos and treacherous prairie dog holes, into which many a saddle horse placed its forefeet, turning a somersault, sometimes seriously injuring its rider. Sometimes the herd circled right back to the wooded sections and dispersed among the trees, becoming lost to the riders and their already exhausted mounts, thus ending a fruitless chase for the day. But when luck was on their side and the horses were driven far from the wooded sections, the chase resulted in the capture of several mavericks, either lassoed on the run or chased to exhaustion. Sometimes the herd was driven into a semi-circular enclosure, that had been previously fenced in by means of felled trees and branches. Inside of these semi-circular enclosures several trees were left standing purposely so that the horses would not notice the barrier beyond. Once inside, the men lassoed as many as they could, the rest breaking through or jumping over the barrier; and there were some fine looking horses caught. A wild horse that has grown to maturity on the range, unhampered by human handling, is a beautiful sight to behold. The condition coincident to its wild life cause it to attain a more lithe body, a sleeker coat of hair, more grace and loose of movement and a keener sensitiveness, in marked contrast to its domesticated kin. The return of the men from the chase was an interesting sight to behold, the young fellows especially, wearing leather chaps, high-heel boots and big sombreros, their red or blue bandanna handkerchiefs knotted loosely about their necks, clinking their spurs as they proudly drove their strings of mavericks, linked together by ropes, in a row, through the winding roads of the village. The following day the mavericks were branded. Then the breaking of some of the horses to the saddle was in order. This was an interesting performance, always watched by quite a number of spectators. To saddle a bronco was a risky proposition, one not to be undertaken except by an experienced hand. Many a time a prancing steed would rear on its hind legs, upon feeling the weight of the saddle on its back, pawing the air furiously with its front feet, sometimes striking even an experienced handler on the thigh or knee, inflicting severe injury.

With the passing of the years, these herds of wild horses finally disappeared from the ranges of Taos County. Most of them were taken by horse-rustlers and sold in Colorado, and the last remnants of them were killed by trappers for use as coyote bait.

The Raiders

by Ernest Prescott Morey

In the southeastern part of Grant County lies the Mimbres Valley. In this Valley is located an old ranch, one of many, which may be found in this spot. The ranch, which I am going to tell you about, is called the White Horse Ranch. It is situated by a small laguna (lake), surrounded by large mimbres trees (from which the valley, Mimbres, takes its name), oak trees and by various kinds of shrubbery. In the year of 1880, this ranch was owned by John McKinne, who at that time was thirty-eight years old. Living on this ranch with him, was his wife, Molly, who was thirty-six and their two small sons, Jim and Martin. Jim was twelve years of age and Martin was eighteen.

John McKinne ran a small spread (number of cattle) and raised their feed, as well as the vegetables for his own table. At this time, there were many settlers from the surrounding country who lived close by to protect themselves from the terrible Apache Chief, Victorio, and his band of braves.

Victorio, in the year of 1879, had left the Mescalero Reservation and gone on the warpath. For the next four years he spread terror throughout this region and also in Arizona. Victorio was killed in 1883, then came Geronimo, another Apache Chief. He had fled from the San Carlos Reservation, in Arizona. He, like Victorio, led a band of Apache braves and outlaws. These Apaches and outlaws knew every trail, water hole and mountain pass in New Mexico and southern and northern Arizona. Both Victorio and Geronimo, with their murderous raiders, had succeeded in beating off and keeping out of the way of American and Mexican forces, many times larger than their own.

In the fall of the year of 1880, the McKinne family and Jim Swartz's wife, were seated at the table eating their supper. It was almost at twilight. The lamps had not been lit, yet. The sun had sunk behind the mountains. The sky had a red, orange and pink-blue glow, that is seen in the sky in the western states. The surrounding valley and slopes of the mountains were tinted with a purple haze, which tints every object that it falls upon, with every color of the rainbow. Young Martin, who was artistically inclined, always appreciated the sunsets and usually made some remark about them. He had just finished describing the colorful outdoors, when looking out of the window from his seat at the table, he saw a large band of Indians coming toward the house. He cried out to the rest of the family: "Here comes Victorio and a lot of his braves!"

Everyone jumped up from the table. The women folks ran out of the front door to a small arroyo (ditch) about a hundred yards from the house. The house, out buildings and corral being between the Indians and the fleeing women, gave them the opportunity to escape.

The two boys sought shelter in the house—Martin, going to a closet in the kitchen, and Jim, to hide under the bed in a back bedroom.

In just a few minutes, the Indians dismounted at the house and began their plundering. Young Martin was soon located and dragged from his hiding place in the kitchen closet. He was very brave and because he defied the raiders, one of the Apache scouts slew him with a tommy-hawk, scattering his blood and brains all over the kitchen floor. Shortly afterwards, Jim was dragged out before Victorio, and shown his brother, who laid dead on the kitchen floor. He was so stunned by the sight that he could not cry.

For some reason or other, the great Chief, Victorio, took a great liking to Jim, and after he and his braves had finished their raiding, he took him away with them.

Several hours afterwards, Mrs. John McKinne and Mrs. Jim Swartz left their hiding places and returned to the house. Darkness had taken control of the valley. Lighting the lamp, they discovered the body of poor Martin on the kitchen floor. They then began the search for little Jim, but both women, after frantic calling and searching, gave up in despair.

Hours after, dawn began to break over this beautiful valley and the frightened and distracted women looked through the window of the kitchen, watching for their husbands. About noon, they saw them returning with twenty, or more, other ranchers, who had been tending cattle in Water Canyon for many days. (This canyon was twelve miles from the White Horse Ranch.)

John McKinne was almost prostrate, when he viewed the body of his dead son, Martin. He and his companions set out at once on the trail of the murdering Indians. For three days, they searched, but were unable to locate them. After giving up the hunt, they returned to the valley. John McKinne was a broken man from that day on, because of the murder of Martin, and the unknown fate of little Jim.

In the year of 1883, he lost his mind completely. In that same year, Victorio was killed. Then, Geronimo seemed to take Victorio's place, as well as his own, in raids.

Three more years dragged on, and then, one morning early in the spring of the year, as Mrs. McKinne was washing clothes outside the ranch house, she spied a mounted Indian approaching the ranch. She gave an alarm to several men, who were working in the corral, branding calves. They came running to her. They drew bead on the lone rider and were about to kill him, when he began to call in Spanish, "Madre," ("Mother,") and at the same time, he held his hands up over his head. The workers held their fire and as the rider drew closer, they recognized him. Everyone was dumbfounded, as the rider kept crying, "Madre, (Mother), I have come home."

It was little Jim, returning after six years of living with the Apaches. His mother recognized him, and then fainted. His father, John McKinne, was brought from the ranch house, but he did not know his son, because of his deranged mind.

There was great rejoicing at the White Horse Ranch and little Jim told the story of his capture and kidnapping.

He was taken to the Apache squaws, who were ordered by Victorio to rear him as an Indian. He told his Mother, Mrs. Swartz and various neighbors about his experience with the Indians during the six years of his captivity. He had learned their customs, and had become a great man in the Apache Tribe. He was considered one of their greatest trackers and hunters. He had even learned to speak their tongue, or language.

The degradations of the wild Apaches had ceased in the Mimbres Valley, in the late summer of little Jim's return. The placid waters of the little laguna (lake) that was close by the White Horse Ranch, was disturbed no more by the feet of the Indian ponies. The purple haze of twilight rested on the quiet cattle and large stretches of waving corn. Today the old ranch stands, a great reminder of General Nelson Miles, of the United States Army, capture of Geronimo and his braves.

This story was told to me by Jessie Swartz. She is fifty years old, having been born in the year of 1888, August 30. Her Present address is Mimbres Valley, New Mexico. She receives mail in Silver City also. Mrs. Jessie Swartz is the daughter of Jim Swartz, who came from Germany a little more than seventy years ago.

Jim Swartz was married to Camelia Swartz. She is eight-eight years old. (She told this story to her daughter, Jessie Swartz.) Mrs. Camelia Swartz is still alive. She lives in the Mimbres Valley. Her address is Mimbres Valley, New Mexico. Camelia Swartz was a half sister to John McKinne.

Both John McKinne and Molly, his wife, are dead. He died in 1907, and Molly died in 1910. Their son, young Jim McKinne, about whom this story is written, is living in Clifton, Arizona. His address is Clifton, Arizona.

Corrections on Ernest Prescott Morey—"The Raiders"

Page 1, paragraph 3

To verify, Section 215, page 182, History and Government of New Mexico, by John H. Vaughan.

Page 2, paragraph 1

Neither John McKinne and Jim Swartz were at home; since they had left their families early in the day to herd cattle, in White Water Canyon.

Page 4, paragraph 6

General George H. Crook (Commander of U. S. Army,) stationed on the Mimbres, asked to be relieved of command, in the Spring of 1886. He had been humiliated by the escape of Geronimo. Then, General Nelson A. Miles was given command by President Cleveland. General Miles had many an engagement on the Mimbres with Geronimo, and during this time, this house of John McKinne was used as a barracks by Gen. Miles. (See Sect. 216, page 183 in *New Mexico History and Government* by John H. Vaughn.)

Lea County and Contiguous Plains: The Role of the Horse on the Southern Plains (Excerpt)

by Mrs. Benton Mosley

Plains Cow Horses: Within a decade of the buffalo's extinction the Texas cattle industry had discovered the grazing possibilities of the southern portion of the Llano Estacado. The dug wells of the original squatters were acquired as headquarter locations for the first ranchers. Tough little Spanish ponies brought many herds here, and followed after them almost continuously. During the next quarter century the country witnessed the peak of its open range ranching.

The ranchers' dependency upon horses can hardly be exaggerated, for to these first permanent settlers he was of prime importance to their very existence. The whole order of their lives depended upon horses to take them here and there. Business, pleasure, and life itself depended upon horses. Often a horse must, in dry or still weather, pump water for both man and beast with that old treadmill, the horsepower. Food came from a hundred or more miles away, freighted by horses or mules. Man was often, in camp, dependent upon his horse for company. Small wonder that there was much sentiment and affection for his horse in the cowboy's life. His horse's welfare was his own necessity. Many more horses were required in the days of the open range ranching then since fences keep the cattle within bounds. Each cowboy had his "mount" of eight to a dozen or more ponies. And there were many extra horses on the ranch besides.

Cutting Horses: The epitome of horse sense and agility and training was reached in the "cutting horse" which would pursue any cow or calf designated by his rider quietly but surely through the milling, jamming, or racing herd till he had succeeded in separating the animal from its fellows, be they hundreds or thousands, all very similar. Roping horses and night horses were often well-trained and trusty; but the good cutting horse was all this and more. He possessed a trained intelligence unsurpassed in the horse world, polo ponies not excepted.

Horse raising in this section was generally carried on in connection with cattle ranching in the early days, though there were a few ranchers who raised horses exclusively. Among these earlier horse raisers were

George Causey, Albert Vincent, Chas. Fairweather; also the Jameses and J. M. Daugherty. Cowden Brothers rode seven Spanish mares to the country which they later turned loose on the range to raise horses, and in a quarter century had raised fifty thousand dollars worth of horses from these mares, merely as a side line, besides many horses used on their ranches. G. M. McGonagill was prominent in the horse industry of this section, as was Mrs. Williams of 7HR and her sons, Sug and Cub Roberts. Though almost all the major ranches of the section raised some horses, the Hat Ranch perhaps produced more good saddle horses than any other not exclusively so engaged. And each of these ranches had its own "Horse Camp" tucked away somewhere, in the sand perhaps, that took care of horses not in use during the winters and where a cowboy or two batched throughout that season. Among later growers of horses, in connection with cattle were: the Taylors, Joe Graham, and Oscar Thompson. The Monument section seems always to have been favored with many horses.

Killing the Lobo Wolf

by Colonel Jack Potter

Back in the early days of the open range a tenderfoot walked up to Uncle Billy Follice, a range boss for fifty years, and asked him how long it would take a fellow to learn the cow business.

Uncle Billy answered as follows: "Son, most anyone can learn how to rope and ride in a few months. This means strength and muscle, but not brains. But to learn the cow business a person—why, why, you never get your diploma."

And Uncle Billy was right. To learn the cow business a person must learn how to class the different ages of cattle from a yearling to mature age. In going to market with cattle the beginner must learn how to take care of them and study their habits, and how to keep them gaining flesh while in transit.

The cowman must also know how to cook, how to butcher, and along with that must come the knowledge of how to shoe your own mount, fight prairie fires or raise a poor cow should you find one down in a weakened condition. And before he knows his business he must know how to trap or otherwise snare the most wily of all prairie animals, the lobo wolf.

In the early 1890s when the wolves in our part of the country were particularly destructive, cowboys had definite orders while on circle to round up cattle, to quit the roundup and use every effort to run down and catch wolves should they come in contact with any.

I believe the greatest wolf man at the time was Wolfhound Tanner. He kept a string of fast horses from which to pick his mount and he always had a string of common hounds. These he used not to catch the pests, but just to follow the trail. Tanner would have an extra man to lead a change of horses while he would run the wolves.

Another interesting wolf killer was Jack Callis. He hunted in a different manner from Tanner following roundups and putting out bait.

Probably the prettiest catch I ever saw was in 1894, after we had made our roundup at the coal banks on the Cienega with Buck Miller in charge. He pointed out a big jaw steer to Callis; after a bit we saw

Callis going up the arroyo with the animal. He took him to the mouth of Alamosites Arroyo and shot him behind the shoulders. Before the animal died he injected strychnine into its veins.

The next morning after starting out on the circle following up a trail at the edge of Rabbit Ear Mesa, we found six Lobos dead. They seemed to be about the same age and must have been from a litter born in the spring.

I suppose the mother wolf must have been visiting because it is very seldom that a mature wolf will taste dead meat or allow its young to do so.

Another incident in my own experiences that comes to my mind was one that happened back early in the 1890s at Fort Sumner on the Pecos in New Mexico.

We had just finished our spring roundup when we got orders to take two roundup crews to The Tu-les a watering place on the edge of the plains and to commence a war on the four-legged bandits, the Lobo Wolf. It was the time of the year that the pups would be leaving their lairs. Our orders were to put in twenty days resting our mounts while we destroyed pups and to shoot the old ones when we had a chance. Our camp was established near a spring and an old adobe house and two posses of ten men each were sent out. The posse I was leading rode out through the sand hills for seven miles until we came to a hardpan flat surrounded by Gypsum bluffs several feet high. We soon found a lair and dug into it with pick and shovel and found seven pups. We killed them and kept the scalps as there was a small bounty on them. After scouting around for an hour or two we found the second lair. Here we unearthed five pups. They were almost old enough to leave the lair and no doubt had received a few lessons from their mother. We killed four of them and one of the boys asked for the last one to keep as a pet. He tied a short piece of worn halter rope around its neck and mounted his horse, carrying the pup on the pommel of the saddle. We got back to camp just before dark.

The pup was tied in the old vacant adobe house near the camp and some beef and a pan of water were placed before him. He refused to drink or eat. As we were setting around the campfire that night a wolf came to the top of a sandhill not more the two hundred yards away and commenced a pitiful howling. She kept it up all night.

The next morning fresh water and beef was offered the pup and again he refused to touch it. When the second night came he still had not tasted his food.

At dark while we set around the campfire the mother wolf started her pitiful howling again from the hilltop again.

After listening for a while the owner of the pup got a rope and stake pin and went and got the pup. He took him out about seventy-five yards from the camp and picketed him with a long rope tied to the original short piece. He said, "I'm going to let him nurse his mother." After he came back to the fire and talked about twenty minutes the mother wolf ceased her howling.

We called his attention to this and he went out to see how the pup was getting along. He found the rope had been gnawed into.

The mother had out-generaled us all and had released her pup.

The Battle at the Box S

by L. Raines

The Box S ranch has been an important factor in the development of the western section of Valencia and the southern part of McKinley Counties.

As Mr. Carr, who owned and operated Box S ranch for many years, was returning home one evening his horse shied at an object lying near the road. Mr. Carr saw the body of a Zuni Indian. He had been on friendly terms with the Indians and therefore as he rode on he merely wondered why the body had not been buried. Again his horse shied and he saw an Indian lying by the trail with his face shot away. He quickened the pace of his horse, apprehensive of the safety of his wife, who was at home. When he reached the ranch house he saw that the forest around the bunk house was full of Indians. A Zuni approached and told him that they would not harm him or his family, but some outlaws fleeing with a stolen herd of Zuni horses had been tracked to his bunk house where they had taken refuge. Warriors from Pescado and Nutria had joined the band from Zuni. They had sent for the soldiers from Fort Wingate and were besieging the bunk house after a slight skirmish earlier in the day.

The next morning Jack Pershing, a young officer, and three companions arrived. So sure were the outlaws that they had only Indians to contend with and that they were safe that they kept no watch as they prepared breakfast. Pershing walked up to the bunk house, pushed open the door and placed the outlaws under arrest. The Indians recovered their herd and the outlaws were taken to Fort Wingate.

Source of Information: Mr. E. Z. Voght, Sr., Morgan, Elizabeth, "Brief Sketches of Regional Tales of Western New Mexico," A. M. Thesis, New Mexico Normal University, 1935.

Cattle Shipping and Trading Posts in the Early Days

by Georgia B. Redfield

From 1885 until the middle nineties, Roswell was the cattle center for all the spring round-ups and spring drives to shipping points.

Round-up wagons and cattle and cowboys in their high-heeled boots, leather "chaps" and "ten gallon hats," would come in from the range from as far north as Fort Sumner, and south as Pecos City, Texas a distance of about two hundred and fifty miles. Some of them often had not seen a woman, or a post office or store, for as long as six months or more. Roswell, the "blow-off-town," with its one adobe store lighted by two kerosene lamps with tin reflectors at the back, which were hung at each end of the store, one near the post office which was in a corner of the store, and the one hotel of the town also constructed of adobe, seemed a "City of Bright Lights" to the care-free cowboys so long away from civilization.

The ones who had not disposed of their monthly wage—from twenty five to thirty dollars—would usually engage a "room" at the hotel, which would be a bed in the attic which was sleeping quarters for all guests. Cowboys, doctors, lawyers and an occasional Territorial Governor (George Curry) would share the conveniences or inconveniences, with no favors shown no matter what their social standing might be.

If there were any church meeting during round-up times in Roswell, or "bailes"—it made little difference which to the cowboys—they would be there literally "with bells on" (jingling spurs) which they never removed for church services or the dance. On one occasion, during the song service at church, when the organist (Miss Mabel Brown, or John Stone's little daughter Emma, they took turns at the organ) started out in a beginning of the offertory a cowboy solemnly rose to his feet—nearly everyone thought to sing—but instead, much to the amusement of the congregation, he selected a clear space and began to jig, or danced the clog. Having had a little too much to drink, after seeing his dance was seemingly appreciated, it was a hard job to get him to a seat, and a chance to "pass the hat." Needless to say, the hat was pretty well filled by the tipsy cowboy as well as his companions, who always contributed the lion's share of the collection.

On another occasion, during a revival meeting conducted by Evangelist Abe Mulkey, which the writer of this article attended in the spring of 1894, the cowboys gave liberally toward the collection for paying expenses of the meeting; then the cowboy who had danced in church some months before, seized the largest of the "ten gallon hats," and took up a collection for the church bell. It became known throughout Chaves County as, "The Cowboy Bell," and may be seen today occupying a place of honor on the lawn of the M. E. Church South, on the high terraced corner of Pennsylvania Avenue and Second Street.

When the round-up came to town, it was hailed as enthusiastically with shouts of joy from the young people—"The roundup's coming!"—as I remember shouting, when a child on the Mississippi River when a boat appeared, "The steamboat's coming!" For the "chuck" wagon dinners or suppers, if one was fortunate enough to stand in favor with the cowboys, and knew they would receive invitations to them, were looked forward to eagerly by both young and old people of Roswell.

The round-up wagon, "chuck," is served at the noon meal on pioneer's day at the end of the trail or parade, during the fall every year in Roswell, and the barbecued beef and mutton, "son-of-a-gun," ice cream and coffee, served to the "old-timers" is hard to beat, but somehow it lacks something in flavor—that cannot be reproduced—of the old chuck-wagon meals of stews, prunes, frijoles and sour-dough biscuit cooked on a camp-fire by a chuck-wagon cook.

"There was a slump in the cattle business in 1887, and during the fall of that year the C A Bar Cattle Company," (J. F. Hinkle being manager) "drove a herd of cattle to Tayah, Texas and shipped them to Chicago and they didn't much more than pay the freight, and for the next few years it was almost impossible to sell cattle at any price," said James F. Hinkle.

"One party about that time shipped a train load of steers to market and they drew on him for the loss. During those years we drove one and often two herds of around fifteen to twenty hundred head to market each year and the average price was eight, eleven and fourteen dollars for one, two and three-year-old steers."

Compared with the price in 1868 that John Chisum received, averaging eighteen dollars a head, it seems that the cattle business was not very promising and comparing John Chisum's average price per head with the twenty-five to thirty dollars per head paid at the present time, 1939, the cattle industry has improved and is far ahead of what it ever was expected to be in Southeastern New Mexico.

Source of Information: J. F. Hinkle, Pioneer Cattleman, from a "Cowboy on the Pecos," 1935.

Cowboys in camp, New Mexico, J. R. Riddle, ca. 1880, NMHM/DCA#076013

Cowboys and Early-Day Cow Camps

by Georgia B. Redfield

Very often in the early cattle roundup days, the cowboys on cattle work would not for six months or longer, see any persons outside of the cattle outfit and the camp cook. However, their days in the saddle riding herd and with roping and branding contests and the excitement of stampedes and "bronco busting" were not boring and there was no time for moping and longing for social life in the cattle towns.

Each of the old cattle "punchers" had their own mounts of ten or twelve cow horses from which they had their chief pleasure and fun. "What time they were not rolling cigarettes or talking brands they were bragging about their pet horses."

The old C A Bar outfit had four hundred saddle horses and the cowboys knew the names, color and description of them all. The old cow ponies knew their masters who rode them and were faithful always to them. Snorting and bucking, pitching off strange riders and doing poor cutting and roping work were the ways of showing their displeasure at being handled by others than their own masters.

One time a favorite old night horse fell down with "Jim" Hinkle during a stampede, and Hinkle, landing in a gully, was stuck fast in the mud. The faithful animal seeing his master's predicament came back and rubbed him with his nose.

Next to their favorite cowponies the punchers took particular pride in their boots which they wore with spurs at all times. Boots and spurs were said to have been the sure badge of a cowman.

One time there was a stranger at the chuck wagon and the cowhands coming in asked who he was. On being told the man was a steer buyer the boys replied, you can't make that stick; he's no cattle buyer we know for he's got on shoes."

Every night around the camp fire, the cowboys would have remarkable tales to relate of the appearance of miraculously increasing herds of the "new comers," who were little stock owners on the range.

It had been the custom on the old open range for each ranch owner to brand all the mavericks (stray calves) found on his personal range. This worked very satisfactorily until many new claims appeared throughout the country. On one claim the owner had one cow he called "Old Velvet," to whose credit twenty mavericks in one year were reported by the cowboys. Another had a yoke of oxen, and he was found by the cowboys with twenty-three mavericks.

Good-sized herds were started from mavericks and drifters by many first settlers in Chaves County and even in the little town of Roswell. Those of the town's people who did not raise cattle were annoyed by strays from the range that lay around on the main streets until it finally became necessary to employ cowboys to keep the cattle driven back. Bob Bond, one of the old range men and a Roswell resident at the present time, was one hired for many years to keep range cattle out of the town.

During the early ranch days antelope and deer shared the range with cattle around Rio Hondo, North and South Spring Rivers and the Berrendo Springs. Thousands of cattle watered at the springs four miles south of Roswell, many of these being the drifters into Roswell. The cowboys delighted in roping the deer but the antelope were too swift for them. The horses were well trained in roping.

In the spring after three or four months rest the horses, remembering old days of fun on the round-ups, would start off pitching. One time in particular Jim Hinkle remembers an old horse starting off pretty brisk one morning with four empty saddles. He spurred up to help out and there were five empty saddles pretty "pronto."

It is said by Jack Potter, once a Pecos cowboy who now lives in Clayton, that the cowboys lay awake at night to think up something specially limbering they could do to a tenderfoot. One in particular they didn't like, with a hard boiled shirt and black stiff hat they determined to get rid of pretty quick. They chained a cowboy to a chuck wagon wheel and told the tenderfoot it was a mad man and not to go near him. When the cowboy broke loose at the proper time, the tenderfoot burned the wind making it to town in short order, leaving his stiff hat behind.

None of the large ranches allowed the cowhands to own private brands or cattle. About all a cowboy owned was his saddle, a slicker and bed roll. However, they were carefree and happy, with their practical jokes swapping yarns and range songs.

An old favorite cowboy hymn sung more often than any other and remembered with pleasure after fifty-five years by "Jim" Hinkle is:

"The trail to that bright mystic region
Is both narrow and dim they say,
While the broad one that leads to perdition
Is posted and blazed all the way.
There, I've heard, there'll be a grand roundup
When the cowboys like others will stand
To be cut by the rider of Judgment
Who is posted and knows every brand."

Sources of Information: Captain J. W. James, pioneer cattleman; *Cowboy on the Pecos*, James F. Hinkle, Roswell.

Pioneer Stories: The Collins Family

by Betty Reich

The Collins family lived at the head of the Mimbres River during pioneer days. They were driven from their ranch home by Geronimo and his band of Indian braves. Mrs. Collins was picking ducks in the duck house. The two older children, Jo Ike, between four and five years of age, and Zona, between five and six, had taken the calves to water. They saw the Indians in the popcorn field and ran and told their mother. The Indians were without ammunition. A large bulldog, belonging to the Collins family, charged the Indians and the family was able to escape. The mother took the eight-months old baby, Carl, on her back and ran in one direction—sending the older children in another direction. The children jumped from one bunch of grass to another to keep from leaving tracks. When they got hungry they returned to their home. On the way they met the soldiers who were in pursuit of the Indians. Mrs. Collins and her baby also returned safely.

Source of Information: Mrs. Zona Collins Liggett, Deming, New Mexico.

Farmington (Excerpt)

by R. T. F. Simpson

History: This section of the country was claimed by the Apaches, although Navajos had occupied it for a number of years. When the whites settled here they had no serious trouble with the Indians, although the Indians had been at war with the Mexicans for a time, until Uncle Sam took them in hand and quieted them down. The cowboys proved worse enemies to the farmers than the Navajos and trouble frequently occurred between the various factions of the herders.

The first trouble was occasioned when a drunken cowboy shot an Indian on the street of Farmington in the spring of 1883. Although the man was not killed, the Indians threatened to go on the war path and in two days several hundred Indians surrounded the town, but Gregorio, a friendly Indian, warned the settlers and said if the plowmen and ranchers stayed in their homes they would not be hurt, for the Indians were after the "tejans" or cowboys. After considerable parleying the Indians agreed to await the arrival of the war chief before they began hostilities, and he decided not to make the attack.

Another time, in 1885, Largo Pete, a sub-chief, turned his horses loose in the grain field belonging to W. P. Hendricks. They held a meeting securing an Indian named Costiano for interpreter. Mr. Henderickson and Mr. Lock sent to Fort Lewis for troops which arrived and finally brought the Indians under subjection, the Red-men promising to behave, which was a relief to the settlers.

History of San Juan County

by Janet Smith

The history of San Juan County, although undocumented, is believed to go back a thousand years. There is evidence that at some distant period San Juan County had an immense population, partially civilized. North of Aztec are the ruins of two large communal villages and across the river from Aztec are the ruins of what must have been a city of great size. Along the Chaco are the well preserved walls of stone pueblos of an architecture which bears but little resemblance to that of the New Mexico Pueblo Indians of today. The most famous of these ruins are those at Pueblo Bonito, which has yielded some of the rarest archeological treasures of the Southwest, and the ruins at Chetro Ketl.

There is evidence that the San Juan Basin was well known to the Spaniards in the 18th century. For example, Adolf Bandelier tells of Don Bernardo de Mier y Pacheco, a Spanish captain of engineers, who went upon a scientific and political mission for the Crown in New Mexico. He explored the ruins of the San Juan country, and the Pueblos of the Chaco Canyon interested him greatly. He thought that the fabulous buried golden city of Gran Quivira was located somewhere among these ruins. This idea spread rapidly until "Tío Juan Largo," an old Indian in Socorro, protested against the idea that Quivira could be found in the Northwest of New Mexico, and insisted that it was east of Socorro on the "Mesa Jumana."

The Spanish Trail regularly followed by both New Mexicans and Americans throughout the middle of the 19th century traversed San Juan County, but it was one of those regions never settled by the Spanish.

In 1860 a special charter for a toll road from Abiquiu through Baker City, a settlement started on the plains of the San Juan River, known as the Abiquiu, Pagosa and Baker City Road, was granted. And in 1861 San Juan County was created. However, the breaking out of hostilities between the North and South stopped all efforts to settle the San Juan country until later, and the act was repealed.

In the late sixties, sheep and cattle men began to move in and take possession of the fine grazing country. They came largely from Lincoln and Colfax Counties, having fled these counties in order to escape the sheriff. They made cattle rustling a regular means of livelihood. The most notorious of the rustlers were Ike and Port Stockton, from Colfax County, where they had belonged to the Clay-Allison gang, and Bill Eskridge. The court records are filled with their escapades. The lawless acts of these rustlers were responsible for the trouble between the whites and the Indians. The first of these outbreaks occurred in Farmington in 1883, when a drunken cowpuncher shot, but did not kill, a Navajo. The tribe threatened to go on the warpath and surrounded the settlement. An Indian named Gregorio came in and advised the settlers to remain in their houses, saying that the Indians wanted only a chance at the culprits. Later there were other outbreaks, but no serious trouble resulted. On one instance the Indians were bought off with a small amount of provisions. The unruly cowboys indulged in this form of devilment simply as a means of diversion. When the first regular preacher came to the county from Texas, cowboys shot up the floor around his feet because he refused to take a drink. At Bloomfield during the performance of the first service, a stereoscopic showing of Bible characters, cowboys shot holes in the screen. The sacrilegious attitude of these ruffians was demonstrated as the firing began when the figure of Christ appeared on the screen.

The first permanent white settlement was begun at Farmington late in the summer of '78. In the spring of '77 a store was opened there and in 1880 an Indian trading post was established in a tent. The land now occupied by Aztec was first owned as part of a homestead and later sold to the Aztec Townsite Company. The town made little progress until 1905 when its growth became marked.

Sources of Information: Bloom and Donnelly, *New Mexico History and Civics*; Twitchell, *History of New Mexico*; Bandelier, *Guilded man and other pictures of Spanish Occupation*.

"De Baca County" (Excerpt)

by J. Vernon Smithson

When Fort Sumner was abandoned as an army post and Indian reservation in 1868, it was bought by Lucien B. Maxwell, who, when he sold the Maxwell land grant in the northern part of the state, came to Fort Sumner with his family to live.

Maxwell, used to doing things in a large way, irrigated and farmed the land that had been under cultivation by the Indians. Soon Fort Sumner was known as the "Garden Spot of New Mexico." Maxwell sold his holdings to a group of Colorado cattlemen in 1884, Daniel S. Taylor, Lonny Horn, Sam Doss and the New England Cattle Company.

These men stocked the ranges with cattle. The land and grass was there for all. The only necessity was that of water or water rights, and one could raise all the cattle he wanted to. There were no boundaries or fences in this country in those days.

Consequently the range was soon overstocked and with the coming of some drouthy years, the cattle was unable to live and the owners' losses were appalling. It is said that one could walk from Fort Sumner to Pecos City on the bones of the cattle that died during the drouthy years. With the depression of 1893 coming on top of their other trouble with the drouths and overstocked range, the cattlemen shipped and trailed their livestock to other regions, mainly to Colorado.

From 1893 to 1900, all the cattle had been shipped out of here, or had died and Fort Sumner was again forsaken. There being no caretaker, the buildings had begun falling down and by 1900 there were no complete buildings left standing at the site of old Fort Sumner.

Ranchers at meal with mess kits, D. B. Chase, undated, NMHM/DCA #056991

A Chuck-Wagon Supper

by N. Howard Thorp

A chuck-wagon arrived at Milagro Springs and the cook who was driving it hollered, "Whoa mule!" to the team of four which had been pulling the load. Getting off the seat he threw down the lines and called to the horse wrangler who was with the remuda, saddle horses, following the wagon, to "gobble them up," meaning to unhitch the teams and turn them into the remuda.

The cook now digs a pit behind the chuck-wagon so that when a fire is built the wind will not blow sparks over the camp and the punchers surrounding it. The horse wrangler, with rope down, drags wood for the fire. The many rolls of bedding are thrown off the wagon and the cook brings forth his irons. Two of them are some four feet long, sharpened at one end and with an eye in the other end. The third is a half-inch bar of iron about six feet long.

Having driven the two sharpened irons into the ground above the pit, the long iron is slipped through the eyes of the two iron uprights and this completes the "pot-rack," or stove. Cosi, as the cook is usually called, which is an abbreviation of the Spanish word *Cosinero*, hangs a half dozen or more S hooks of iron about six inches long on the suspended bar and to these are hooked coffee pot, stew pots and kettles for hot water.

The chuck-wagon is always stopped with the wagon tongue facing the wind so that the fire will be protected by wagon and chuck-box. The rear end of the wagon contains the chuck-box which is securely fastened to the wagon-box proper. The chuck-box cover swings down on hinges making a table for the Cosi to mix his bread, cut the meat upon and make anything which may suit his fancy.

There is an unwritten law that no cow-puncher may ride his horse on the windward side of the chuck-box or fire. If he does the Cosi is liable to run him off with pot-hook or axe. This breach of manner would only be committed by some green hand or "cotton picker," as the Cosi would probably call him. This rule is observed so that no trash or dirt will be stirred up and blown into the skillets.

The Cosinero, having built his fire, takes a pot-hook, an iron rod some three feet long with a hook bent in one end, and lifts the heavy Dutch bake-oven lid by its loop and places it on the fire, then the oven itself and places it on top of the lid to heat. These ovens are usually round, about eight inches in depth and some two feet in diameter, but come in all sizes, being used for bread, meat, stew, potatoes, etc. The coffee pot is of galvanized iron, holding from three to five gallons and is left hanging on the pot-rack containing plenty of hot coffee for anyone who wants it.

The Cosi with a huge bread pan begins to mix his dough. After filling the pan about half full with flour, he adds sour dough poured from a jar or tin bucket which is always carried along. Then he adds salt, soda and lard or warm grease, working all together into a dough which presently will become second-story biscuits. After the dough has been kneaded he covers it over and for a few minutes lets it rise. A quarter of beef is taken from the wagon, where it has been wrapped in canvas to keep cool, and slices are cut off and placed in one of the Dutch ovens into which grease, preferably tallow, has been put. The lid is laid on and with a shovel red-hot coals are placed on top. While this is cooking, another skillet is filled with sliced potatoes and given the same treatment as the meat.

Now the bread is molded into biscuits and put into the oven. These are much softer than those made with baking powder and as each is patted out it is dropped into the hot grease of the bake oven and turned over. These biscuits are placed in the oven right together until the bottom of the container is full. Now comes the success or failure of the operation. The secret is to keep the Dutch oven at just the right heat, adding or taking away the right amount of hot coals from underneath the oven or from the top of the lid. If everything goes right you may be assured of the best hot biscuits in the world. Sometimes a pudding is made of dried bread, raisins, sugar, water and a little grease with nutmeg and spices. This is placed in a Dutch oven and cooked until the top is brown.

This is the usual cow-camp meal but if there is no beef in the wagon, beans and chili are substituted.

Along in the evening as the men are through with the day's round-up or drive, tired horses are turned into the remuda and the Cosi hollers, "Come and get it, or I'll throw it out!"

The punchers in their chaps, boots and spurs flock to the chuck-wagon and out of the drawer get knives, forks and spoons and from the lid of the chuck-box a plate and cup which have been laid out by the Cosi. Then they go to the different bake ovens and fill their plates which, like the cups, are made of tin.

Lots of banter usually passes between the punchers and the Cosi, though he generally gives as good as he receives. Plates filled, the boys sit around on the different rolls of bedding, on the wagon tongue or on the ground with their backs against the wagon wheel.

As the boys finish their meal, plates, cups, knives, forks and spoons are thrown into a large dishpan placed on the ground underneath the chuck-box lid. If some luckless puncher should place his "eating tools" on top of the lid, he would be sure to be bawled out by the Cosi. All the eating tools when washed are put on shelves or in drawers of the chuck-box, while the heavy Dutch ovens, coffee pot, etc., are put into a box bolted underneath the wagon bed at its rear end.

This is the real chuck-wagon and way of eating as found in New Mexico though some of the northern outfits have a different lay.

From the Cimarron river north as far as grass grows many outfits have quite elaborate lays. Those that have a large tent or tarp spread over the wagon extending out on both sides are called by read punchers "Pullman outfits," and old hands will inform you that they are used so that the punchers won't get sun-burned and usually add, "bless their little hearts," further explaining, with a very straight face, that these Pullman boys usually wear white shirts and are obliged to shave and shine their boots every morning before starting work.

Along the Rio Grande

by N. Howard Thorp

For miles on either side of the Rio Grande are mesquite and cat-claw thickets, these are known as the torral while the Tornillo thickets are known as the Tornial, Tornillo being the Spanish name for screw. These thickets are dense, the Tornillo bushes growing from ten to fifteen feet in height.

The branches are thorny and at certain seasons of the year bear screw-shape pods containing seeds.

These tornials grow in clumps or motts, and vary from a few acres to miles in extent. These were the haunts of wild cattle, horses and other animals, and was the last place of refuge in which the wild animals made their stand against the inroads of civilization.

The ranch-men lost many cattle and horses on account of their gentle stock taking up with the wild ones, a gentle animal sometimes becoming more hard to handle than those who for generations had been wild.

There is an old Spanish proverb used by the Mexicans here which seems to apply to the cow and horse thieves, "Lo que cantando viene cantando se va." "Easy come, easy go."

This tornial was a regular clothes-snatcher, an ordinary outfit would not last a mile. Men wore leather leggin's or chaps on their legs, taps or tapaderos on their stirrups, heavy canvas brush jackets, leather cuffs and gloves, and the barbequejo, or chin string to their hats.

We protected our horses breasts with a reguarda or shield of raw-hide, and also raw-hide leg coverings, but as these were always getting out of place soon were discontinued.

Running parallel with the Rio Grande at a distance of from one to ten miles are ridges which are known as sejas. The wild cattle and horses lay up in the Tornial during the daytime and at night feed towards the sejas. If the weather is cold, some of these cattle lay out in the roughs of these sejas for two and three days, and graze back to the Tornial at night.

In the fall when the Tornillo beans are ripe, the stock get as fat as they would on mesquite. We usually made our camp at one end of a Tornial so as not to give the wild cattle a scare.

On moonlight nights we would watch the trails that came out from the thickets. When cattle showed up on the flats we would wait until there were at least one quarter of a mile between them and the brush they had just left. Then, riding like hell-a-beaten tanbark, we would build out loops as we went, and dab our lines on anything we could get to that had a long ear, and that was most any of them.

We usually worked from one camp about four nights before moving, as the cattle we had caught, necked or hobbled out by then had to have water. Just before moving camp one of the boys would go to the ranch, and bring back some gentle work oxen. We would then neck up our mavericks to them and turn them loose.

During idle times at the ranch we would make up a lot of these twisted raw-hide neckings so as to have them handy when the mavericking season began.

The old gentle oxen would graze along towards the ranch leading the captives with them. Sometimes it would take three or four days grazing, and watering at the different pot holes, to make the ten or twelve mile trip, but eventually they would enter the home corral where we would find them licking salt.

After we had all our catch necked to the gentle oxen, and had given them a start towards the ranch, our outfit would hunt a new campground near where there were well defined trails coming out of the Tornial and leading to the open range.

By the time we had our second catch made, one of the ranch hands would bring over gentle oxen, and we would neck up our second lot of mavericks.

Some maverickers lost many of their catch by necking two wild ones together. These would get running, tugging and fighting, 'till they overheated themselves and died.

If we were short of oxen, and especially if we had a muley "hornless animal" or yearling, we would neck him to a gentle burro who without fail would graze him into the ranch. Often when an animal necked to a burro refused to lead or "sulled," the little canary would blaze away with his heels at the steer, who wouldn't be long in obeying orders.

Though in those days we had a few wire fences, we usually managed a small rail fence pasture for saddle horses, which in an emergency we could use for the cattle.

After gathering some Mavericks one man would stay at the ranch, to cut and roast the thorns or "espinas" off the prickly pear plant to feed them. A good many of the ranches were located at the mouths of rocky canons, where there were potholes which held water the better part of a year. These would often be made permanent waterings by building earthen dams below them.

On either end of the dams would be large spillways or openings to allow the flood waters to pass. During the heavy rains when water came rushing down these rocky canons, the tanks above the dam would be filled with fresh water for another year.

Most of these canons had vertical cliffs on either side, too steep for stock to climb. By fencing each end with brush or fallen timber the ranchmen had a natural horse pasture at little cost.

The main corral was usually built above the dam or reservoir, so saddle horses coming into water would have to pass through the corral gate and were, when needed—by closing the corral gate—easily caught.

Working wild horses or cattle within the limits of the Tornial was quite different from roping them on the outside. While working the brush we would split up. If a bunch of twenty men were working together, half would go to the end of some big Tornial, and start everything, we will say, north. A couple of miles further ahead the other men would take stands some quarter of a mile apart and on the side of the thicket opposite to where they wished to turn the drive into the open.

Most of the hands, Mexican and American, rode little mules, though a good many rode horses. The little mules whose mammies were burros and daddies were horses are very smart, and usually better reined than those bred from a jack and mare. They have smaller heads and ears and are more intelligent. They can easily out-dodge—as the Mexicans say—their own shadows. They will save themselves from thorns and brush swiping, whenever possible, but get as wildly excited as an old brush horse when once the chase has begun.

Some of these brush peppers, as we used to call them, take a lot more chances than any other riders going.

Take your stand on a brush horse along where you think the drive will pass, and he will seem to be asleep, you can't hear anything but the drone of flies or hum of mosquitoes. Presently one of your horse's ears will commence to point forward, then his other ear; he has heard something which has not yet reached your ears. Then, listening, his head will raise, maybe in the far distance you can catch a high pitched yell, not unlike an Apache Indian. Your old brush horse works his bit with his tongue, and sort of fishes for it, the while tightening his reins. Another yell of the drive coming closer and closer, and without warning he is off.

Somehow you are swinging your body from side to side, dodging the limbs with an arm you are warding off the thorny brush, rip! goes a pocket of your brush jacket, as a stiff limb tears it off, buttons and button holes are torn out, the tail of your slicker — rain coat — is left in a bush, your fast-flying horse lands you beside the racing cattle and you and the other men who have taken stands try to crowd the bunch into the open.

But they split on you, you have crowded them too close; you drop in behind the split and head them again towards the main bunch. If you are not side-swiped off your horse or forked in a tree, you stand a chance of again throwing them together.

Some of the old experienced brush horses depended more on breaking their way through the brush, and you could, by "riding Indian" all over them and they didn't take the bit in their teeth and go cold jawed with you though full of thorns, scratched and bleeding, you would find yourself still on your horse when the run was over. Though your horse's front legs and flanks might be full of thorns, he would seldom fall with you.

Yes, if you want real excitement, get a good brush horse, and join some old hands on a cow hunt in the matorral. Pigsticking, Polo Steeplechasing, and Fox Hunting, are very tame compared to it; your horse may not be as pretty as some of the well-groomed eastern ones, their knees are probably covered with bumps from past bruises and old thorns having entered and broken off. For the first few miles after saddling, he may go stiff, but when warmed up, you have got a horse under you. There is no other class of horse that can equal him at his task. You will be going fast, in fact seems you are flying, the matorral or Tornillo is whipping you and your horse at every jump, half the time he is high in the air as he clears big branches he can't break through.

Here is a big limb, you throw yourself over on your horse's side so it won't beat your brains out, with your right hand and arm you are turning the thorny brush aside, as at racing speed he clears a badger's den.

Maybe your horse jumps sharply to the right to avoid a tree; you throw your weight and swing low in the same direction, and when clear maybe the next jump will be a sharp turn to the left, he makes the whole in a cock-screw leap. It is then your blood is up and fine electric needles play up and down your spine, while the short hair at the back of your neck turns into boars bristles an inch long.

It is a trade of its own. Riding a good brush horse will give you more thrills than bull-dodging steers, the rest of your life.

In the prairie lands you will find many of the men using a bridle knot tied in their lines, but never a brush hand, for if a limb should catch the lines above the knot in a bridle rein, it would be liable to jerk their horse over backwards or break his jaw. Brush hand and horse have to be raised to the job, yet take them outside on the flats and they make good hands, where as a prairie hand and horse in the Tornial would be useless.

As you ride towards camp the sight of the pot rack, the smell of hot coffee, dutch oven biscuits, frijoles ("beans"), and the call of the cook, Vengen a comer, "Come and eat," makes you forget the tough day you have just had in the matorral, and the food tastes like the finest meal you have ever had.

Sitting around the campfire at night, everyone talks about the drive, and all the smallest details are recalled. Your bedroll coaxes you to lay down, and you sleep until someone calls "daylight, and let's go," and another day of brush-popping has begun.

Aztlan (New Mexico) Outlaws

by N. Howard Thorp

Order from Governor Lionel S. Sheldon, Santa Fe, June 1882.

"**W**henever information shall be received by Officers of my troops, that there is a riot, mob, or demonstration of violence in their vicinity, or any 'rustlers' or other desperados shall commit depredations upon the person or property of Citizens, such officers will at once pursue, and capture such offenders at any cost, turning them over to the proper civil authorities, and restore all stolen property to its owners.

"It is expected that these orders will be executed with such promptness and vigor, that bad men will take warning and avoid New Mexico as a field for carrying on their criminal occupations."

From the above order it may be seen that the mounted Militia of 1882, were practically mounted Police, and were expected at all times to furnish the Sheriffs of Counties, and Constables of Precincts, the necessary force to execute all writs or process of law, civil as well as criminal, when called upon by Sheriffs or Constables.

One evening late in May 1882, a ranchman named Mason, upon returning from a trip to Mesilla in Dona Ana County, drove his team into his corral, and was confronted by three men, who covered him with pistols and guns, and ordered him to hold up his hands. He, of course, complied. All the members of Mason's families and the employees about the ranch were then locked up in a room and the robbers stripped the house, taking everything of value, including the clothing of the men and women. They also carried off all the goods in Mason's store, likewise all bedding, and what provisions there were in the house. They packed the plunder on Mason's horses and drove them off, together with what cattle they could gather about the ranch. They were supposed to have headed for Uba Springs, about twenty miles northeast of Mason's ranch, and about nine miles west of the town of Colorado, Dona Ana County.

The gang was supposed to have numbered about twenty outlaws.

Colonel A. J. Fountain of Las Cruces hastily assembled some men and took the trail.

Just before he started, a report arrived that a band of thieves had been seen, driving a herd of cattle south of Las Cruces. Fountain's men overtook the thieves, eight miles south of Las Cruces near old Fort Fillmore. There were over twenty-five head of stolen cattle, and three men were driving them toward the Texas line.

When ordered to throw up their hands, two of the thieves opened fire. One of the posse had his bridle reins cut in two by a bullet, and another received a bad scalp wound. Two of the thieves, mounted on splendid horses, made their escape, although both were wounded. They were recognized as Santiago Cooper and Aldrete, who lived at Ysleta, Texas. Armienta, the captured thief, claimed to be an employee of the two men who escaped, and disclaimed all knowledge of their names or of where they got the cattle.

These three men were a part of the gang that robbed the Mason ranch, and the cattle came from the Ubas, the headquarters of the gang. Armienta the prisoner took no part in the shooting, as he was disarmed before the firing commenced.

Another lot of the Fountain men started after the main body of the thieves who had robbed the Mason ranch. This body of men, under Colonel Bull, left from Mesilla and headed directly for the Mason ranch. The morning after their arrival, the trail of five of the gang was found, headed towards Old Mexico.

The trailers followed the horse sign across the waterless plain in a direction of Las Palomas, just south of Old Mexico border. They reached Palomas lakes the following night, having ridden over ninety miles across a country without water in thirty-six hours. The following night the posse camped on the Janos river, where the fugitives had camped two nights before. Here was found part of the plunder taken from the Mason ranch, including some woman's clothing and letters with Mason's address on the envelopes. The following day the trailers reached the town of Ascension, in the State of Chihuahua, Mexico. The fugitives had gone around the town and Lieutenant Bull was obliged to report to the authorities and obtain permission to pass through.

The Authorities, offering every assistance, refused to let so large a number of armed men go further into the interior of the State, but consented that Lieutenant Bull, and not to exceed five of his followers, might continue the pursuit. Couriers were sent ahead, and the whole country was aroused.

While all this excitement was going on, word came to Ascension that a suspicious-looking American had been arrested at Casas Grandes who might be one of the thieves, but he did not turn out to be any of the men Lieutenant Bull was after. In the meantime a party from Ascencion took up the trail of the outlaws, following them to the town of Valispe in the State of Sonora. On June seventh, a messenger reached Lieutenant Bull from General Reyes of Sonora, with the news he had caught the fugitives. Other information received at the same time satisfied Bull that the fugitives were beyond reach of human punishment; in fact, they had gone to a place where a writ of extradition would not be likely to reach them. Upon the receipt of this information, the Couriers were called in, and the posse left upon its return journey to the United States.

In the spring of 1883, what were known as the Farmington gang of outlaws, finding northern Sheriffs too alert and pickings too slim, moved down into the Black Range in Sierra County, and were soon busily engaged in stealing horses and cattle, in fact, anything of value they might run across. Among the best known of these thieves, were Joe Asque, Cooper, Celso Morales, Estevan Morales, Faustino Lopez, Moro Saiz, and many others, all indicted rustlers, whom the Sheriffs of the different counties were unable to cope with. The difficulty the mounted Militia had in running them down was due to the fact that the movements of a body of Militia was easily noted and reported to the outlaws through the medium of friends, whereupon, being advised, they would scatter like a flock of quail, to meet again at some distant point. This is the way things worked. A reliable stockman guided the Militia to the alleged place of rendezvous of the Farmington gang. A nearby ranchman said the Farmington gang had now in their possession a big bunch of horses and mules, recently stolen. The trail to their hide-out was over a very rough country, and when the posse arrived there, the thieves and their stock must have smelled a rat and were gone.

The rustlers had all the advantage in the broken and rough country known as the Black Range. Then again, most of those living in the Range were friends, and in many cases relatives so consequently would harbor and protect them, and especially against the Militia.

Jose Asque, "already mentioned" narrowly escaping from a Sheriff's posse at Lake Valley, headed his horse northeast, and the second day camped at Indians tanks on the Carrizozo flats. At this point there was good water, and watching the many head of stock coming in to drink, Joe's itching rope longed for action.

Finally, a bunch of five head of fat saddle horses came to water, and as they started to leave, Joe fell in behind them and headed them east. Not knowing the country well, or who ran certain brands, was the cause of his downfall. In some fifteen miles he came to the wooded canyon called Nogal on the road to Roswell, which Joe thought would be a good place to dispose of his stolen stock. At the head of the canyon, the road climbs a steep hill and then falls down another sharp grade into the Rio Bonito. The horses by now were strung out along the road which entered the timber.

Looking ahead, Joe saw a wagon approaching with two men in it. Thinking nothing of it, he was prepared to give a greeting and pass the time of day.

As the team got abreast of him it stopped, and Joe was gazing into a black hole in the end of a Winchester. "Put them up!" one of the men called, and "Don't dally." Joe did. "Get down," the men told him. Joe, who was armed with only a six-shooter, obeyed. He was disarmed, his hands tied behind him and placed in the wagon. His own rope was slipped over his head, and the wagon was headed for the nearest tree.

With the rope tied to a limb, he was forced to step off the wagon and left hanging with his toes just clear of the ground.

His saddle was put on one of the horses, which belonged to the two men, and wagon and stolen horses started back to the range from which Joe had brought them.

Joe was very small and light, and this fact probably saved his life. The knot in the rope happened to have been under his chin, so although it was hard to breathe, he did not actually choke. After sometime he managed to get his hands loose, got out his pocket knife and cut the rope.

Joe said the hanging wasn't so bad, but riding his old horse bareback, for a hundred miles back to his home range with only a rope around his neck, certainly made him mad.

Mexican Version, Dogies, Dogal

by N. Howard (Jack) Thorp

Assuming a ranchman is milking two cows, the calves are left in the milk pen and the cows turned out to graze. In the evening the milk cows enter the big corral and one of the calves is turned in to nurse. The milker puts a rope around the calf's neck (this the Mexicans call Dogal, to tie by the neck) and holds it back, only letting it nurse one teat. If grass is good the calves are turned out at night and their mother left in the corral. The Americans have probably corrupted it to Dogie; as most of the lingo we use about horses, saddles and cattle, etc. is borrowed from the Spanish, this is probably the explanation.

American Version, "Dogie"

All Dogies are pot-bellied and stunted—reason: mother probably died and calf had to raise itself on grass or weeds and eat an abnormal amount of food to sustain life and consequently had a large belly. Years ago, the punchers called such calves dough-bellies, then doughys, then Dogies. Stand a naked Mexican boy of 4 or 5 "en profile" and you will see his little tummy sticking out—"too many beans and not enough milk." Take another who has nursed a goat, he will have quite a different figure.

Old Time Ranchmen of the Pecos Valley

by N. Howard Thorp

The Pecos river is quite a different stream today, to what it was before sheep and cattle were brought there.

At that time—the Old Mexicans tell us—it was a narrow and deep stream with but few crossings, and those dangerous. The stock, going to and from water, broke down the banks and the stream, in consequence, as it filled up with the dirt, broadened out and became shallow. The same thing happening from its tributaries on the west, sent still more dirt and sediment to the mother stream, filling it up, and widening it in consequence.

Few buffalo bones have been found on the east side of the Pecos, as they were afraid to cross the stream, and consequently the caravans of buffalo hunters, who yearly went in search of meat, traveled to the Llano Estacado and the Canadian river to hunt.

The first man we have any record of who drove a herd and established a ranch was John Chisum; this ranch was located about the year 1868, near Bosque Grande.

With the exception of a few trappers, traders and adventures, who made no settlement, Chisum should be given the credit of being the first ranch-man to locate there.

Pope's Crossing, at where the Delaware river enters the Pecos, was named in 1856 after a soldier; this was where the Butterfield Stage coach, which ran from San Antonio Texas to California, crossed the Pecos river.

At this time Lincoln county was some two hundred miles square, and the only towns were Lincoln, White Oaks and Seven Rivers, and which today are practically dead.

Eventually several counties were created from Lincoln, but nevertheless it is still a sizable county. It was some fifteen years after John Chisum founded his first ranch at Bosque Grande before the L. F. D. cattle company came. This was in 1882; they had a headquarter ranch at Bosque Grande, and was known as the Littlefield Cattle Company, and Mr. J. P. White was the manager. After the L. F. D. many others came, and either located directly on the Pecos or on some of the streams to the west, whose waters emptied into that stream. The brands of a good many of these outfits I remember, but of the owners and managers there are but few that I can recall. Some of them I remember were the Eddy-Bissell Cattle Company, the C. A. Bar, the W T, the Holt cattle company, The Hash Knife, The Bush, The V. V., The Blocks, Diamond A., C. A. Bar, The L. E. A., The F. H. C. and many more outfits I do not mention, and several individual owners, with large cattle holdings. John Chisum alone claimed a hundred and twenty-five, to a hundred and fifty miles of the Pecos river front, on both sides. There was many a good cow-man that rode the range in those days, and among these I recall are, Tom Catenhead, George Wilcox, Morgan Tom Livingston, John Dunaway, Hess, Walker, Todd Barber, Jim and Jake Gould, Bill Mack, the Jones boys from Seven Rivers, Dow, Bass, Clabe Merchant, Forehand, and Tom Fletcher. Si and Green Ursher, Bill Harmon, Jack Potter, Ballard, Charley Perry, and hundreds of others, and one of the best of them was old Governor Jim Hinkle, one of the very few of those mentioned above who is alive today.

One of the big outfits worked a bunch of colored hands, mostly southern Texas brush hands, and the kingpin of them was one named Ad, and some comical stories are told of him.

Just after the spring horse work, two of the top horses of the Boss's mount were missing, and though there had been a very clean work, no sign of them could be found. Ad was sent one place and another, to isolated waterings and ranches, but to no avail. Finally the Boss told Ad to saddle the best horse in his mount, and go get those horses, no matter how far he went and never come back without them. "Yes," Ad responded, "Mr. Boss Man Ize gone."

As grass was late that year, so was the horse work, and it was not until the middle of May that Ad left. He headed south and east, and after several days brought up at the Trinity river in Texas. As most every night he stopped with a different cow outfit his board cost him nothing. He carried a letter, stating that he was working for the outfit that ran the brand his horse wore. On leaving, his Boss Man gave him some expense money, and Ad was saving it to make a splurge, when he hit his own country. Ad, who had not been home since a boy, told his folks plenty. How his Boss Man was the richest man in New Mexico, had almost a million cattle, so many the cow-punchers couldn't count them, and they had to hire school teachers to do the job. His Boss Man also owned all the land on both sides of the Pecos river, from Texas to Colorado, and he, Ad, was foreman of the whole outfit and the Boss Man had given him a thousand dollars in cash, and told him to go home for a few months and enjoy himself.

Ad bought fancy clothes, and took in all the church festivals, camp meetings, dippings, and dances and soon had all the girls he could lug around. Directly green corn, and watermelon time came around, and Ad qualified as a real hand; there wasn't a patch of melon he had not befriended.

At the Dallas State fair, Ad won both the calf roping, and bronc riding contest, and his reputation was made. Next he married the prettiest yaller gal, on the Trinity river. By now Ad's money was about played out, so he decided to check on the Boss Man.

As outside of reading brands Ad could neither read or write, so he got a friend to write a letter. He told his boss where he was, and on account of having chills and fever and ague, and getting married, he was alright but had been much delayed. He was now close on the trail of the stolen horses, and would try and be home in a month; he also said he had made out a check on him, and please send the money, so he could get back home. The check was made out in the form of a draught, his friend signed Ad's name to it, and Ad, who had once worked for the O. K. outfit placed this brand under his signature, and under that the ranch brand, the same as on his horse L. F. D.

The money came alright, and as Ad had heard of some horse works on the Canadian river he headed there, thinking if horses had not been stolen, they might have drifted to and down the Canadian river with stock horses.

The third night after leaving he landed at a chuck-wagon. This wagon was on a horse round-up and was working east on the Canadian. He was told by the foreman to unsaddle and grab a plate. As he was hobbling his horse out, the foreman asked him what outfit he was riding for. Ad told him, and pointed to the brand on his horse. "I think we caught a couple of horses in that brand, when we were working about a hundred miles up the river," said the foreman, "and they were such good ones we have been riding them a few saddles, and have still got 'em." "A big roan and a bay?" asked Ad. "Yep," answered the foreman. "Thems the horse I'm after and a-hunting," said Ad.

"What are you doing making your bed down here?" he roared.

"Mr. Boss, youse got to step over Ad every morning till youse hire me back."

Ad worked on for the outfit many years, until on account of old age he could ride no longer.

The Mustangs of New Mexico

by N. Howard Thorp

Wild of eye and fleet of foot were the tens of thousands of Mustangs, which—prior to 1870—roamed the plains and Mesas of New Mexico. Descendants as they were of the pure Arabian Barb horses brought over by the early Spaniards, they had all the bottom and endurance of their ancestors.

A great many of the isolated bunches became badly inbred, but under conditions where vast numbers came in contact, this was not the case, and many an animal taken from these herds became fine cow and saddle horses.

In colors they ran the gamut, their progenitors being of chestnut, sorrel, grey and bays, with a few blacks and duns. These crossings often produced Grullas—a mouse color—and Palominos, a creamy dun with white main and tails; also the various Pintos, with either black, bay or yellow spots. These were often termed scrubs or off colors, but were the result of crossings of the different colored Arabian Mares and Stallions.

These bunches of Mustangs were of various sizes, but a fair average was some twenty-five to forty to the Stallion.

Many years—when water holes went dry—one could see a thousand head of wild horses at one watering, made up of many different manadas, or small herds of Mares.

At these times the various Stallions heading the manadas would fight for supremacy, the victorious ones stealing the vanquished ones' mares. In fighting, a well directed kick on the hock might place the receiver out of the combat, or too tight a grip on the jugular vein might mean death, the latter, as a result of these desperate combats not being unusual.

The Mustangs of New Mexico were not ruthlessly slaughtered, as was the case in some other States, but great round-ups of them, by the ranchmen and "Mustangers"—as the professional wild horse hunters were known—were made whence the "catch" was trailed to market.

Among the best known of these old Mustangers were Horse Evans, Pony Bob Campbell, and Wild Horse Gould. These men in their line were Artists. Various were the methods used to catch the Mustangs. Some built stout corrals at the edge of a mott of timber, with wings extending a quarter of a mile in either direction, then run their horses between the wings and into the corral. Sometimes this worked, and other times it didn't, as a very wary bunch will seem to sense danger, and will break back into small bunches, and disappear in the brush.

If a Manada while in the open country happened to sight a horseman, they would at once head for the densest timber or thicket they could find, and splitting up, would again get together after they were well out of danger.

It was particularly interesting to watch a wild bunch of badly scared horses, how when frightened they run towards another bunch of animals, were they Antelope, wild cattle or another bunch of Mustangs, and how when they had overcome their fright, the Stallion would separate his Mares from those of the other bunch into which he had driven them. Also to watch how he ran behind the laggards of his Manada, biting their rumps, and making them hurry, and how after he got them all started, he would gallup proudly ahead and take the lead.

Some horse hunters tried catching the wild ones by placing snares or loops suspended along certain brushy trails used by the horses when going to or from water, but very few were caught.

Three brothers, just starting as wild horse hunters, conceived the scheme of digging a pit across a trail much traveled by horses; this they did, and after a week of hard work completed it—it was very similar to a bear pit—and carefully covered it with leaves and branches. They then took turns watching.

Presently a Manada of about thirty head came along, with the Stallion in the lead jog-trotting down the trail to water. When the Stud came to the side of the pit, he stopped, sniffed and led his bunch carefully around it. An exuberant colt, dashing around its mother, fell into the pit. It then took several men the best part of a day to fish him out, so the net result for a week's hard work was one small bay colt, which, as the boys could not raise, turned it loose to join its anxious mother. Shortly after this they had to fence the pit, so that stray cattle would not fall in.

The two most successful methods were either making a round-up of a manada of gentle Mares and colts, and heading the Mustangs towards them. After they had run a while the entire bunch could be checked up, and if there were plenty of men on the work, they could all be corralled. After being put in the corral the Mustangers made a circingle of a piece of rawhide, and with a short piece around the front ankle, tied one foot to it, or else they would cut a piece of rawhide some six feet long and four inches wide and fasten the end around the ankle of a front foot, so if the Mustang started to run he would step on the rawhide, and either trip or fall. Both of these methods were used to keep the wild ones from running away after they were put on herd in a gentle bunch.

One of the greatest troubles after catching and breaking Mustangs was to keep them, for no matter how gentle they became, unless moved away from their home range, they would at the first opportunity disappear, and eventually re-join their companions.

In early spring—during the breeding season—the old Stallions are continually battling and whipping all young Stallions and males out of their manadas, who immediately upon being put out would endeavor—it seemed in retaliation—to steal a mare or two from their former bunch.

No matter how fiercely two old Stallions might be fighting, if they saw some young Stallion trying to purloin one of their mares—for the time being the combat would cease until the thieving Stallion could be run off, after which, the dispute would be resumed.

Tall old tales are told by some of the old Mustangers, and although they sound a little fishy, I believe the most of them to be true.

Wild mules become mightily attached—at times—to horse colts, though some of the big native eastern mules, if loose in a pasture with colts, will often chase and strike at them, and sometimes cripple and kill one.

Old Pony Bob Campbell tells of a little "yaller" lion back mule, whose mammy was a Mustang, and who always ran until he was five or six years old with the remuda in which he was raised. On account of the wariness of this mule, his bunch had never corralled. One time on a big wild horse round-up, his manada had been pressed so hard, the little mule had split them up in spite of the Stallions efforts to keep them together, so all, with the exception of one mare and colt, got away in the brush. This mare and colt was taken with the round-up and penned in the huge winged corral previously built.

The next morning, one of the boys saw the little buckskin mule standing on the flat about a quarter of a mile away, making some mule noises, and the little colt we had caught with its mammy nickering in reply.

We kept the bunch in the corral for three days, while working them over, and on the fourth day put them out under herd to graze. By this time the little mule seemed to have disappeared, although at times the colt would nicker.

After we turned the horses out of the corral, I noticed the mare and colt on the nigh point of the herd, but at the time thought nothing of it. Before we got to good grass, we had to pass through a patch of post oak. Just as we entered it we saw a small yellow flash dart between the mare and colt and the herd, cut the two of them out, and disappear in a cloud of dust. And every word of that is so, said Pony.

Another way of handling Mustangs was to walk them down. Full moon was the time usually chosen, for with this help you could keep them going night and day, never letting them graze or rest. We use to make our camp in as near the middle of their range as possible, for they would rarely leave it.

When we first jumped the bunch we were after, they probably would break and run for three or four miles. After the Mustangs got to the end of their range, they would double back, and as they passed camp, one of the other boys would take over the job of following them, while the first man rode to camp, caught up a fresh horse and got something to eat. This method of slowly following them we kept up, until usually at the end of the sixth or seventh day—having had no rest and nothing to eat—they would begin to weaken; then throwing them together with a bunch of gentle stock, we would have no trouble driving them into a corral.

Historic Ranch House on the Gila

by Clay W. Vaden

The large Adobe ranch house was purchased some time ago by Ed Otero from Cole Railston, one of the late Eugene Manlove Rhodes' cowboy cronies of early days in New Mexico, now living near Magdalena, for $100,000.00. It was purposely built by a spring and at a distance from nearby mountains to meet the danger of surprise attacks of Indians, Mrs. Jacob Dines, widow of one of the first owners of the ranch, declared recently.

The famous old ranch is on the headwaters of the Gila river about 130 miles west of Socorro. The Adobe ranch house contains six large rooms almost surrounded by balconies or "portales."

Johnny Dines, her son, was the hero of that name in Eugene Manlove Rhodes' western novel, "Stepsons of Light." When he was about seven years old, Mrs. Dines recalls, they sold the ranch in 1886 to Mitford and Hardcastle, Englishmen. They remained on the ranch a few months while the Englishmen were becoming accustomed to western life.

One day Johnny galloped in to report to Hardcastle: "I saw some mean looking men leading off your gray horse just now."

Hardcastle and two other men at once took up the trail and found the thieves were a band of Chief Geronimo's warriors on their way from San Carlos reservation in Arizona to the Mescalero reservation in New Mexico. A few miles farther on and near the old mining town of Grafton, the Indians killed Charley Stevenson, Harvey Moorland, and Frank Adams, three neighbor cowboys employed by the Anchor X ranch which had headquarters at Ojo Caliente.

A short time after the ambushing of these cowboys, settlers for miles around met at the Adobe ranch and decided to go to Fairview (now called Winston) for protection until the Indian uprising could be suppressed. Mrs. Dines recalls that 63 men and about 10 women and children, with 300 horses, trailed out from Adobe ranch to Fairview during this danger period in 1886.

Mrs. Dines also recalls having seen droves of 50 or more antelope, which are nearly extinct in parts of the state now, come to the ranch spring to drink.

Cowboys Near Las Cruces, New Mexico, Unattributed, 1904, NMHM/DCA #000610

RANCHING

In the winter of 1888, or 1889, the cattle that died were so many that cow-men said that the dead cattle along the Pecos River were so thick, that if they had been placed side by side, they could have walked from Ft. Sumner to Roswell on dead cattle.

From "Melrose (Excerpt)" by Dad DeGraftenreid
and Mrs. Ida G. Boyles

"Just two things that cowpunchers were afraid of—the Pecos River and Rattlesnakes."
—From "Early Days of a Cowboy on the Pecos"
by James F. Hinkle

From Hackett's "Historical Documents"

by Lorin Brown

In the establishment of settlements in New Mexico the ordinances governing same as issued by the members and chamber of the Royal Audencia of Mexico and confirmed in the city of Mexico, September 1577, were followed.

That much interest was taken in the proper care and propagation of livestock is evinced in that portion of the ordinances which treats of the amount of land devoted to enclosures for livestock and for farms devoted to stock raising. The parts of the ordinances which deal with these provisions in Hackett's Historical Documents Relating to New Mexico are given below. The ordinances are headed in part as follows: "Land ordinances and regulations for measuring *sitios, criaderos de ganados mayores* and *menores, caballerias* and other lands; etc. (Confirmation of said Ordinances, with corrections and additions.)

"In the City of Mexico of New Spain, on the nineteenth day of the month of September of the year 1577, the most excellent lord, Don Gaspar de Peralta, Marquis of Falces, Count of Santiestevan, *mayordomo* of his Majesty in the kingdom of Navarre, his viceroy, governor, and captain general in this New Spain; president of the royal Audencia during the time in which it was governed by his excellency in the name of his majesty:

"There has been conceded and granted a large quantity of farming land, for *sitios de ganado mayor* and *sitios de ganado menor, caballerias* and other lands but the proper method, and procedure have not been completely enunciated for locating setting up the boundaries, measuring and giving possession to these *sitios* and other lots of land, (where for the viceroy) commanded that these ordinances be corrected," —etc.

The Measuring Yard

The ancient measuring yard is the same as that used by Solomon, which consists of five spans (*tercias*), which is not now used, it is to be noted that the measuring yard named here for measuring all kinds of land is the ordinary common yard, called the Castilian yard, which has four hand-breadths, and is that which is used by merchants.

The *Cordel*

It should be notes that the *cordel* with which all kinds of land are to be measured must be fifty Castilian yards in length, and it must be drawn straight and as taut as possible.

The *Sitio de Ganado Mayor*

A farm site for large cattle-raising (must measure) three thousand paces of the measure of Salomon; each pace contains five spans (it is understood that this dimension is from east to west); and from north to south it must also measure three thousand paces. From the centre to any of the four sides or edges, it must measure fifteen hundred paces of Salomon; reducing these measures to the common yard, the *sitio* measures five thousand yards from east to west, five thousand from north to south, etc.

If such a *sitio de ganado mayor* is reduced to *caballerias* it contains forty-one of the latter, with 14,272 yards left over, which makes a dwelling site of 119 and a scant one-third on each of the four sides.

The *Sitio de Ganado Menor*

A farm site for small cattle-raising (sheep, goats, swine) measures two thousand paces of Salomon (each five spans long) from east to west, and two thousand paces (also five spans each) from north to south; from the centre to anyone of its four sides one thousand of the same paces of five spans length.

If this *sitio* is reduced to *caballerias* it must contain eighteen of them, and a building site of 366⅓ yards.

In like manner the area and method of measuring a *Criadero de Ganado Mayor y Menor* (stock farm for both small and big livestock, cows, horses, mules, and sheep, goats and swine) were specified and made mandatory, and provision made here also for division into *caballerias*.

As has been stated before, sheep were raised in larger numbers because they could be more easily controlled in compact herds pastured close to the settlements; cattle were raised but confined for the most part to areas close to the settlements because of the ever present danger from the predatory Indians. However a *mesta* or grazers court functioned in New Spain for the promotion of cattle raising in the settlements of New Spain.

Kit Carson Ranch

by James A. Burns

Kit Carson made two attempts to settle down as a ranch man in the Cimarron Valley but was interrupted by exploration trips, Indian wars, etc.

The first attempt was on Cimarroncito Creek about 1850, which he abandoned to go to California with General John C. Fremont. After a disagreement with Fremont he returned to Taos a couple of years later and later located another ranch on El Rayado with intention of raising hay for the cavalry at old Fort Union. This project was interrupted by the trouble with the Navajo Indians and later by the Civil War, so that Carson finally abandoned the idea.

Source of Information: Frank T. Cheetham, Taos, New Mexico.

Cattle Industry of Otero County

by F. M. Casey

We very often hear the old time ranchers speak of "the good old days" when referring to the days of the "pool wagon." That was in the early settlement of the county, when a number of the ranchers would "throw in together." They would set a date and starting place for the Spring or Fall Round-up, appoint a Wagon-Boss whose duty it was to see that each rancher was represented, and calves and strays properly branded. Each rancher in the pool would bear his share of the cost of "Chuck-Wagon," furnish his share of help, and see each Brand drifted back to the proper range. The most important man in the Round-up was the Chuck-Wagon cook, as being able to handle a bunch of hungry cow-boys was an art within itself. Chuck-wagon was always supplied with water barrel, coffee-pots, frying-pans, and Dutch-ovens with a plentiful supply of chuck. When convenient, camp was made near a stream or spring.

In those days the cattle were rounded up on the open range and in lieu of corrals, night-herders were used to keep the herds from straying until all were ear-marked and branded. Each rancher prided himself on at least one expert cutting and roping horse, as this was necessary to cut out his cows and calves in order to brand the calves.

As a means of diversion on these Round-ups some of the cow-boys usually had a few good bucking horses in their string with which to entertain the crowd. Also in all these outfits you would find one or more horses, and many a horse race took place on these Round-ups. Expert roping and tying was an everyday occurrence, such as we seldom see in this day and time even at a Rodeo. The pool-wagon system was done away with in the late nineties, and many of the small ranchers sold their cattle and holdings to larger outfits who continued the use of chuck-wagons of their own. These larger outfits took over The Cattle Industry on an improved system, fences were built, watering places established, either with tanks or wells, and corrals and branding pens were built at each camp or outfit and in some cases well-built homes; some of the most pretentious houses in Otero County are ranch homes. Usually two or three men were stationed at these camps to look after the water and brand any calves found in this particular part of the range. It was also their duty to vaccinate the calves for black-leg, a system unknown to the early day cattleman.

For a few weeks each year the chuck-wagon was used when gathering cattle for shipping to market or to Northern pastures in the spring, and the branding of strays which had escaped the cowboys at the established camps. In these round-ups each cowboy had from seven to nine ponies in his string; he had to change mounts frequently as these horses were without feed except what they obtained through grazing. A wrangler was in charge of the horses and his duty was to see that the horses were picketed and were brought into camp at certain times.

Source of Information: Shelby Davis, Pioneer Cattleman.

Cattle, Estancia Ranch, J. R. Riddle, ca. 1886, NMHM/DCA #076110

Cattle Industry in Lincoln County, New Mexico

by Edith L. Crawford

The first settlers who came to Lincoln County in the early days brought small herds of mixed cattle and sheep. The Jinglebob outfit owned by John Chisum was the first to bring in a large herd of cattle. They were all sizes and colors. The headquarters ranch was near the head of South Spring River, about two miles south of Roswell, New Mexico, which was in Lincoln County at that time. The first record found on the files of Lincoln County of the brand of John Chisum was dated December 17, 1869.

Some of the other large cattle companies operating in Lincoln County about the same time were, The Lea Cattle Company, The Feliz Cattle Company, The Carrizozo Cattle Company, Three Rivers Cattle Company, The El Capitan Land & Cattle Company, (better known as the Blocks) and The Bloom Cattle Company. The V V Ranch was also a well known ranch but was established much later, about 1886 or 1887. All the ranges were wide open in those days and the cattle roamed from the Texas line on the south and east to the Rio Grande River on the west.

At round up time the cattle companies started the wagons out with a cowboy from each outfit, to look after the interests of the company which he worked for. One crowd would work the east side and one crowd the west side of the Pecos River. Other wagons would start from the Texas line and work up until the two crowds would meet. Then the cattle would be cut out and the cowboys would take the cattle wearing the brands of the company that he represented and take them to their home ranch. This procedure would be gone through each year as long as there were open ranges. In the early nineties some of the larger companies, wanting to improve their herds, imported bulls from different places. The V V Cattle Company imported the black Poll Angus Bulls directly from Scotland and put on his range in Lincoln County. The El Capitan Land and Cattle Company bought 100 thoroughbred Hereford bulls (white faces) from Kansas to improve their herds. Other cattle companies too, went in for heavier type beef cattle and now some of the very finest beef cattle to be found anywhere come from Lincoln County.

Mrs. Susan E. Barber, of Three Rivers, was called the cattle queen of New Mexico at one time. She managed her own ranch herself and was very successful in her undertakings. This lady was the wife of Alex A. McSween during the Lincoln County War, and lived in Lincoln, New Mexico, at the time of the war. She later married Geo. B. Barber, a lawyer. Her last days were spent in White Oaks, New Mexico, and she is buried there.

The Carrizozo Cattle Company, better known as the "Bar W Ranch" belonged to the first governor of New Mexico after it became a state, Governor W. C. McDonald. This ranch is still owned and operated by the son-in-law of the governor, (T. A. Spencer) and his grandchildren. The V V Ranch is still owned by Gerald and Charles Cree, whose grandfather established the ranch. The Bloom Land & Cattle Company is still owned and operated by members of the Bloom family who established this ranch in the early days. These three ranches are the only survivors of the ranches established in the very early days of Lincoln County.

Some of the larger ranches in Lincoln County today are owned by W. R. Lovelace, of Corona, both sheep and cattle, G. A. Titsworth, of Capitan, both sheep and cattle, L. D. Merchant Ranch near Capitan, (cattle), and the Block and Bar W Ranches, owned by the Spencer family.

The report of the Assessor for Lincoln County for the year 1889, show 11,621 horses, 362 mules, 253,111 cattle, 128,592 sheep, 10,078 goats, 167 burros and 895 swine.

The report for the Assessor for the year 1939, shows 31,934 cattle, 2,734 horses, 97,712 sheep, 18,373 . . . .

Indian Story

by Edith L. Crawford

I had to take some money to my Uncle Shafer, who lived on a ranch about thirty miles from Cimarron, New Mexico. My brother, who was younger than I, and my girl chum Annie Crocker went with me. In those days we rode side saddles. We stayed all night at my Uncle's ranch. The next morning when we were getting ready to leave we found my brother's horse was lame and he couldn't go back with us. So my girl chum and I started out alone for home. When we got on top of Riado hill we looked back and saw an Indian riding fast towards us, and it scared us nearly to death. So we started out to gallop our horses, and the Indian would ride faster. So we ran our horses just as fast as they could go the rest of the way home.

Mother came to the door when we arrived, and said "Girls, what on earth is the matter, just look at your horses?" The horses were covered with sweat and lather from riding them so hard. But we outrode the Indian.

When my mother helped me down from my horse, I could not stand on my right leg. I had gripped the horn of my side saddle so hard in my ride for my life, so I thought at the time, that in some way I injured my leg and have been a cripple since that day. I had to give up dancing and I did love to dance.

Source of Information: Mrs. Mary E. Burleson, age 78, Carrizozo, New Mexico.

Retold from the Probate Files of Lincoln County, New Mexico

by Edith L. Crawford

Statement of Sue E. Barber Administratrix of the Estate of John H. Tunstall deceased, as to the receipts and disposition made of said estate up to date October 30th, 1880.

Received of Geo Kimbell Sheriff, 138 head of Cows and calves—Received from Isaac Ellis 28 head of Cows and calves, making a total of 166 head of Cows and calves belonging to said estate turned over to me—I sold for cash Cows and calves at $10.50 per head around, that is to say all cattle of one year of age and upwards brought $10.50 per head with the calves thrown in, of the above mentioned cattle received at time of sale 93 head were classed as yearlings and upwards and brought in cash $976.50. The cost of gathering, driving and herding the cattle received from the aforesaid Sheriff, was immense, owing to the following reasons—

1st. Said cattle was in the possession of thieves who held them in a remote part of the County, and at the time I recovered these cattle a state of lawlessness prevailed in the County, consequently I had to pay large sums for labor performed in gathering and herding the cattle up to the time of making the sale of said cattle as stated above; following is an account of the expenditures made by me for recovering, gathering and herding said cattle up to the time they was sold, to wit; Paid Charles Scase $75.00 for going to Seven Rivers to find out where the cattle were located and who had possession of them—Paid Samuel Smith $50.00 for going to Roswell to identify, prove and swear to the cattle as being the property of the Tunstall estate this proceeding being necessary to get the cattle from the Military Authorities who had possession of them at that time—Paid Sheriff Kimbell $61.70 for bringing the cattle from Roswell to Lincoln—Paid Todocio $62.50 for herding 2½ months, the 28 head of cattle received from Isaac Ellis—Paid two boys $5.00 for assisting in herding the cattle I received from Sheriff Kimbell, prior to removing said cattle to Brewers Ranch—Paid one boy $5.00 for assisting in driving said cattle to Brewers Ranch—

Paid two boys $10.00 for assisting in driving said cattle from Brewers to Copelands Ranch—

Paid $105.00 board bill of herder and boys who assisted in herding and driving said cattle during a period of 4 months and 24 days—Paid Samuel Smith $75.00 per month for 4 months and 24 and ½ days work herding and taking care of the cattle till sold, making $361.25 (note) and my utmost endeavors could not procure another man to do this work for the same price or more for the reason that their lives would be in great danger.—Paid Geo. Washington & Jose Romero $32.00 for searching for stray cattle reported to me as belonging to said estate, they failed to find any cattle.—Paid $60.00 for a horse for Sam Smith to use in herding said cattle, said horse was stolen from Sam Smith at Lalones Ranch. Paid $25.00 for making out papers and taking acknowledgements for the recovery of said cattle from thieves, making a total of $842.45 expended up to time of selling said cattle, which leaves a balance of $134.05 now in my possession.

In the matter of the store owned jointly by the Estates of John H. Tunstall and A. A. McSween, I have received $574.33 rent from said building and the appurtenances thereto belonging, up to October 1st, 1880, and have expended out of this amount for repairs $572.00, for repairing said store building which is now in good repair and rents at the present time for $40.00 per month. At the time of being appointed Administratrix of the two estates last written and upon taking possession of the effects of said estates, I found them in a confused state and thought it necessary to employ an Attorney.

I employed H. I. Chapman, deceased, and paid him $146.00 in each estate for his services. I now have José Marie Aguyia employed in making collections for the Tunstall estate.

Respectfully submitted by Sue E. Barber, Administratrix.

To Florencio Gonzales, Probate Judge of Lincoln County, New Mexico.

In Probate Court Lincoln County Territory of New Mexico at the May Term A. D. 1881.

In the matter of the Estate of John H. Tunstall Deceased.

Supplemental Report to the one made November 6th 1880.

Collections made since January 1st 1881 up to April 30th 1881 as follows to wit Cash $17.50 Corn 1419 Lbs & one pony Horse. Notes taken in settlement of accounts due said estate in the aggregate $296.23. Judgments obtained against different parties on notes and accounts amounting to $400.12. Money paid out for said estate: G. Gauss $29.90. Cash paid for Corn sacks, $3.00. José Ma Auggia for collections, Cash $10.00. Corn 227 lbs. Amount received for rent of Tunstall Store from Oct. 1st 1880 to March 31st 1881 $240.00.

Statement of Sue E. Barber Administratrix of the Estate of John H. Tunstall and A. A. McSween.

This within statement was approved this 14th day of May A.D. 1881 except that she is to account for 48 head of Cattle undisposed of in this report.

— J. W. Tomlison, Probate Judge.

Filled with supplement this 6th day of May A.D. 1881. Ben H. Ellis, Clerk.

Cattle, Horses and Men

by J. H. Culley

Introduction by Nelson C. Crow

In any true history of the western range, due credit must be given the men of British and Scotch descent who were so active in the development of the cattle business. Most of these men from the tight little British Isles were men of means. It was their money that capitalized much of the beef cattle development in the United States. Any man who understands livestock breeding knows that from the British Isles have come the foundation for most of our improved livestock in this country. The British Isles developed the Hereford, Aberdeen-Angus, Shorthorn, Galloway, Devon—all beef breeds—as well as our popular breeds of sheep and horses in this country. America owes a great debt to the British Isles for the improved livestock its breeders have passed on to us; and for men who came over to the North American continent to pioneer the development of our vast livestock industry.

In 1893, Mr. Culley and his wife went to the famous old Bell Ranch in San Miguel County, New Mexico, Mr. Culley becoming ranch manager. This ranch is still one of the largest in the United States, and is now under the management of Albert Mitchell, one of America's best known and highly regarded cattlemen. A section in this book is devoted to this celebrated cattle ranch.

The Bell Ranch was a Mexican Grant and in 1893 comprised a total of 750,000 acres.

Chapter 3. The River (The Old Canadian)

But they weren't all grim, my recollections of the old Canadian. I will try and show you now, why I have some pleasant memories of the river, too.

The title to the Bell Ranch, or to give it its official name, the Pablo Montoya Grant and Baca Location, was perfect. Nevertheless, the Northern part of the river from the mouth of Las Conchas to the grant fence contained several little plots of land and ran their goats and milk cows in surrounding brakes.

However, a short while after the new ownership came into effect it was decided to start a movement to get settlers off the grant and it fell to me to take the principal hand in this proceeding. There were one or two things that were of help to me in this task. To begin with, I had a good working knowledge of the Spanish language, both to speak and write it. A second point in my favor was that I did not have the full prejudice against Mexicans that prevailed almost universally amongst the cattlemen of the west. I had, I must confess, something of that contempt for what we are pleased to consider "inferior races," which is characteristic of all Anglo-Saxon peoples: I remember sharply resenting being arrested, once, by a Mexican peace officer. But, raised in one of the older countries, I never felt that active animosity against the "greaser" that characterized almost all western Americans.

This attitude and state of feelings spread over west from Texas, along with the cattle business which originated there. Its roots were in the Alamo. Numbers of the good people of the east have never heard of the Alamo. But for the Texan of those days—it is even true of the present generation—the memory of that spot with its record of Mexican savagery kept alive a never failing flame of hatred and contempt for everything Mexican. As a consequence, the range men of those times treated the entire Spanish-American people as if they had no rights at all, refused to have any social relations with them—although some were of proud Spanish blood—killed them, dispossessed them of their lands, scattered their sheep and drove off their cattle. The Mexicans, being without means of self-defense, became completely cowed and browbeaten.

Chapter 9. A Little Grant History

The Pablo Montoya Grant, which constitutes the Bell Ranch, was made Nov. 8, 1824, three years after Mexico achieved her independence. It is, therefore, a Mexican, not a Spanish grant. There is only the evidence of one old Mexican that Pablo Montoya himself ever occupied the property. The land comprised by it formed until 1868 part of the Comanche and other plains Indians' buffalo hunting grounds.

In 1851 Fort Union was established, a powerful post thirty-one miles north of Las Vegas. The outpost of Fort Bascom, located within the actual limits of the Montoya Grant, came into existence in 1864. (Fort

Bascom played an important part of checking westward movements of the Comanche Indians and protecting the cattle trails.) Yet still—and even after 1868, when the treaty with the Indians was concluded—the Bell country remained a dangerous one. Nick Dillon, who was at one time trail boss for the famous Texas cowman, John Hittson, and who is still living near Las Vegas, went up the Goodnight Trail from Central Texas to Colorado with a herd in 1872. He says the Goodnight Trail followed the course it did because it was impossible to take the direct route across the Staked Plains and the Bell country at that time on account of the Indian threat. Instead the trail drifted southwest by Abilene and Concho (Tex.) till it struck the Pecos at Horsehead crossing, about ninety miles south of Roswell, New Mexico, thereafter following the Pecos, North, past Fort Sumner to the Rimrock, fifteen or twenty miles from Las Vegas and leaving the Bell ranch well to the east. Nick relates that some years later than this, while driving a herd over the same trail, his outfit came upon Jesse Hittson (son of John) in a fight with Comanches, who ran off his horses, burned up his wagons and shot arrows into some of his cattle.

It was not till 1875, says Evetts Halley in his admirable book *Charles Goodnight*, that Goodnight opened a new trail which, turning east at the Cuervo (tributary of Las Conchas) and passing Tucumcari Peak, crossed the Canadian close to the Montoya Grant south line. Thereafter to follow the east side of the Grant up Ute Creek, eventually entering Colorado at a crossing of the Dry Cimarron.

Source of Information: U.S. Agriculture Library

Spring Roundup at Head of North Spring River near Roswell, New Mexico,
Phillips and Sheek, 1892, NMHM/DCA #005330

Melrose (Excerpt)

by Dad DeGraftenreid and Mrs. Ida G. Boyles

In 1882, my father and mother came through here, and there was not a white family anywhere, only at Roswell and Santa Rosa. Everybody were Mexican.

It was two hundred miles from Ft. Sumner to Pecos City, and we made that round up, to gather up the cattle, which had strayed away. They would drift that far away.

In 1902, the year that Horn died, the farmers began coming in, and taking the land, which was until then open range. Then was when the cow-men had to go out of business, and was the end of cow-ranches.

In 18__ there was no water in the Pecos River, and as before related, lots of cattle died of thirst. The weak cows and calves could not go ten or twelve miles to grass and back to water. Horn had about 3,000 cattle; Doss, his brother-in-law, had 8,000 or 10,000. Taylor his other partner had 6,000 or 7,000. He came in from the north (Colorado).

I made a study of brands. The pig-pen brand was used different ways. I studied my brand, the X (X-bar) from every angle. I decided it could not be changed. I got it for my brand. It was my stock brand. I had another brand for my steers: the lazy "B." My stock brand went along alright for awhile, and one day I found a cow that I thought was mine, with a moon-star brand. I studied the brand and finally decided that my brand had been changed, and later I found several of my cows in the hands of another. The thief was finally caught and imprisoned for seven years. He stayed six months and I signed a petition for his pardon. He was turned loose. The "Lazy B" was my steer brand. The letter B, upside down on the shoulder (?) on the yearlings. The "Leaning B," leaning about the 45 degree angle; on the second-year calves, the "Straight B"; on the three-year olds, and the Lazy B, was down-side up on the four-year old steers.

"Brands" is the most interesting thing among cowmen.

I came down here, in these alkali lakes, when there was no water in the Pecos, and made water down there. I dug springs, made boxes, and sunk them, and water would rise in them, and I dug ditches, for cattle to have water. And saved cattle that we would have lost, if we hadn't gotten them water.

When I came here, in 1882, there was only two counties, in Eastern New Mexico. Chaves, and San Miguel.

Horn was also a banker in Kansas, and he was rated as the only million-heir cowman in Kansas.

The "Horn" ranch was established in 1887, or 1888. I worked for Horn first, in 1888, or 1889—I think it was. Horn lived in Denver, Colorado, and in 1900, he moved his family down to his ranch. In 1902, I moved my family out. My family lived in Portales, and my wife sent the children to school while I worked on the ranch.

I came out with Mexicans, in 1907 or 1908 and I put down a well.

"Old Batchelor Blanton" had a sheep ranch on East Tulia Draw. This draw is a tributary to Black Water Draw.

The Mexican boy, Salidone Trujillo and I came over from Ft. Sumner, and stayed and heeled cattle (rode line on cattle) and the others went back to Ft. Sumner. We had to get our supplies and our mail from Ft. Sumner.

When Mr. Horn came down from Colorado, he claimed he had more cattle than either of his two partners, who were Mr. Taylor and Mr. Doss. They ran the cattle all together after they bought the old Ft. Sumner grant, but they had separate brands.

In the winter of 1888, or 1889, the cattle that died were so many that cow-men said that the dead cattle along the Pecos River were so thick, that if they had been placed side by side, they could have walked from Ft. Sumner to Roswell on dead cattle. There were too many cattle for the grass. The grass was all eaten from the banks of the Pecos as far as the cattle could go, and get back to the river for water. This was the reason for the death among the cattle that winter. They had grazed out so far, they were not able to walk so far back to the river for water.

I left the Mexican to take care of the cattle through the summer, and I went over on the Pecos and worked from Pecos City, Texas back to Ft. Sumner, and I brought in something like fifteen hundred cattle, that I had gathered on the "round-up."

The Mexican and I dug and made a "dug-out," and boy! We lived high that winter in a real good dug-out.

There were no buffalo in this country, at that time, but thousands and thousands of antelope, as they would drift in off the north plains, down here in the sand hills. I have seen thousands of them in a bunch, drifting back after a storm.

The most trouble we had was watching our saddle horses, to keep the young mustang studs from stealing them. The old mustang would whip out and run off every spring, the young studs, and they would steal anything in the horse-line.

In 1888, I think it was, we started to build the old Ranch House, as Mr. Horn had come down, and wanted to move his family. We hauled the lumber, or had the Mexicans to, rather, from Ft. Sumner. Old Alexandra, an old carpenter, or supposed to be, from Ft. Sumner, came out and made the adobes, and the dimensions of the wall. I asked him: "Why are you so particular in different rooms, and shape of the house?"

He says: "We have to make the house, or walls, to fit the lumber." The lumber was out of the old buildings, at Ft. Sumner, of Pete Maxwell's, where "Billy the Kid" was killed.

"Billy the Kid" was killed in the east room of Maxwell's house. The kitchen that we used on the ranch was built of the same lumber, doors and windows, of the house that he was killed in. The bullet mark is in the window yet, I suppose, as it was when I left the ranch. Anyone can see plainly it is a bullet mark. The bullet mark in the window and one in the ceiling was put there by Billy, after Pat Garrett had shot Billy.

In 1900, Mr. Horn moved his family down from Denver and only lived two years afterward. He died in 1902. Then New Mexico went to the bad.

As now and then, dry-land farmers began to drop in. Mr. T. N. Clayton and our present W. O. O'Donald, who is janitor in high school, were the first to file. They filed north of the old Horn ranch, what we call the Horseshoe range, owned by the Curtises. They filed in 1903.

In 1902 or 1903, Henry Moss filed east of the Horn ranch and Will Krenshaw and Bob Krenshaw, his brother, also filed there. From then on the country began to settle up.

Then they built the railroad, the Belen cut-off. In 1906, was the big rush. That's when all the cow-men lost their heads and commenced going broke.

About the year ____ when Otero was governor of New Mexico, we had just bought a big bunch of cattle, and put up miles and miles of fence, and before the cattle had acquainted themselves with the place an order had been issued by the government to "take down all fences" Why? When settlers began to come, the ranch, as was other ranches, was at a loss to know what to do. They finally decided to see the governor and talk to him personally. They wanted some time to dispose of their cattle, so the governor listened with a compassionate ear, and he gave the cattle men a year to adjust themselves. The year finally went by, and no one said anything against their using the land. Another year went by, and no one seemed to care. The governor won some people to him, who will never forget him.

Salidone, a Mexican who worked for me, was out one day and he saw a deer. He told me about it afterward and says, "Dad, I saw the biggest deer today I ever saw in my life." It was an uncommon thing to see a deer here so we supposed it drifted this way from ____ with a storm.

A while after that, I was riding along one day thinking about the deer, and wondering where it was, when I rode close by a bunch of trees and there lay the deer in plain sight. He had the biggest horns and was the biggest deer I had ever seen, too. I knew if I made the least noise, it would be gone in an instant, so I reined my horse to a stop, and I pulled out my six-shooter and fired, killing him instantly.

I removed his entrails and hurried away to the ranch house about three miles away, and got a man to come help me with him. It was all we both could do to load him on the horse. I had to hurry for I knew if the wild animals got to it before we got back, that they would soon eat all of it. The wild animals were thick.

Edith L. Crawford,
Carrizozo, N. Mex.

Dated: June 16, 1939.
Words: 154
Topic: Brands
Source of Information:
Brand Book, on file in the
office of the County Clerk,
Lincoln Co. N. Mex.

JUN 1 8 1939

BRANDS.

In checking over the earliest records of brands in Lincoln County, I find the brand of Lawrence G. Murphy & Company. This brand was used "for the purpose of marking all horses, mules and cattle" belonging to the company and was filed for record June 28, 1869. The brand was

-----

On June 28, 1869, the brand of Antonio Torres was filed for record. His ranch was on the Hondo River.

On December 17, 1869, the brand of John Chisum was recorded as follows:

Alexander A. McSween recorded his brand on May 3, 1877.

A record of the brand of Jas. J. Dolan & Co. was filed on April 8, 1879.

J. W. Olinger's brand was and filed for record May 23, 1879.

All of these men were large cattle owners and very well known in the early days of the cattle industry in Lincoln County.

Brands, Edith L. Crawford, June 16, 1939, NMFWP, WPA #115b, NMSRCA

Folklore and Folkways: A Horse's Love for His Home

by W. M. Emery

One often reads or hears of dogs who have traveled for months to return to a home which they have loved, but it is seldom that a horse is credited with the same intelligence and homing instinct as a dog. But all horse lovers know that a horse will grieve for his old home, and try to return to it if he has a chance.

Hank, a pet saddle horse on the YH Ranch, showed his mixed ancestry of thorough-bred and cold-blooded stock by his tall slender body, and dainty little feet, his unusually thick black mane and tail and his speed and endurance.

Matt was about seventeen years old the first time he saw Hank, and he immediately wanted him to add to his string of good saddle horses. His father was reluctant in giving his consent to the trade, but Matt was not to be denied.

"Daddy, if you could only see him! Why, he can go like the wind, and stop and turn on a dime."

The father finally gave Matt permission to trade a cow and give ten dollars to boot for the much prized horse.

Hank was all Matt had said and more. He could run, stop and "turn on a dime" as Matt had said; had a good saddle gait, and would frequently "break in two" and do a good job of pitching, much to the delight of the boy and his friends. But he soon became one of the best cow horses on the ranch.

A few years later Matt was married. His wife, a town girl who knew nothing about horses or cattle, found ranch life a little lonesome at times so she spent a great deal of time winning the friendship of the saddle stock which was kept at the ranch headquarters. It wasn't long until every horse on the place was eating out of her hand, and quarreling with one another trying to see which one could get to her first.

Hank soon became her special pet, and she could go out in the pasture and catch him at any time. Although the first time she saw him and tried to pet him—thinking he was one of the other horses—he tried to kick her, and the first time she rode him he nearly bucked her off.

One day Matt rode Hank when he was going to the pasture to look after his cattle. That evening when he came home he was riding a strange black horse. Jane ran out to meet him and ask where Hank was.

"Well, I met a horse buyer over at Lane's ranch, and he wanted Hank. He was buying horses to train for Polo. I traded Hank to Ben for this horse and Ben sold him to the horse buyer. He will take him up on a ranch near Walsenburg, and train him for the game. In May, when he sells the horses to a California outfit, he will pay Ben a hundred dollars a head for the horses. I wouldn't trade with him on those terms, so I traded with Ben and let Ben trade with him. This is a good horse though; you'll like him."

Yes, Midnight was a good horse, gentle, reliable, and easy gaited, but that didn't prevent Jane from missing Hank.

Now and then someone would stop at the ranch who had seen Hank in a Polo game in Trinidad or Walsenburg, and tell what a fine polo pony he had made. He was considered one of the best in the bunch.

But when the time came for the California buyers to take over the horses, they broke their contract and the horse buyer was left with over a hundred head of horses on his hands. These he returned to their original owners. Ben did not want so many old horses and soon traded Hank to a horse trader for a yearling colt.

Hank was taken over near Wagon Mound and put out in a pasture about two hundred miles from his old home. A short time later his new owner was sent to prison for stealing horses.

Over a year went by. One day Jane had been washing and friends stopped in for dinner. As she was hurrying to prepare the meal, Matt came in and said, "Jane, you can't guess what's out here."

"No, what is it?" asked Jane.

"Come and see," replied Matt, and went back out, followed by the curious Jane and her friends.

"Oh! It's Hank!" cried Jane, "Hank, Hank, do you know me?"

Hank came into the yard and up to the door to rub his nose against Jane, and tell her in every way a horse could that he did know her and was just as glad to see her as she was to see him. Jane got a few hands full of corn and fed him. Hank had brought another horse with him, a big grey saddle horse. This horse ate out of Jane's hand, too.

It was later learned that the horses had gotten out of their pasture near Wagon Mound, and Hank had left for his old range at once, even though it had been over a year since he had been there.

The next winter when the horses were turned out into the winter pasture, the grey horse was stolen, but Hank remained on the ranch and received the best of care as long as he lived.

William F. Sumpter

by W. M. Emery

When W. F. Sumpter went to his eternal reward, March 21, 1935, Union County lost one of its oldest pioneers, and one of its best authorities on the history of Union County.

In recent years Mr. Sumpter had been visited by men from Kansas, Oklahoma, Colorado and New Mexico who were interested in gathering data on the early history of the cattle industry in these States, as he had a reputation for giving accurate and dependable information.

W. F. Sumpter—more commonly known as Bud—was born at Leavenworth, Kansas, June 5, 1857. He spent his first birthday in the arms of his mother as she walked across the plains toward Denver. The family was traveling by ox train to Denver when they were put on a blind trail by a dishonest store-keeper and all their stock was stolen by a band of renegades and they were left afoot 200 miles from Denver.

Shortly after reaching Denver his mother married Madison Emery, and Bud was better known as Bud Emery by the men with whom he worked.

The family moved from Denver to Old Fort Bent, on the Arkansas, then over to the San Luis valley, which they were warned to leave by the Indians. Then moved to the Maxwell Grant where they lived five years.

In 1865 they moved to Madison, on the Dry Cimarron river.

Here Mr. Sumpter received his schooling at the small country school house. At the age of ten Mr. Sumpter and his mother assisted the soldiers from Fort Union in capturing the notorious and elusive outlaw Coe.

When Bud was thirteen he killed his first bear, this made him one of the proudest and happiest boys in New Mexico, even though he was one of the sickest from eating the bear meat without salt.

At the age of fourteen Mr. Sumpter began working for the Hall Brothers, original owners of the now well known Crossell Ranch. He later became foreman of the ranch.

After working for the Hall Brothers for several years Mr. Sumpter went into the cattle business for himself, on the same ranch on which he was living at the time of his death, and a few miles west of the Crossell holdings.

When the Hall Brothers sold out to the Prairie Cattle Company in 1881, a Mr. Green, representative of the Prairie Cattle Company, came to Mr. Sumpter with the following offer.

"Sumpter," said Green, "William Hall speaks well of you. He says you are a good cowman, and that you have a creditable bunch of cattle. We are forming a new, great, cattle company, financed by Scotch capital. We want more stock. I am here to offer you $135,000 for your cattle. If you will sell out to us, we will make you range manager of the new company, at a salary of $2500.00 per year. Will you take the offer and accept the position?"

Sumpter promised to think the matter over. At the time he owed $40,000.00 on his cattle, which he had bought on time from his friends. He could have paid all of his indebtedness and had $95,000 clear. But for some unknown reason he turned the offer down, a decision which he was soon to regret. In 1884, the price of cattle declined. Then the hard winter of 1885–86 came on with severe losses, and Sumpter was forced out of the cattle business, with one old black cow all that was left from the $135,000 herd.

Mr. Sumpter worked as foreman for several of the larger cattle companies of northeastern New Mexico. He rode the range from the Arkansas river to the Canadian river, and made numerous trips to Denver, Dodge City and Coolidge with trail herds.

At the age of twenty-seven Mr. Sumpter was married to Miss Minneta Darling. One child, a girl, was born to them, but died a few years later.

During the '80s Mr. Sumpter spent one year in South Park, Colorado; the only year of his entire life spent out of the State of New Mexico.

In 1896 he re-married, this time to Miss Daisy McLaughlin of Folsom. They made their first home on a ranch near Capulin, New Mexico, later moving back to the old home ranch on the Dry Cimarron.

To this union seven boys were born; they are Lewis F. of Great Falls, Oregon; Leonard H., who now owns and operates the home ranch near Folsom; Robert F., manager of one of the Doherty ranches near Officer, Colorado; Raymond P., of Kenton, Oklahoma; Benjamin F., Folsom; William Homer, of Fort Gibson, Mississippi; and Howard B., who is foreman of a Doherty near Trinchera, Colorado. He also has a sister, Mrs.

Sarah Jane Gleason, of Folsom. His half-brother, Matt Emery, died in 1915.

During his career Bud Sumpter at one time was owner of one of the largest cattle ranches in this part of New Mexico. He formed partnerships at different times with various persons, among them John Milliken; J. M. Johns, and Dr. Owens, in livestock and ranching interests.

He took an active part in all movements for the betterment of the community, and served several terms as a director on the school board.

The Sumpter ranch, on U. S. Highway 64, was widely known for its old time Western hospitality. Its doors were ever open to friends and strangers alike.

Source of Information: S. J. Gleason.

An Unusual Log House

by Kenneth Fordyce

A nineteenth century six-sided log house of unusual interest is located on the Whistler Ranch in northern New Mexico. The house itself is peculiar; the builders of the house were strange people.

John Matthew, his wife, a very educated and intelligent woman, his son and his daughter (Walter and Nina) came to northern New Mexico from Deadwood, South Dakota in 1891. Matthew, with his family and the herd of cattle which they drove into the country, located on the Unade Gato River (Cat's Paw River), near Johnson Park, a few miles north of the T O Ranch. After a year in the park Matthew decided to move out onto the flatlands south of the mountains, along the lower Sugarite River; today the spot is a quarter of a mile to the south of the new highway 87, which has just been completed.

Matthew cut the pine logs for his new house in the canyons below Johnson Mesa and hauled them to the grove of cottonwood trees where the new home was to be erected.

The wife and two children had had a peculiar experience before they left South Dakota which greatly influenced the style of the new home. The three were extremely frightened each time that the wind blew. At their former home near Deadwood a few short months before, they had been caught in a cyclone, picked up bodily, and swept along for a half mile to a spot where they were caught in a wire fence. The three were found after the storm nearer dead than alive, but they recovered. It is little wonder that the wind of the flatlands, strong but not dangerously severe, put terror into their hearts. As a result of this experience, Mrs. Matthew wanted a house that the wind could not sweep away, and in which she and her family would be absolutely safe.

The new house was made of logs, twenty-one logs high from the ground and it had six sides instead of four. The floor of the first story was one step lower than the ground. The floor of the second story which was even with the eleventh log, extended out two feet farther than the walls of the first story, on four sides. The overhanging second floor gave the log house the appearance of an old-fashioned blockade built for protection from the Indians in the Colonies of the east. There was one room downstairs, used for a general living room and the entire upstairs was a bedroom. There were windows on three sides of the second floor bedroom and two outside doors on the lower floor. Having six sides, the house was almost round; there were no corners for the wind to catch on. Two adobe lean-tos were built at the rear, the one to serve as the kitchen and the other as a spare bedroom. Mrs. Matthew felt certain that this heavy log and adobe house without corners was safe from her dreaded enemy, the wind.

Mr. Matthew ran his cattle on the prairie for four more years and then moved to the southern part of the territory. Mr. Matthew had the misfortune to contract smallpox, which proved fatal to him. Mrs. Matthew became discouraged with life and shot herself, according to the general report.

Back up in northern New Mexico, the log house had new occupants: Mr. and Mrs. G. C. Whistler had moved into it with the purpose in mind of homesteading the place. They lived in the log house until a few years ago when they moved into a new home on the ranch.

Afterword: A Deadwood, South Dakotan traveling through New Mexico in the late nineties was asked if he knew John Matthew from near Deadwood. His reply astounded those who heard it. He said that he did not know a John Matthew in South Dakota but that he could remember a John Matthew Wood who worked for a rancher back there named Fairchilds. According to the traveler's story, South Dakota people believed that Mr. Fairchilds had been murdered and his body burned in his ranch house in about 1890. However, the body had been so badly mutilated and burned when dug out of the ruins of the burned house that it was impossible to be positive about the matter. He stated that they did know that John Matthew Wood, Mrs. Fairchilds and the two children and all of the Fairchilds' cattle had been missing since the fire.

Mr. G. C. Whistler—Raton did not want to be quoted on the information in the last paragraph, so perhaps it should be omitted.

Source of Information: Mr. G. C. Whistler, Whistler Ranch, Raton, New Mexico.

Pioneer: "A Remarkable White Steer"

by Kenneth Fordyce

'Lige Johnson lived at Johnson Park almost up to the Colorado–New Mexico State Line back in the days when cattlemen had to drive the herds which they wanted to sell in to Dodge City, Kansas. New Mexico was an excellent place to fatten steers and many seasons 'Lige drove his salable cattle through.

'Lige Johnson had a white steer that developed quite a reputation as a leader. When the drive to Dodge was ready to start this white steer was placed in the lead and the steer would remain there leading the cattle all the way. It made the driving exceptionally easy for the "punchers" for the white steer could and did lead without error.

The most remarkable part of the white steer's performance was that when the cattle were delivered in Dodge, the white steer was turned loose and would return to the ranch, arriving there almost as promptly as the drivers. The white steer led the herd through, three different years.

Source of Information: Ed Popejoy, Raton, New Mexico, February 11, 1937.

**Branding Cattle in Southern New Mexico near Deming,
Unattributed, 1890-1900?, NMHM/DCA #012711**

Early Days of a Cowboy on the Pecos (Excerpts)

by James F. Hinkle

Roswell, New Mexico 1937

Chapter One

While this is more or less personal, still it is in a way a history of the old cattle days never to return. The writer was on a cattle ranch near Colorado City, Texas, in the spring of 1885 and in the winter and early spring of that year a great number of cattle drifted across the plains to the Pecos River from the head of the Conchas and Colorado Rivers.

At that time there were very few ranches or cattle on the then called Llano Estacado or Staked Plains. Several outfits, two hundred cowboys or more, were sent across to bring the cattle back and this was my first knowledge of the Pecos. Then later in the year the C A Bar outfit which I was with began to move cattle to New Mexico, where they had bought and established a ranch on the Rio Penasco, a tributary of the Pecos River.

The first of these cattle were shipped to Tayah, Texas, and trailed from there, but the great numbers were driven across the plains following along the line of the then new Texas and Pacific Railroad.

Then I landed on the Penasco in old Lincoln County in October, 1885—and now, October, 1935, just fifty years afterwards, I am writing this.

At that time all southeast New Mexico was solely and strictly a cattle country—there were no other interests—and there were large herds. The Chisum ranch at South Spring River was the oldest ranch on the Pecos and claimed the range on both side of the Pecos from Seven Rivers to Bosque Grande—a distance of 125 miles and claimed something like sixty thousand cattle. This outfit was one of the first on the Pecos. John Chisum brought cattle into New Mexico as early as 1868. Their cattle were trailed from eastern and southern Texas to the various military forts in New Mexico and some as far west as Arizona. Afterwards the South Spring ranch was started.

In 1882 the L F D moved in on the Pecos and established ranch headquarters at Bosque Grande. This was known as the Littlefield Cattle Company and was managed by J. P. White, who was in the cattle business on the Pecos continuously for more than fifty years.

But the real cattle drive came to the Pecos from 1884 to 1890 and at that time, in addition to the Chisum and L F D outfits, there were the Eddy-Bissell Cattle Company, the Holt Cattle Company, the W T outfit and the Hash Knife, all below Seven Rivers. The C A Bar outfit, the Diamond A, the Lea, the Milne Bush, the Blocks, the V V, the F H C and the Holy Cattle Company—all of these on the Pecos or tributaries to the Pecos and in what was then Lincoln County. This county was about two hundred miles square in area, almost one-fourth of New Mexico.

The principal towns of southeast New Mexico—in fact the only towns of any consequence—in Lincoln County at that time (1885) were Seven Rivers, Lincoln and White Oaks, all since practically abandoned.

All of the outfits mentioned had herds of from thirty to fifty thousand cattle; also, there were some smaller herds. But one can see from this that every interest was cattle.

Roswell at that time was just a cattle trail point of a post office and one store, and Carlsbad was not located or started until 1889. Later on the counties of Chaves and Eddy were created from Lincoln and organized and in effect January 1, 1891.

At the session of the legislature in January, 1889, was my first visit in Santa Fe. I was there on this county division with Captain Lea and George Curry. Jas. J. Dolan was the member of the Council and Frank Lernet the House member. Ross was Governor. I was chairman of the Board of County Commissioners of the remaining portion of Lincoln County in 1891 and made the settlement with Chaves and Eddy Counties.

From 1885 and for about ten years thereafter it was just cattle, nothing more—only a fight to hold your own. The roundups started with the first green grass, usually in April, and continued until November and it was ride and ride hard all the time. We would send men out on the outside work and they would often be away for six months. They would work with the outside wagons and throw the cattle back towards the headquarters ranch. Often they would work as far south as Pecos town on the Pecos, and sometimes below that, and as far north as old Fort Sumner, a distance up and down the river of two hundred and fifty miles.

Roswell during this time became the cattle center. The spring roundups from all directions would wind up there, clean up their herds and start their trail herds. During this time it was two hundred miles or more to any railroad, and all marketable cattle had to be trailed to some shipping point. I had herds trailed to Engle, Las Vegas and Springer on the Santa Fe, to Clayton and Amarillo on the Colorado Southern, and Midland and Tayah on the T. P.—all around the circle, any place to sell them or ship to market.

There was a great slump in the cattle business in 1887 and during the fall of that year we drove a herd of 700 three and four year old steers to Tayah, Texas, shipped to Chicago, and they did not much more than pay freight and expenses, and for the next few years it was almost impossible to sell cattle at any price.

One party about that time shipped a trainload of steers to market and they drew on him for the loss. He answered, "no money. will ship more cattle."

During these times we drove one and often two herds of around fifteen to twenty hundred head each year and the average price was eight, eleven and fourteen dollars for one, two and three year old steers. So while the cattlemen barely got by during those times, their only gain was in increased numbers in breeding cattle; still, none seemed to fare as badly as the party who wanted to ship more cattle.

However, along in the nineties I was interested in a herd of horses and, becoming over-stocked—for there was hardly any sale at all—we shipped two carloads to Kansas City. The commission house drew on me for eighty-five dollars for loss. I didn't offer to ship more horses but I felt like it.

The L F D outfit during this time drove two thousand head of two and three year old heifers as far north as the Arkansas river in Kansas and could not sell them, and returned with them. They were four to five months on the trail going and returning. This goes to show what a hard time the cow men had in those days.

The ranches at that time owned only the living waters, that is the rivers, creeks and springs, and all was on open range, no fences or wells or windmills. This was the case on both sides of the Pecos; from Fort Sumner down to the New Mexico line each outfit claimed range according to water front.

Roundups usually commenced in April and continued until late fall. Each particular district had a corporal in charge and all the outfits worked in harmony. The spring roundups were for putting up trail herds and throwing cattle back on their respective ranges. The summer roundups were for branding the calves.

Some winters the cattle would drift south very much. I call to mind one roundup on both sides of the Pecos from Seven Rivers to the Berrendos, just north of Roswell, when there had been a great drift of cattle from as far north as the Canadian. Our outfit was on the west side of the river and was one of twenty-two wagons on that work. It took about thirty days to do that work for we would have large numbers of cattle in each roundup. The cattle were largely on out waters, that is, surface water holes and lakes, and the drive would have to go out each morning twenty miles or more to get around the cattle. At the clean up at Roswell there were fifty thousand cattle under herd to be taken back to the various ranches.

On this work, on account of so much out water and the distance of the cattle from the river, many cowboys rode as much as one hundred miles each day. Now to one of this day this does not look reasonable. But those who went on the outside circle had to ride out twenty miles or more to get around the outside cattle. They were off as soon as it was light enough to catch horses and the roundup would be thrown together from ten to twelve o' clock; then work the cattle and brand until dark—and stand guard one-third of the night.

Each cowboy mount consisted of ten or twelve horses and he rode four each day. There were no fences or corrals at that time and all branding was on the prairie; also, the saddle horses were night herded, as well as the cattle. So one can readily understand that a cowboy in those days had to ride and ride straight up sixteen hours a day.

In the late eighties some of the larger outfits, such as the L F D's, moved out on the plains and established ranches there. Up to that time only some small herds were on the plains. The J A L outfit was on the lower plains near the corner of New Mexico and the Newman outfit where Portales is now.

The days of the buffalo had passed at this time, but the antelope were in vast herds on both sides of the Pecos, but especially on the plains. One could often see them in herds of two or three hundred. Also in the foot hills of the Sacramento and Guadalupe mountains were many black tail, or mule ear deer. We seldom killed the deer or antelope in the early days, except by a little practice once in a while with our forty-fives, but we could rope the deer, and often did, but not the antelope, they were too fast on foot for our best horses.

Chapter Two

For a decade, from '85 to '95, it was truly the old longhorn cattle days. It was indeed then:

"Home, home on the range,
Where the deer and the antelope play,
Where seldom is heard a discouraging word
And the skies are not cloudy all day."

During this time it was all open range. The cattle outfits owned or otherwise claimed all the living or natural waters, the river fronts, the creeks and springs and all the surrounding lands that this controlled. They were lords of all they surveyed and if anyone settled on their range, they were considered intruders or trespassers.

And then in the late eighties and early nineties came the covered wagons and a little later the sheep men. They stood the covered wagon fellows pretty well but it took them a long time to even get on speaking terms with the sheep men. This was largely on account of the fact that the sheep owners at that time were mostly trespassers, as they were not land owners, and drifted about over the government land and watered their sheep on privately owned land. This brought on the trouble. The Legislature finally passed a law that a sheep herd traveling—and most all had to travel or move for very few had ranches—must move six miles a day. This helped but did not cure.

At that time the outfit that I was running owned forty miles of running water, the Penasco River. All of this was fee land. Several with large sheep herds came in, would water and graze out three miles on one side; then next day they would go back and water and go out three miles on the other side, making the six miles a day.

There was another case. A party from Texas drifted in with a large number of sheep and was grazing on first one range and then another. Finally he found a pretty good place and decided to stay. He was ordered off by the cowboys of that ranch. He explained that he couldn't move as his wagon was "broke down" and he showed them the wagon with a wheel gone. As it was fifty miles or more to any place where he could get another wheel or have one repaired, the punchers were very lenient, but on looking around they found the wheel hidden in some mesquite brush. Of course that party then moved and that P. D. Q.

However, the sheep men, like the cattlemen, had a hard time getting along at that time. This was on account of low prices and adverse conditions.

One Johnnie Martin, who was in the sheep business, or had been, but was in the early nineties running a small store up in the Sacramento mountains. During the political campaign that fall we were after Martin to help out and get active for the Democratic ticket. He said, "No, I won't. I am a Democrat but I voted for free wool and came within four cents of getting it." With four cent wool and sheep at seventy-five cents to one dollar per head value and not much market at that, like the cattlemen it was indeed hard times. But with all, there was not much complaint.

Most all the cowboys we only knew as and called "punchers." They were young and active and willing. There was a great fellowship feeling, a common union, among them. But it was work and hard work. There were no union hours. It was from daylight until dark, except the three winter months.

One time I had a puncher who complained; said he was tired of two suppers every night, so he quit, packed his bed on his pack horse and left. In about three months he was back and had no bed. He said he had had a job over on the west side of the Sacramento Mountains. "Well," I asked, "where's your bed?" "Oh hell," he said, "I didn't need a bed over there. Just a lantern."

During those days a puncher would stand for almost anything except to catch another puncher riding one of his pet horses. That was one thing they would not stand for. Each man, that is, the regulars or old hands, had mounts of ten or twelve horses. The outfit I was with had around four hundred saddle horses and we knew the name, color and description of every one. Many were remarkably well trained. Like the owners, they had good and bad points.

I had one old cutting horse named Carnello. He was not much for looks but was considered the best cutting horse on the range. One day a tenderfoot was at the roundup and I remarked that Carnello knew marks and brands. At the time we were cutting out cows with unbranded calves for breeding. This party said he would have to be shown so he bet me five dollars, but I had to cut out three C A Bar cows with unbranded calves before he gave up the money. However, it was easy. All we had to do when we rode up to a cow of our brand with unbranded calf was to touch the horse with the spur or in some known manner drop the bridle reins and the horse could cut them out.

The horses were as well trained in roping. But in the spring, after three or four months rest and in good condition from off the ranges, the best trained old horses would not forget the art of pitching and, when first starting out on the spring roundup, we often had many empty saddles.

An old cow pony was as faithful as a dog to the one who rode him. One could go in the remontar at any time without a rope and walk up to his horses—but go in with a rope, and they were gone. They knew it was their time on duty.

One time my old night horse fell down with me in a stampede and I landed in the bottom of a gully in the mud. Soon the faithful old pony came back in the dark, found me and rubbed me with his nose.

One very noticeable characteristic of the cowpunchers of those days was that they did not talk very much. Whether this was on account of life on the open range or being alone so much, no one seemed to know, but it was a fact. It was a common expression on the plains to say: "One could see farther and see less; more cows and less milk; ride farther and talk less."

In the early nineties I was nominated and running for the legislature. My opponent on the other ticket, as his acceptance speech when nominated at the convention said, "Thanks; I'll do my darndest to be elected." Nothing more. Anyway, I was elected. Probably because I said less.

Also, many years afterwards and when statehood came I was again running for the legislature—this time the state senate. My opponent challenged me to a joint debate. As public speaking was clean out of my line, this stumped me. However, we had the debate and my opponent, the challenger, was to make the first talk, and did for one hour and a half. The hall was densely crowded, many standing. When my turn came I said, "You folks look tired but if you want to remain longer and listen to a debate between a second class lawyer and a first class cowpuncher, here we go." This broke up the meeting and somehow I was elected. I give these as examples, for in those days any real cowhand was of few words and for action.

Mr. Casey, the president of the cattle company I was running, came out from Missouri and, after an all day's drive, we reached the roundup chuck wagon very late. The boys were all on night herd, as they were holding two herds, or asleep. Mr. Casey had brought a phonograph or talking machine so we unpacked it and turned it on. We didn't stampede the cattle but did stampede the punchers. Very few of them were used to this kind of music. They could all sing, or rather hum "Sam Bass" while on night herd. "Sam Bass" was the old Texas song known to every range man in the southwest. First and last I think there must have been at least two thousand verses, according to the variations of the cowpunchers.

However, sometimes they would break loose on the old cowboys hymn, which was something like this:

"The trail to that bright mystic region
Is both narrow and dim, they say,
While the broad one that leads to perdition
Is posted and blazed all the way.
Then I have heard there will be a grand roundup
When the cowboys, like others, will stand
To be cut by the rider of Judgment,
Who is posted and knows every brand."

Chapter Four

In 1896 was the beginning of a new era in the range cattle business; more settlers, smaller herds, pastures and fencing and watering by wells and windmills.

Many of the larger herds began reducing. The first of these was the old Jinglebob outfit, one of the first and the largest herd on the Pecos. John Chisum located on the Pecos in 1868, first at Bosque Grande and later South Spring, near Roswell. He drove the first trail herd into New Mexico and established what was known as the Chisum Trail. This was from the Gulf Coast of Texas to the head of the Concho River; thence across the staked plains to the Pecos River, near old Fort Stockton; thence up the river on the east side to what is known as Pope's Crossing, the mouth of the Delaware Creek, a tributary of the Pecos; thence on the west side to old Fort Sumner; also west to Fort Stanton and to points in Arizona. Chisum delivered beef cattle to these various military ports and Indian reservations and this route was known as the Chisum Trail.

The first white man to enter what is now New Mexico was the Spaniard, Cabeza de Baca. With three others he made his way from the coast of Texas to the Rio Grande and over practically the same route as described as the Chisum Trail.

Pope's Crossing was named for an Army lieutenant, afterwards General Pope, who made that location in 1856 and it was then the route of the Butterfield stage coach and mail line from San Antonio to California.

Cabeza de Baca described the plains, the Pecos and the mountain ranges so well that without doubt he traveled about this route and reached the Rio Grande about where Las Cruces is now. More than likely he went up the Rio Penasco and crossed the Sacramento Mountains about where the Mescalero Indian reservation is now, and thence across the San Andreas Mountains to the Rio Grande.

Up to the great cattle drive to the Pecos, which was in the eighties, the Pecos River was a very narrow, crooked and deep stream. There were very few crossings and cattle seldom crossed the stream. And the cowpunchers did not if they could avoid doing so. Just two things that cowpunchers were afraid of—the Pecos River and Rattlesnakes. It was known and often said that the buffalo were never found west of the Pecos and there were immense herds east of the Pecos. This is borne out, for in the latter eighties many buffalo bones, horns and skulls could be seen anywhere on the east of the Pecos and very few on the west side.

Cabeza de Baca mentioned crossing a stream narrow, deep and swift, often seeing many buffalo (cows he called them), and then in sight of the mountains. This was the Pecos.

The great cattle drive and stocking of the ranges on the Pecos naturally wore down the banks and, by floods and erosion, widened the stream. Flood waters did not reach the Pecos until then. There was soft soil, well sodded, and the waters did not run off until after the cattle trails were made. Then came floods. There was no evidence of floods or records of them on the Pecos or tributaries, such as the Penasco, Felix, Hondo, Mora and others, until the cattle days.

Beginning in 1896 range cattle prices were better and all the outfits began reducing their herds. During the next few years most of the larger herds were about closed out.

Also, the old hands began to scatter, some to other occupations, but it was a trial to forget and leave the old range.

One fellow tried South America. He was in the cattle business there for a while and became stranded there, but finally returned and, when sailing into New York harbor, looked up at the Statue of Liberty and said, "Old Lady, if you ever see me again, you will have to turn around."

Some others went to British Columbia—the Alberta country—but they mostly froze out there. Anyway, the days of the old open range cowboys were drawing to a close, never to return.

The C A Bar outfit finally closed out in the spring of 1901. They had been selling and delivering cattle wherever possible for two or three years and, when the final books were closed, we had in that time sold and delivered forty-one thousand cattle. I had been with the outfit seventeen years. And thus ended the open range cowboy life for me.

I was again a member of the Territorial legislature in 1901. This time a member of the Senate (Territorial Council as it was called then). My district was the ninth and consisted of six counties, all of southern New Mexico; Otero was Governor during this session and Colonel J. Frank Chavez was President of the Council.

Well, the old life and habits were still with me and I soon was in the cattle business again. Mr. J. J. Hagerman, who started the first reservoir irrigation project in New Mexico, at what is now Carlsbad, and who built the first railroad in the Pecos River country, had acquired a large tract of land east of the Pecos River in Chaves County and was stocking it with cattle. This was known as the South Spring Cattle Company. I went in as manager. This was strictly a windmill and pasture project. The open range and the days of the roundup and the corporal and the Remontas were over. Handling cattle was quite different at this time from on the open range. One of the new regulations was dipping the cattle for sanitary purposes. We had to build vats and dip all the cattle. In the old open range days we often had to dip some of the cowpunchers, but not the cattle.

We had in this ranch about two hundred thirty thousand acres, all owned or leased land, and about one hundred seventy-five miles of fence. The ranch was stocked with high-grade Hereford cattle. I was with this company for eight years but when they began to round up and herd cattle with Ford cars I thought it no place for an old range cowpuncher. So I quit in 1911 and turned over, in round numbers, fourteen thousand cattle.

This ended the twenty-five years I was active in the range cattle business on the Pecos. But I couldn't or wouldn't quit political or public office and was elected the first full term mayor of Roswell and served two years. That was in 1905 and 1906.

During that time, and before, we had wide-open saloons and licensed gambling. We put a very high license and strict regulations on the saloons and cut the licensed gambling entirely. This was the first ordinance of this kind in New Mexico.

I was elected to the first State Senate when New Mexico came in as a state in 1912, and served in the three sessions of 1912, 1913 and 1915. I was elected Governor and served in 1923 and 1924 and, cowboy-like, of few words, I delivered about one of the shortest messages on record to the legislature when they met. That was "to pass laws that an average layman could understand and that would not have to go to court to interpret what was meant, and to cut out putting whereas and dictionaries at the beginning of the laws." Looking at it now and at the present practices, it would be well if Congress and the various legislatures would simplify their acts. There would not be so much necessity of the courts working overtime.

Stories of Old Timers by Tom Gray

by Carrie L. Hodges

A big lake surrounded by hundreds of miles of rolling grassland— that was the beginning. Then cattle drivers began to camp overnight near the lake, some enterprising fellow put up his tent and started selling groceries and supplies, a railroad passed by, and low and behold, the town of Clayton was begun.

That is the story of the beginnings of Clayton as told by Mr. Tom Gray, and he should know, for he is the oldest citizen, in point of residence, now living in Clayton.

Mr. Gray with Mr. T. E. Mitchell came to this section in 1882 and located on a ranch 65 miles south of Clayton. At that time the scenery was unmarred with any trace of human progress. It was possible to ride from Arkansas to the Rio Grande without seeing even an adobe hut to signify the presence of human beings, Mr. Gray says.

Only two methods of transportation were possible, horseback or by covered wagon. However it wasn't necessary to move around much, Mr. Gray said, because all ranches were large and were completely equipped with everything that one might need. It was only necessary to leave the ranch once or twice a year when cattle were being driven to market. Cattle was practically the only industry.

Large herds of cattle were allowed to roam at will over this vast section of prairie. And the gala time of the year came at "round up" time when the cattle were all gathered in and sorted according to brands. This was followed by the big social event of the season, the round up dance. A certain amount of gun play always seemed necessary at these affairs, Mr. Gray declared.

"Money was free," said Mr. Gray, "and a great amount was spent on ammunition. Cowboys didn't wear overalls as they do now, but insisted upon the best of materials. They spent fabulous sums for Stetson hats and big, dangerous looking gun belts."

"Buffalo roamed the prairies by the thousand, but Indians were not especially common," he continued. "The last Indian raid of any importance was in 1878. After that, only an occasional tribe would pass through, en route to their villages, on their way wandering either east or west in search of uninhabited lands."

In 1886 Mr. Gray moved to a ranch now known as the Bushnell ranch, 40 miles southwest of Clayton. The post office there was then known as Benham. He remained there for eight years when he moved to Clayton following an injury in a round up.

"Prior to 1887 there were no settlers in this immediate section. Not even a post office marked the site of the town of Clayton. In that year a few tents dotted the hill side, and in the following year the Colorado and Southern railway built its lines through here, and Clayton enjoyed several years of rapid growth," Mr. Gray said.

"The first house in Clayton was brought from the Tri-Angle Ranch," he explained, "and placed on the grounds where the present Isaac's Hardware company is located. It was used as a hotel and a livery stable was located near by," he said.

It was not unusual to find from 100 to 150 saddled horses in the town of Clayton overnight. Often five or six cow outfits would stop overnight in the village at the favorite watering holes. These were two big lakes, one located just north of town and the other in the present part of the city, lying south of the post office. These outfits were composed of a chuck and provision wagon, a cook, about fifteen men to a wagon, each man having about ten horses.

Mrs. Ada F. Love, resident and property owner of Clayton, was the first school teacher here. The school house is now being used as a residence. Only a very few students were enrolled in this one room school, but it was at least a start. John Hill Jr. was the first white child born in Clayton. He made his home here until a few years ago when he went to Amarillo, Texas, to live.

Mr. Gray left the ranch in 1895 because of an injury which made it impossible for him to continue as a cowboy. The last year he rode the range, he shipped 17,000 head of cattle from Des Moines, then nothing but a corral.

He made Clayton his home from 1895 to the time of his death which occurred April 24, 1936.

Source of Information:1. Related to Reporter of the Union County Leader and published in the same publication October 8, 1931, and submitted for publication by Mrs. Leah Gray Wilson, daughter of Mr. Gray. 2. Data furnished by Mrs. Leah Gray Wilson, October 19, 1936, Interview.

"The Snowstorm of 1889"

by Carrie L. Hodges

"The fall of 1889 had been mild with no premonitions of severe or sudden storms." A number of cattle companies had driven their herds of cattle to within a short distance of Clayton, New Mexico, awaiting shipment. The roundup wagons started on their return trips, bound for the Pecos River country, a long and tedious journey to Puerto de Luna, Ft. Sumner and Roswell, wagons loaded with a winter's supplies.

"The afternoon of October 30, 1889 showed signs of inclemency and later in the evening snow began to fall. With increasing severity which next morning portended to blizzard proportions, the storm raged, nor did it let up for several days. The wind piled the falling snow in drifts and drove sleet in cutting, blinding, impenetrable clouds against whatever it met. Cowboys, on guard about their cattle, held out against nature's assault for some time, but blinded by the gale which hourly increased in fury, the riders finally abandoned their charges, let the cattle go, and sought such protection as they could reach. Some of the men found shelter in ravines and canyons, others, left at the wagons, their horses gone before the gale, found what solace as they could in their tents.

"All communication with the outside world, was, for a time, cut off for Clayton. For eighteen days it was without train service from the north and probably from the south. All efforts of the railway company to clear their track were unsuccessful, as wind blew the cuts full of snow as fast as it was removed.

"Reports finally began to reach town through incoming persons who made trails and paths through the snow, of lost flocks of sheep, some of which were buried beneath drifts or had been swept away before the storm, of abandoned herds of cattle, and of dead cowboys. The following is a copy of a telegram sent out from Denver to the eastern press, a week after the storm:

'Denver Colo., November 7, 1889!'

'A special from Clayton, New Mexico, says, unless the snowstorm which has been raging for eight days soon comes to an end, next summer will show a country as thickly covered with dead bodies of animals, as the old Santa Fe trail of the fifties. The depth of snow is not less than twenty five inches on a level and in many places is drifted seven feet high. When the storm struck this section seven large herds of cattle numbering from five hundred to two thousand each, were being held near this place, awaiting shipment to eastern markets. The rain of a week ago was followed Thursday morning by a blizzard of snow and sleet, which sent the herds drifting off in a southern direction. In vain did the half frozen cowboys try to check the march of the cattle through the increasing storm until finding it utterly impossible to hold their charges, they let them pass, and rode their exhausted horses into canyons and sheltered places, to spend many hours without food or fire. Two cowboys drifted through the storm into a deep gulch, where they found a tree in which was a rat's nest. They made a fire of this. During the second night one of their horses died from cold. Having no food, the men cut pieces of flesh from the dead animal, which they roasted and ate without salt. After remaining in this asylum for sixty hours, the men started out and, weakened from suffering, finally reached a ranch house, where they were cared for. Five cowboys are known to have perished in the storm, Henry Miller, John Martin, Charles Jolly, and two men, names unknown. Two Mexican sheep herders have been found frozen to death. Three men coming to town this morning, report drifts in some places, seven and eight feet deep. In many of the drifts, horns of cattle which have died, were seen protruding from the snow. In one drift thirteen dead cattle were counted, and another, ten head. In a bank of snow, several head of steers were seen which, though alive, were unable to move or free themselves. Bands of sheep are completely wiped out. No roads to Clayton are open, though trails have been made through the snow to this point. At Texline, nine miles south of Clayton, two passenger trains have been snowbound for several days. Here, provisions are reported running low. It is thought a snowplow will reach the imprisoned trains tomorrow, and that the railroad will be opened in a few days. The storm is by far the worst ever known in north eastern New Mexico, where the loss of life cannot at present be estimated.'"

After days of sunshine and clear and warmer weather, normal conditions were restored in Clayton and vicinity, but stock shipments were practically discontinued for the winter.

"The southern trail men made no attempt until the next spring, to gather their lost livestock, though local workers finally got their demoralized organizations in order, and gathered small bunches of cattle for shipment to market. Flock masters told of exhuming from their sepulchers of snow, sheep which had been buried two weeks. A considerable number of sheep from one of Christian Otto's flocks were rescued alive after twenty days imprisonment and found little worse for the ordeal. Herders felled cottonwood trees, and dragged them to their hungry animals, which ate the bark, buds and twigs and were thus kept alive until the snow melted, and grass was again exposed. Fortunately cattle and sheep were strong in October 1889, which was greatly to their advantage.

"Across the span of forty-three years there arise no visions of hardships, experienced by those of us in Clayton who were temporarily cut off from the outside world in the fall of 1889.

"The snowfall of this storm of early Clayton's will go down in history as the heaviest perhaps, to be recorded in northern New Mexico."

Colonel Jack Potter relates the excitement and hilarity he caused when he came into Clayton at the time of this storm, wearing four or five shirts with only a vest over them to protect him from the bitter cold. He was trail boss for the New England Live Stock Company of Ft. Sumner, and his herd of some two thousand cattle was marooned a few miles south of Clayton, trapped by the snowstorm. Colonel Potter made the mistake of letting fair weather and glorious, warm sunshine play havoc with his better judgment; therefore, when the unexpected storm hit, he was without a coat, and sought warmth in the various shirts at his disposal.

Bibliography:1. Data taken from *The Story of Early Clayton,* Albert W. Thompson, *New Mexico,* 1933, pages 35–38. 2. Interview, Colonel Jack Potter, Clayton, New Mexico, June 9, 1936.

Description of a Ranch: G.O.S. Ranch

by Mrs. Mildred Jordan

The G.O.S. Ranch, a famous ranch located in Grant County, New Mexico, about 44 miles west of Silver City, being one of the largest in the state, could far more appropriately be called a park. U. S. highway #260 leads to the ranch.

The ranch was founded by George O. Smith (G.O.S.) being his initials and named for him. Mr. Smith came to New Mexico in 1874, a brother Dave Smith preceded him, they located and opened up the Commercial silver mines in Georgetown about twenty-five miles from Silver City and while working these mines in 1883, purchased his first ranch property, known as the Turkey Cienega ranch, which is a part of the present G.O.S. ranch, owned by a different party at present.

At the period Mr. Smith purchased the ranch and for a number of years after, it was the custom of the cattlemen of New Mexico to locate water among streams and at springs in order to control the water supply, and the livestock was grazed on the public domain.

Mr. Smith introduced on his ranch the white-faced cattle and was one of the first to breed up high grade stock in New Mexico.

At the time of the sale of the G.O.S. ranch, it was considered the largest in its locality and had ten thousand head of cattle, besides a large number of riding ponies. The cattle ranged over the Black Range, the Pinos Altos mountains and the Gila forests reservation, and sometimes strayed a hundred miles from the ranch houses.

When Mrs. Smith (still living) was a bride in 1879, the Santa Fe railway had been constructed to Lamy only, and it was necessary to travel by stage the several hundred miles to Silver City.

The old "Jerky"—the old Concord stage coach, with its leather and steel springs—was not the easiest mode of travel, as it swung back and forward and from side to side, but in that day was considered about the best that could be had.

Travelers in that day when making the trip would look forward to the end of the trail, after a long ride over good roads and bad ones behind fresh teams of horses which were relayed from time to time along the trip, and were traveling rather fast for horse transportation over rocks and around sharp curves, up hill and down, in a wild rush to cover the ground, but somewhat to the discomfort of the passengers, coming to the Black Canyon where Victoria, an Apache Indian Chief, with his tribe had attacked and massacred a number of freighters in the Canyon and carried off several such articles and food as they wanted and scalped the victims, burned their wagons and killed their oxen, all left lying on the roadway and at the side of the highway.

At that time the Government had established an Indian reservation at the present Mescalero Apache Indian reservation and was preparing to move them from the Hillsboro County near Silver City which was contrary to the wishes of the Indians. They threatened that if the U. S. Government insisted on transporting them, which it did, that they would go on the war path, and make it unsafe for even a coyote to pass, and they kept their threat and raided and killed freighters, stage drivers and passengers, ranchers and settlers in general.

Among others, they raided the G.O.S. ranch and drove off about one hundred head of cow ponies. When a horse had been ridden down, it was usually speared by the Indians and left to die.

Victoria, during the Indian war between his tribe and the U. S. Government, was killed by the troops and Geronimo succeeded him as the chief of the Apache Indians. Chief Geronimo was captured and placed as a prisoner with some of his followers on an island along the coast of Florida. . . .

"Pinon Country"

by Haniel Long

Like Coronado, Oñate brought stock along. But he brought a great many more and particularly females for breeding. He started out with 7,000 head of cattle, sheep, goats and horses, and 83 team of oxen. When the caballeros and the colonists entered the southwest driving along their stock they brought with them the source of most of the little wealth their descendants have ever known. For generations sheep and steers were to be the only export of a people who needed to import tools, clothing, equipment. The Spaniards came to find wealth, they found none in their cattle, sheep and goats. They merely brought their grub along. The way the Navajos welcomed horses and sheep and changed at once into a nation of horsemen and shepherds makes it seem possible that the Spaniards obligingly restored to them what their forefathers had been forced to leave behind, on the uplands of Mongolia centuries before when they came across the Bering sea on the ice.

Peon, Vaquero, Ranchero and Caballero

by Bright Lynn

The Spaniards who came to New Mexico during the eighteenth and early nineteenth centuries from Europe were of two principal classes. Many had been favorites of the Spanish court or the protégés of such favorites and had exiled themselves for longer or shorter periods to occupy high and lucrative posts in the new land. But by far the greater number were men who had left home in their youth, poor but robust and energetic.

With little difficulty, such immigrants found places in mercantile establishments or on large estates. Soon many of them owned land or businesses of their own. They became, intrinsically, the strongest element of the population by the middle of the nineteenth century and very often wealthy.

This class was formed by the vaqueros or cowboys, rancheros or small land owners, and caballeros, those who possessed some lucrative business which enabled them to become well-to-do citizens of the various settlements. The peons were the very lowest of this element, usually only half-breeds and very often held in bondage for a part or for all their lives.

Better than the peons or Indian slaves by breeding, education or natural ability were the vaqueros. Because of their peculiar labor, they soon formed a picturesque class of their own in regard to costume. This evolved naturally from their necessities and the type of work they performed.

Vaquero

Riding over land covered with cacti, brush and tough evergreens many months at a time, it was necessary to have sufficient protection which would also withstand the rigors of weather and long hard usage. The burning rays of the sun and the dust blown by the steady wind also demanded certain protective clothing of a different type not needed by the farmer or townspeople.

The vaquero, therefore, exhibited his ingeniousness and soon became distinguishable from the other inhabitants by his tough leggings, leather trousers and small rectangular shawl or serape which fell over his shoulders, back and chest allowing his head to protrude through a hole in the center. This was usually so tightly and firmly woven it was waterproof as well as warm and, consequently, served a variety of purposes. Fashioned in stripes and designs of all kinds in the gayest and gaudiest of colors it added a very festive touch to the costume.

The large sombrero or hat was worn constantly as a protection against the sun's rays and heat. It might be of felt, but more often was of straw as that was cheaper and more easily obtained.

At his saddle horn hung the inevitable lasso and bag of chico (parched corn) and jerked meat from which one meal a day was all that he required.

His chief interests in life, however, were gambling and cock fighting and he was quite capable of losing all his worldly goods, his wife and even his pony at the national game of monte, and then lighting a cigarette, go sauntering off without the least sign of regret.

At the latter accomplishment he was usually very proficient. A mounted vaquero could take out his guagito (his little tobacco flask), his packet of hojas (prepared husks) and his flint, steel, etc., make his cigarrito, strike fire and commence smoking in a minute's time—all the while galloping at full speed, and the next minute would perhaps "lazo" the wildest bull without interrupting his smoke.

Cibolero

Another native of the country who must be classed with this group of intrepid cowmen is the cibolero or buffalo-hunter:

"As we were proceeding on our march, we observed a horseman approaching, who excited at first considerable curiosity. His picturesque costume and peculiarity of deportment, however, soon showed him to be a Mexican Cibolero or buffalo-hunter. These hardy devotees of the chase usually wear leathern trousers and jackets, and flat straw hats; while, swung upon the shoulder of each hangs his carcage or quiver of bow and arrows. The long handle of their lance being set in a case, and suspended by the side with a strap from the pommel of the saddle, leaves the point waving high over the head, with a tassel of gay parti-colored stuffs dangling at the tip of the scabbard. Their fusil, if they happen to have one, is suspended in like manner at the other side, with a stopper in the muzzle fantastically tasseled."

Peons

The peons were, no doubt, the least attractive of the laboring class. Usually dressed in cotton shirt and trousers, open from the hip down, with very wide full drawers underneath and frequently barefoot unless their work required some kind of foot covering, commonly a straw moccasin, they made little impression in the gaily dressed group of other citizens. A hat was worn, if needed, of straw, but of nondescript size and design.

Caballeros

The caballeros were, by far, the most attractively and romantically garbed. Their costume consisted of the sombrero with medium high crown and wide brim, covered sometimes with cloth and at others fashioned of felt and surmounted with a band of tinsel cord nearly an inch in width; a chaqueta or jacket of cloth gaudily embroidered with braid and fancy barrel buttons and cut in the popular bolero style; curious trousers, called calzoneras, with the outer part of the leg slit from hip to ankle with a gaily colored inset and the borders set with tinkling filigree buttons, and the whole fantastically trimmed with tinsel lace and cords of the same material. As suspenders were not worn, the shirt and trousers were held together with a broad sash which was drawn very tightly around the body, adding to the picturesqueness of the costume.

The Women

The wives of these men were dressed according to their station just as much as their husbands. The peon women, usually house servants, wore a sacklike garment of cotton, either sleeveless or with short sleeves, reaching to the calf of the leg and usually belted with whatever was at hand. Straw moccasins were worn with this and it was a fortunate slave who possessed a shawl of whatever material could be obtained. This was worn as both cloak and head covering.

The Ladies of the Caballeros

The wives and daughters of the caballeros dressed as nearly as possible like the ladies of the haciendas and the women of the government posts. All these were passionately fond of jewelry; and were usually seen with their necks, arms, and fingers loaded with massive appendages of a valuable description. As there was heavy duty on any imported trinkets even as early as 1790, articles of native manufacture, many of which were admirably fashioned, without alloy or counterfeit, were generally preferred.

The ladies never wore hats except for riding. Those who could afford it, were always seen with the mantilla, but those of the poorest class wore a rebozo or shawl usually seven or eight feet long by nearly a yard in width made of diverse materials—silk, linen or cotton, and many times figured or variegated in the warp by symmetrically dyed threads woven through it. Many of them were very beautiful and highly valued, some as high as fifty or a hundred dollars. But the common cotton ones were never worth more than three or five dollars. The length of fringe of these usually denoted the wealth or rank of the wearer. Many of them were woven at home and were examples of the skill and taste of the maker.

The hair was piled high on the head and held there by a comb. The custom of ornamenting it with a flower as well was very popular among the rancheras and villageras.

Shoes were of leather and most of the women were very proud of their small feet. Heels were high, adding to their gracefulness.

It is from this early middle class population that the present day cowboy and provincial costume originated and many of the modern articles of wearing apparel used in New Mexico can be traced to their beginnings in this period.

Source of Information: Gregg, *Commerce of the Prairies*, p. 53.

Place Names: Bell Ranch, San Miguel Co.

by Bright Lynn

Headquarters ranch located about 2 miles north of Campana. Established about 1870 by Wilson Waddingham, a wealthy man from the East who came here for the health of his daughter. The ranch became the headquarters of a large sheep and cattle company. The ranch is at present owned by the Red River Land and Cattle Company. There are three possible origins of the name of the ranch: (1) The ranch was originally laid out in the shape of a huge bell and was called the Bell Ranch because of this. (2) The name was given the ranch because a family named Bell lived on or near the ranch when it was established. (3) The leading cow in a herd of cattle is called the "bell cow" because the owner places a bell around her neck in order that he may locate his herd. For this reason the Bell Ranch was so named because it was the headquarters of the surrounding sheep and cattle companies, and was consequently the "bell cow" or the leader of the sheep and cattle outfits.

(Note: Of the three possible origins the first is least likely.)

Source of Information: Joseph Danziger, Las Vegas.

Mexican cowboys loading cattle in Southern New Mexico near Deming, Unattributed, 1890–1900?, NMHM/DCA #012714

Customs and Conditions of Early Ranch Life (Lea County)

by Mrs. Benton Mosley

Frontier Hospitality: People were so few on the Staked Plains and the early rancher so eager for conversation, companionship and news that anyone passing his way was made welcome—even the stranger—to come in, stay awhile, eat dinner, spend the night—or several days if he chose. No one was ever too busy to extend the common courtesy of entertaining those passers-by who stopped for their own convenience as considerately as if they had been specially invited guests. Where one man met another on the prairie there was visiting—an hour or two at least. To have passed on by with only a greeting would have been the boldest of effrontery, an open insult.

The hospitality of welcoming all passers to one's habitat was not entirely or merely a social function, it was an obligatory custom born of necessity, for—save where the traveller had full camp equipment—he journeyed at the mercy of such hospitality. There was not a place where lodging and food could be bought in the whole broad land, a section which with the mode of travel of that time required a week to cross.

The host rancher knew he too would be travelling some day and have the same needs. And since he must do unto others as he would have them do unto him, he entertained graciously and heartily, enjoying the social contacts thus brought about. To refuse such lodging in such a locale would have been unthinkably inhuman. It was also customary if there were no one home at the ranch or camp for the traveller or visitor to go in, cook and eat, or sleep as the need might be, wash up his own dishes and go on his way. A locked house in such surroundings was an insult to humanity.

When "woman company" came the way of the lonely ranch wife, though they might be strangers, she dropped all work save that of entertaining and extending courteous consideration to her uninvited guest. Larders were raided, beds were made down, and men marvelled at their conversation and enjoyment. Under the circumstances guests could hardly be critical of even the most meagre accommodations and fare. Ranch houses on the Llano Estacado were never large—particularly when one considers the number of persons they housed—but those small camp-like affairs of the early day were in some way large enough for all "comers and goers." If the ranchman's bed consisted of but two blankets he gave his guest one—and slept closer to the fire. If he had gotten down to bread and coffee he insistently shared that with whoever passed his way, and loved doing so. What flavor such hospitality lent!

Regardless of how long one's guests chose to stay, to accept pay—even from a stranger—for food and lodging was beneath the dignity of the poorest rancher. To offer such pay was the grossest of insults; and for him to have accepted would have—for some peculiar reason—been a disgrace. His hospitality was as genuine as his guest's need. The interdependence of the plainsman's hospitality seems to have welded many friendships.

Though there were usually the two phases mentioned above in ranch hospitality there was at times—particularly the earlier times—another and little realized phase due to the fact that not all the cattle and horse thieves which worked across the Plains were Indians (then removed). Because one's livestock was at large on a range too immense and too isolated for any protection by law, outlaws or travellers with a shady or questionable reputation were often entertained as well or better than one's best friend, that they might be so won and placated—as some Indians had been—by your hospitality as not to "steal you out." A small rancher seldom dared do otherwise.

Where Food Could Not Be Bought: Travellers through this section, when it was wholly a ranch country, often wondered why, with money in their pockets, they could not buy food from the ranchers. If you were out of bread, the rancher, though he might have a thousand pounds of flour, would not consider selling you so much as a pound. He would, however, loan you all you needed if you were a neighboring rancher, or give you enough to appease your hunger if you were a travelling stranger.

The difficulty of hauling commodities the hundred or more miles from the railroad, and the long intervals between times that "the wagon went to town" account for this custom. And also explain why "paying back what you borrowed" was the crucial test of Plains morality and religion.

If the rancher loaned you any of his comestibles and you didn't pay them back "in kind" before he was out, it meant he himself would be without for weeks perhaps. And if he sold foods to you he could not in the emergency so created eat your money. His freight wagons would never hold all the commodities he needed; why should he haul flour for you?

Another reason why selling food was taboo was that often the owners of the ranch resided elsewhere, and the manager or ranch-keeper in charge was a custodian and not an authorized seller of the ranch supplies.

Cash A Negligible Factor: Actual money was of so little use in the ranch country that very little was kept on hand, or seen. The rancher or cowboy didn't think of needing any till he got to town, which was once or twice a year. (His simple everyday needs—if he had any—were supplied by the ranch company and charged against his wage account.) The rancher with property and credit might not have a dollar about him for weeks or months. The traveller often found his bankroll more of a care than a comfort. It wouldn't buy—or wasn't necessary for—food and lodging. There was no place to spend it. It wouldn't even buy transportation— unless one chose to own a horse.

About all the cowboy knew to do with the loose change left in his pocket when he reached the ranch from town was to give it to the ranch-keeper's kids (who hoarded such contributions), carry it in his pocket till it wore through and escaped, or lose it in a poker game. The latter opportunity did not present itself as often as may be presumed; getting up at daylight or before usually made sleep a preferred pleasure.

No Near Neighbors—And None Wanted—was the rule in the settlement of these parts, not just a coincidence. With the Indian menace removed there was not the need of pioneers settling close together for protection as on many frontiers. With the grazing of herds the only industry, the greater the distance between ranches the better for all parties concerned. The new rancher on the public domain usually realized and observed this as well as the old. To settle within five or ten miles of another ranch was considered a most unwelcome infringement. The newcomer was considered a most unwelcome infringement. The newcomer would likely be treated with coolness—occasionally colder—for some time. He might at some time, when hard pressed, receive offers to buy him out. Oddly enough, though his coming had been sorely resented, if he stayed on and was a fair neighbor he was in a few years accepted by the ranchers as one of them.

(Settlers in the general homesteading, which came years later—and who settled anywhere and everywhere—were resented by the rancher much as a city dweller would resent a stranger pitching camp on his well-kept front lawn. The rancher held no title to this land, of course, but it had been his right of usage so long that he felt much as the Indian had when white men drove him out; he not only coveted the land, he loved it.)

Though, for economic reasons the rancher did not want his neighbors too near him, the distance between them, and their fewness, seems to have made neighbors doubly appreciated. It is doubtful if mankind has ever been known to do more for one another than here, at that time.

Women on the Early Ranches led a more isolated life than the most isolated of farm women. Yet it was distinctly different from farm life. The ranch woman met all sorts of emergencies, many of which demanded extraordinary fortitude and resourcefulness, but her work in general was confined to the household—often a household so small and simple that, with no social life offered, she was left with much leisure. There was not the endless toil of the farm, no arduous outside chores nor field work. (Not until the homesteader began farming and the population created a demand for produce.)

With so few women among many men, she received more chivalrous homage—seemingly was more cherished—than in many sections, and subjected to less drudgery. Only the domestic woman with a keen interest in her ranch home and the welfare of its inmates could graciously accept and adapt herself to ranch life.

The aloneness of her situation is hard to imagine. There were weeks at a time—often months—when she saw no other woman, in fact almost forgot there were other women. Many such women will tell you that the most boresome factor in such existence was to hear nothing save the cow-and-horse, boots-and-saddle, riding-and-roping conversations of the men about the ranch, who seemingly knew no other topic. Ranch wives sometimes made a house guest welcome for months for feminine companionship.

If she was the cook—and she more often was—there were meals to be cooked and served at any hour of the day or night that hungry men arrived. At times she got out of bed after retiring to cook meals for men she had never heard of before—just travellers passing that way who must be fed. Naturally she learned to keep something cooked on hand, and never to throw out left-overs from one meal until the next.

On many ranches the men on the place cooked breakfast, which was very early, and also some of the emergency meals mentioned above, but left all other kitchen duties to the housewife. In other instances the men or some boy did all the dishwashing. Any seasoned cowboy knew how to cook the simple food he ate. But only a few of the ranchers employed men cooks regularly at the headquarters ranches.

With most of the cowboys away on the "works" through much of the summer and fall, "headquarters," even of the larger ranches, resembled ordinary family life, but when the chuck- wagons and their following of workers got in, it more nearly approached a hotel. At such times the chuck-wagon cook often came into the ranch kitchen and cooked for the crowd. Besides being cook and housekeeper, the ranch wife was always the nurse, often the doctor, sometimes the school teacher, generally the bookkeeper, post master, and banker, and on occasions the confidante and counsellor, for those about her. If she were the wife of a hired ranch-keeper, though she toiled ever so devotedly, she rarely received ought for her labors but her board and keep, and that of her children, if any; the wage paid a ranch-keeper and wife being little more than that of the single worker.

Unlike the farmer, the ranch woman's husband was not greatly bound by regime or meticulous chores; when he was pretty well up with his work or felt the need of a holiday (seldom though this might be) he just turned out the calves—if there was no one to leave at the ranch—and took the two or three days off necessary for him and his family to properly visit some neighbor—possibly without any especial invitation other than the general understanding that, since visitors were so scarce and came so far, they were always welcome.

No Post Offices: The fact that it was a hundred miles or so to the nearest post office—and one went only once or twice a year—was not so bad as it may sound. Bringing out the mail for all ranches along one's way and for those still farther out constituted a most sacred obligation. One which no rancher dared forget or neglect. Such mail was too eagerly expected. And if one were going toward town, to mail all letters entrusted to his care—or relay them to the next ranch—was a similar obligation. To do less was an unforgettable misdemeanor. Fortunately for such voluntary postmen this was before the parcel post era, and a gunny or flour sack sufficed to carry the mail either on horseback or by freight wagon.

Once a month, or sometimes oftener, some one would ride to the next ranch toward town, carrying all letters to be mailed, and to see if any mail had been brought out. If so he brought back all for his home ranch, those round about, and those farther up the line. Thus, by this friendly relay system, it was rarely over two or three weeks or a month between mails; but the mail received might have been twice that long en route.

Letters were generally posted by the "first passing." If one had been negligent and did not have his letter written, the "first passing" customarily waited till the correspondence was—perhaps laboriously—completed. It was customary, too, for the party mailing all such letters to see that they were properly stamped, gratis. If there was small change about the ranch, and no stamps, a nickel a dime or a quarter might be offered for the stamping; this was more often generously refused. Stamping and mailing such an accumulation of letters was not an unimportant task when one reached town.

No Schools: The early rancher usually moved his family to town, for a few years at least, when his children reached—a rather late—school age. Other ranch children learned the rudiments of reading, writing, and arithmetic about their mother's knee, and were later sent away to school. Governesses were employed in some instances (until cowboys married them).

One of the first attempts at having a school on the plains was made in the 1890s when Miss Annie Adcock taught the Medlin, Causey and Dunnaway children in a bedroom of the Jerry Dunnaway ranch home. Though the ranch child's educational advantages were so exceptionally meagre, if at all attracted to learning, he often brought an interest so fresh and eager that his advancement was speedy.

The Prairie Child had little but leisure. In emulating his elders he played all day perhaps at breaking broncs, roping, riding. Rocks, horns, wild gourds all became cattle that must be branded, penned, etc.; wells must be dug. The little girls were almost always tomboys—and out in the open, too; though they of course found time for innumerable dolls, often homemade, and for dishes. Children were so few in the ranch country that they were invariably teased and indulged by the cowboys; neither of which improved their dispositions, but seemingly increased their spunk.

Isolation and loneliness of ranch life seems never to have bothered children, since they knew nothing else. Lacking playmates and toys, and having so much time on their hands, they were especially addicted to pets. Pet horses, cows, burros, dogs, antelope, rabbits, coyotes, lobo wolves, cats, prairie dogs, chickens, and birds served as playmates and playthings. Perhaps from his association with these the prairie child could not help being a little wild. When taken to town or thrown with crowds he was usually beside himself in excited play, or else suffered from a pathetic timidity equaling torture.

From his environment of the range he took self-reliance and resourcefulness, and was robust. And though he possessed a marked ability at getting along alone, he often lacked the faculty of getting along with others—at least to the extent of fitting into the pattern of the modern business and social world. The freedom and leisure of early ranch life had a strong tendency to make one almost incurably individualistic—to resent and suffer from long hours of regular indoor employment almost as the Indian suffered from such confinement.

Sources of Information: Mrs. E. C. Causey, 534 Brett Street, Inglewood, Calif.; Mrs. E. H. Price, Palma, N. Mex.; Mrs. Nancy Dunnaway, Lovington, N. Mex.; Mrs. Annie Brunson, Stanton, Tex.; Mr. Jake Owen, Carlsbad, N. Mex.; Mrs. C. C. Medlin, (now deceased); Mr. Chas Fairweather, Lovington, N. Mex.

As It Happened in Curry County

from New Mexico Federal Writers' Project

In eastern New Mexico or what is now Curry county from 1887 to 1938 the early settlers have related what has taken place. The ranch land extension and activities have been told as follows by Messers. John Manning, J. J. DeOlivera and wife, Rhea Brothers. This is from the old settlers firsthand. Therefore, it can be relied upon as authentic.

The 3 T Ranch extended from Texas line on the east, beyond Plains, New Mexico, on the west, the breaks on the north, to the sand hills on the south. In the beginning the heart of the 3 T ranch was in Curry county. The stock that grazed this region watered from wells, one four miles north, one two miles southwest, one seven miles southeast of Grady. The three original wells on Running Water Draw, Three on Frio Draw and lakes filled by rain or melting snow. This ranch has become a memory of the past for small ranches and filings of settlers have taken its place.

Mrs. J. J. DeOlivera's history of the ranch change runs like this— Thomas Carson sold to Mr. Trammel who in turn sold to Joe Rhea & brother the eastern portion of Running Water Draw. This today is known as Rhea Ranch. The Rheas dug a well and built a stone house nineteen miles north of Clovis. This is still occupied.

The homesteaders of Hollene and surrounding country hauled water six to ten miles from these wells and paid $2.00 per month. This was fair for wells had to be kept up. Supplies then were high.

Supplies of flour, sugar (little of this), tobacco, salt, coffee and oats for emergency horses from 1887 to 1900 were freighted from Las Vegas by ox and burro teams. They had no roads. They followed the shortest trail across the country. Santa Rosa was the rest station. No meat was freighted for the game of the prairie served the people. Antelope plentiful. No law against killing quail. Cottontails, jackrabbits, beef and mutton were to be had for the going after. Badgers, coyotes, and lobos called loafers (larger than coyotes) were killed for their hides and for sport. The rattlesnake, an enemy to man and beast, did not escape.

Travel was by wagons and a few had buggies. The wagon served a double purpose for passengers and freighting the long distance on hot summer days and the cold short ones in winter made it hard on man and beast. But the people in general were happy and murmured very little. They came here to make a home and expected these hardships. Some would go away to work but when the harvest or cotton picking season was over they would come back to their families they had left behind. Most of those who went back to stay in a few years would come trekking to the old community.

There were very few landmarks. Just two wells between Grady and Texico. Most of the time, one out of commission caused the travelers to haul drinking water. Some took stock water along. Often at night travelers would get lost. After hours of winding about, beasts worn out were halted until sunrise. Many times people would discover they were near their destination. In summer this was not so bad. Toward morning the atmosphere would be real chilly. But in winter getting lost was dangerous. If blizzards or strong winds came up, people would likely freeze.

Mr. DeOlivera, the father of the DeOlivera boys, in 1887 bought a portion of 3 T ranch that lays to the west of Rhea ranch. In 1889 his son, J. J. DeOlivera and his young wife came. They built a stone ranch house, dug a well in the yard and lived there until 1898. Sold out to Mr. Sid Boykin who in turn sold out to Mr. Alex Shipley, then to Mr. Craig.

West of DeOlivera ranch in 1901 Mr. Jack Lewis established a small ranch. These ranchmen extended hospitality to many weary and storm-overtaken travelers. Nothing unusual for twenty-five to collect at Rhea's ranch for the night. Some had money to pay. The ones who did not were fed just the same. When beds were not enough the children, the sick, and the older ones were put to bed. Others counted themselves lucky to have a warm fire to stay by.

The better soil of these ranches became homesteads. Today crops are raised on this. Every farm has a well, if the driller could find water. Water runs in veins here.

The new ranchmen were advised to build corrals on the south sides of lakes or hillsides so the snow would not drift. Those who deemed it wiser to build on the north side often had to free the stock from snowdrifts five to ten feet high. In 1898 a blizzard came that froze the legs of cattle. Some survived because there was plenty of range and they could move about to exercise.

Only drift fences were put up by cattlemen to hold the cattle. The U. S. Government sent out inspectors from Amarillo to make ranchers take them down. They did as was ordered. These same fences were in place again by the time the inspector made his three-day horse and buggy drive back to Amarillo. The inspector's last order was in 1906. . . .

Governor's Report to the Secretary of the Interior, 1890:
Gradual Change in Cattle Raising Methods
by Governor L. Bradford Prince

from New Mexico Federal Writers' Project

Quoting J. E. Saint, a member of the Cattle Sanitary Board:

"I think there has been shipped to Kansas and Nebraska pastures this year nearly 125,000 steers from our territory. This large shipment was caused by short pastures here and by the success of this method of maturing cattle in the States, which was begun in 1888 and continued in 1889. It was demonstrated that to ship steers direct to market from our short ranges was unprofitable, as the long haul of from 1,000 to 1,200 miles made them wholly unfit for beef and generally undesirable except for canning purposes, and this grade of cattle brought the lowest prices.

So the theory of shipping cattle to cheap food, near market, to mature, was the outgrowth of necessity."

From Colonel Dwyer of Colfax Co.:

"Six years ago in Colfax County was the wealthiest of the counties in range cattle, but as in other localities, the owners have so reduced the number of their holdings that today there are scarcely one-fourth of the number of cattle that were then in the county.

After years of experience the owners of cattle have demonstrated that the business of cattle-ranging on open ranges is not profitable, and there is a disposition toward smaller holdings and to confine the cattle in smaller pastures. Prominent ranchmen express the opinion that 500 cows confined in a pasture will produce more profit than 5,000 on the open range. Hereafter many of the large properties will be subdivided and small ranches will be the rule."

Quoting Mr. Daniel Troy of Colfax Co.:

"The history of the industry for this portion of our territory for the last fifteen years has shown a steady improvement in the care and quality of our sheep, while at the same time the number of sheep raisers has gradually decreased by the closing of small owners, augmented by the increased demand for mutton sheep for the last four years."

Old Cow Outfits Near Gallup
Gallup Gazette, **March 14, 1940**

from New Mexico Federal Writers' Project

The livestock industry may be said to have had its introduction at the now ruined Zuni village of Hawikuh, 12 miles southwest of the present pueblo, and about 60 miles from Gallup.

It was here that Coronado brought the first cattle from Compestela, Mexico. The animals were brought principally for meat for Coronado's soldiers and trail hands. Oñate, the first real colonizer, brought 300 horses and 7000 cattle in 1598, twenty-two years before the Pilgrims landed at Plymouth Rock, using the Rio Grande as his entrada.

The first cattle in this country were brought up from Texas and Mexico, but the real cow business did not begin here as early as in Texas. Though sources of information are rare and memories of old cowmen are getting dim, the cow business does not seem to antedate very many years the coming of the railway in 1880.

Franz Huning, father of Fred of Los Lunas, whose home ranch was in the Rincon north of the Rio San Jose, within the Antonio Sedilla grant and only several miles east of Suwanee, was a large cattle owner. Further west to the south of the present overpass, Jose Antonio Luna ran cattle at Lucero Spring. The Laguna Indians went in more for sheep. So did the settlers of Cubero, San Rafael, Seboyeta and Juan Tafoya.

Don Silvestre Gabaldon, still living at Tinaja, still recalls well the days before the iron horses began to puff passengers and freight through the country. He packed the mail from the now ruined town of El Rito, east of Mesita Negra, to Bluewater when there were no cow ranches in all that country. At Bluewater, known as Agua Azul, the Provinchers, Damacio, Stephen and Eduardo, ran a stage station, making the money with which they bought cattle and later moved to the Atarque region.

At San Mateo, Roman Baca was building up his herds, which reached many thousands. An ex-soldier who located scrip on the open land at the El Rito ranch near San Mateo and who brought in some fine Guernseys was done away with. His cattle soon wore the Roman Baca brand and the ranch became the Roman Baca home place. Don Manuel

Chavez was also a figure in the livestock business in San Mateo but the rest of the natives were "pociteros."

Somewhat later Joe Saint, now an attorney, established a large cow outfit, the Acoma Land and Cattle Co., with headquarters ranch (walls still standing) east of the overpass east of Grants and north of the highway, on ground now owned by Eliseo Barela of San Rafael. The Saint outfit brought in 5000 Mexican longhorn cattle. Their summer range was at Seboyita, east of the Mal Pais and at Agua Fria, the Gallinita and the Gallina in the Zuni mountains, which had been settled before the railway came.

Later, at Bluewater, the 7 Bar L's headed up by Judge Latta of Chicago, Wm. H. Hulvey, manager, ran a strong outfit. Their summer ranch was at Lancaster's, now the Nick Hausner place, in the Zuni mountains.

South of present Ft. Wingate and above Nutria village was the Box S ranch owned by army officers and managed by Capt. Clark M. Carr, who went there with his St. Louis bride. His father, General E. A. Carr, and other officers used to make the Box S the center of picnics and parties, which they reached with army saddle horses or the mule-drawn ambulances. For a time the Box S, with its 10,000 head of cattle, claimed the Nutria Spring, which ultimately fell to the Zuni Indians. Their cattle ranged into the mountains and over the Seboya valley, where Ramah now stands.

East of them at the Seboyita ranch, above the present Vogt ranch, at El Muerte and Tinaja, the Jesus Mazon and Epitacio Mazon outfit ran cattle as well as sheep and maintained none too cordial relations with their Box S and other neighbors. In those days Judge Colt, range official carried on every cowboy's hip, settled many a dispute without resort to courts.

To the north of the Chaco mesas the American Cattle Co. had 5000 head of cattle in the Myers Wash country where Ed Thomas ranches now. But they only came to grief through hard years, scattering herds and hungry natives. Navajos soon learned to run calves with their sheep. Ewes actually allowed calves to nurse the milk from their bags. Some old-timers claim the Navajos got their start with cattle by stealing calves, just as many others did.

At Pueblo Bonito the Hyde Exploration company ran cattle,

excavated the great ruins, and even attempted to make leather. They used the canaigre plant for tanning purposes. This was years before Dick Wetherill was shot there as he rode out of the arroyo one evening.

The Atarque country was settled about the time the railway reached Gallup in 1881 and '82, by the Garcias, Landavazos and Provinchers, who all had cattle. To the south and west of them Sol Barth, father of Jake Barth of St. Johns, was the Rey of the country. Nathan Barth was also a large owner but limited his activity mostly to sheep.

Before Gallup was started, the railway roundhouse was at Coolidge, once called Guam. The principal settlement here was at the mine north of Gallup, named after Bob Gibson, mine foreman. Wiley Weaver, Charley Kennedy, mine operators of Gibson, and Aleck Conrad owned the Triangle Bar ranch north of Thoreau and west of the Bluewater Lake. Here one Henry Dorsett was foreman and Herman Techlinburg, custodian of the Gallup high school, was a young cowboy. Mr. Techlinburg states that when he went to work for the Triangle Bar in 1884 there were no less than 60,000 head of cattle between the Arizona line and the present McCartys and the grass was stirrup deep all over the country.

For a time, at Bacon Springs, east of Coolidge, Crane and Foster were cow ranch partners. Foster is said to have been the best man with cattle but Crane excelled at poker, which he played with the soldiers at Ft. Wingate.

Other activity near Gallup included the McIntire cattle at the present Rehoboth, followed by George W. Wells, who later bought out the stage station (a part of it still standing at All States Camp) which had been operated by Tom Dye. Wells, who was the father-in-law of Palmer Ketner, watered his cows in the little lake north of the highway and east of El Rancho where skaters enjoyed the ice this winter.

Doctor Sawyer and John DeLong ran their cattle at their ranch east of the hogback.

When Frank Rich ran short of water at the Lorenzino ranch two miles west of Gallup, he built a tank where the present cemetery stands and filled it with water from the old Aztec mine. Rich afterwards sold a half interest in his cow outfit to Murray, Allen and Tom Johnson.

The first whitefaced cattle are thought to have been brought in by Dave and Tass Harrington to the 6A ranch south of Coolidge in about the year 1905. The first registered Herefords were introduced in this region by the Smith brothers, Wales, Wade and Leon, about 1916.

Charley Paxton ran a few cattle at the Prewitt ranch north of Casa del Navajo at Coolidge. At the Milk Ranch, John Bloomfield bought out a man named Fleehive and north of there against the red mesas where McPhaul's ranch is now located at the North Star, Charley Baker preceded Billie Morris and L. W. Kirk.

At the site of Holbrook, a native by the name of Barazo ran a stage station before the Hashknife or Aztec Land and Cattle Co. got strong there with their sixty thousand cattle. Their headquarters ranch was south of Joseph City. John T. Jones was their first foreman though J. E. Simpson was foreman the summer of the Pleasant Valley war in 1887. Cowboys who fought in the Tewksbury-Graham cattle war were Tom Pickett, Tom Tucker, Buck Lancaster, George Smith, John Paine, Robert M. Gillespie, McNeal, Roxy and Peck.

At Emigrant Springs, Jim Bennett, still living in Lupton hale and hearty, ran cattle for many years. Ed Bargman of Winslow, and Commodore Owen, sheriff of Apache county, who cleaned out the Blevins gang near Holbrook, were cow foremen for Bennett, who ran up to 2000 head of cattle. He bought Navajo Springs about 1880. Burgess Brothers, Canadians, followed there but became disgusted with dry years and stealing, sold out to Jim Houck, who built what became to be called Houck's Tank. Mr. Bennett bought this and ranched there for 35 years. Mr. Bennett also owned Tulapai ranch south of Houck where Billie Hawthorne and Billie Free lived for years.

The Long H ranch was a strong outfit, with Tommy Tucker, who had worked for the Box S outfit, at its head.

Down on the Zuni river, Lorenzo Hubbell and Dan DuBois ran cattle and horses and other outfits had holdings.

Cook's ranch and stage station on the old Zuni–Ft. Defiance road south of the present Manuelito, was built by Bennett, who with his partner, George Peters, dug the well by hand. But this was more of a trading center than a ranch.

In an account of this sort one might well mention the founding of the Joseph City stockade by the Mormons in 1882 or '83 and old Fort Moroni, afterwards Fort Rickerson, nine miles north of Flagstaff, where

John W. Young ran cattle. This outfit was absorbed by the Arizona Cattle Co., branding the AIBar, the largest cattle company in Arizona.

Lack of space draws the curtain down on the past of the old days. Perhaps the information given, though very incomplete, may help some researcher who could trace, through memory, brand records, spoken and written accounts, a complete story of the cow days of yore.

One should mention the Roberts, Dwight Craig, Old man Miller at McCartys, Henry Brock, Joe Cox, Tom Talley, Harry Coddington, Box S Charley, who was killed near Danoff by his nephew, Sam Winston, and many others.

The writer is indebted to Palmer Ketner, Wade Smith, J. W. Bennett, John Bloomfield, Silvestre Gabaldon, D. O. Garcia and Earl Forrest, Washington, PA, for helpful information.

Branding S Ranch, New Mexico, Ben Wittick, ca. 1880–90, NMHM/DCA #015608

Santa Fe Weekly Gazette: Comancheros, Important Military Orders, March 6, 1869

from New Mexico Federal Writers' Project

General Sheridan has issued the following orders in reference to the illicit trading in cattle in the Indian Territory:

January 21, 1869—General Field order No. 8.

—111. Brevet Major General George W. Getty. Commanding District of New Mexico, is hereby ordered to make every effort to break up and punish the bands of New Mexican Traders who have been and are still trading for captured stock with hostile Indians; and if hereafter such traders are found at any point east of the Eastern line of New Mexico their goods will be burned and their stock killed.

March 13, 1869. Comanches.

Last week our humble city was honored with a visit from some nine Comanche Chiefs. They, innocent souls, who had never been at war with the Whites, and who had never done anything wrong in their whole lives, came up here from Texas to negotiate a treaty of peace with General Getty, Commanding the Military District of New Mexico.

March 27, 1869

President Grant has requested the Society of Friends to furnish him with a list of persons they can recommend of Indian Agents. This is truly a novel beginning, and a revolution as complete as was ever seen in any department of the government.

May 15, 1869

Advertisement. Supplies for Navajos

1,000 head of beef cattle (steers or dry cows) nothing under four years old.

300,000 pounds of shelled corn.

The Grant County Herald, June 2, 1877:
"Wholesale Slaughter of Cattle by Indians"

from New Mexico Federal Writers' Project

We recently learned that forty or fifty Indians raided the lower Gila settlement and that south and near the bridge over the stream, they killed twenty-five beef cattle belonging to Peter Morris and helped themselves to beef. Five others are missing and supposed to have shared the balance of the herd. This wholesale slaughter occurred four or five weeks ago and is supposed to have been the act of the band who killed the mail rider near Camp Bowie on the 28th or 29th, and who subsequently repulsed Lt. West's handful of men, who were sent out from that post with orders to punish them.

The Grant County Herald, June 30, 1877, No. 17
"Lincoln County Cattlemen Threaten Violence
Warrants Issued for the Arrest of Wylie, Chisum, and Higshaw"

Before giving credence to the following statement which we copy from the NEWS (and which for aught we know may be true) we advise readers to wait until the Chisum & Wylie version is given to the public. They can then come to an intelligent conclusion and place the blame where it properly belongs:

Mesilla, N.M.
June 15th 1877
T. F. Catron, U.S. Attorney
Sir: In accordance with your request I give you the facts of the Chisum War on the Pecos river: John S. Chisum claims to have about 40,000 head of cattle grazing on the Pecos river, also D. R. Wylie has about 3,000 head, these two stockmen concluded they wanted all the Pecos to themselves from Pope's crossing to Fort Sumner, a distance of 200 miles.

A man by the name of Richard Smith, Wylie's foreman, was killed by a herder, James M. Higshaw, on March 28th, in camp, shot in the back five times with a colt's improved 45 calibre six-shooter, Chisum remarking that the war had commenced; he had six more men to kill; (The Seven River thieves), Viz: Lewis Paxton, Underwood, Chas. W. Woltz, R. W. Beckwith, Johnson and Buck Powell. These men having each from 200 to 1,000 head of cattle which they were herding in the neighborhood of Seven Rivers; Lewis Paxton happened to go to Lincoln city on business April 8th, when he was informed by Maj. W. Brady, sheriff of Lincoln county, that John S. Chisum was hiring men to kill him and others. Mr. Paxton got his horse and rode home as fast as possible to let men know what Chisum intended doing; these men then left their camps and came up to Seven Rivers to the house of R. W. Beckwith for self-defense.

On April 10, James J. Dolan came down to Seven Rivers for some beef cattle which he wanted for the use of the U.S. Troops at Fort Stanton, a party of men started to go down to Paxton and Underwood's camp to get the cattle when they met six of Chisum and Wylie's men on the public road near Wylie's cow camp, who upon seeing the party, coming down the road, got off their horses and got down into a water course and prepared to shoot at them, which Mr. Underwood's party seeing, charged down on them; they fired a few shots on both sides, nobody hurt; Chisum's men then got on their horses and rode into their camps remarking that they got whipped; Chisum then rode off to Fort Stanton to try to get soldiers and arms to assist him in killing these men, the commanding officer told Chisum it was none of his business; he was not there to kill citizens but to protect them. Chisum then tried to get the sheriff of Lincoln county to assist him, he also would not do it.

On April 20th, Chisum and Wylie got all the men that would join them together, some thirty men, went to Seven Rivers, took what horses and mules these other men had out grazing, went up above Mr. Beckwith's house about a mile and cut off the water in the ditch which supplied the house saying he would starve them out and when they have to come out to get water they would waylay them and shoot them down; that night two men Chas. W. Woltz and Buck Powell rode out past them and went to Mesilla, the county seat, to get warrants to arrest Wylie, Chisum, and J. M. Higshaw for the murder of Smith.

April 21st. Chisum sent a Mr. & Mrs. Gray who live at Seven Rivers, to Mr. Beckwith's house to tell the women and children to leave, that he did not want to kill them but wanted to kill the thieves that were in there.

Mrs. Stafford, Miss Helen Beckwith and two of Mr. Beckwith's younger children were all the family who were present at Mr. Beckwith's; they refused to leave the house as they would not trust themselves to Chisum's men, Mrs. Stafford replying that she had all the protection she wanted at home.

April 22nd. Chisum advanced to carry out his threats into execution telling his men that they would try and take the walls on the other party, and kill all who were in there; they commenced shooting at about 700 or 800 yards distance, the besieged returning the fire; Chisum's men lost courage and would not advance any closer saying they were going to get killed for $30. a month, that they had hired to herd cattle and not fight; Chisum then raised a flag of truce, and sent in a man to tell Mr. Johnson to come out, that he wanted to compromise and let everything go as it was; Johnson told him that he would not compromise for any person but himself, as men were there who Chisum & Wylie were owing money to, and they wanted their money before the business was settled. Chisum then said he would turn the water on and give back their horses; he withdrew his men and went down the river to round up his cattle along with Wylie. They were going to round up together and separate their cattle when they got above Wylie's ranch; there Chisum took the smallpox. May 7th Buck Powell, having got back from Mesilla with the warrants, and with a posse of 14 men rode down to the Chisum and Wylie camp to arrest Chisum, Wylie, and Higshaw; they having learned that we were coming after them had gone to south Spring River Ranch (Chisum's) which is fortified against Indians, there to resist the law — fight if necessary. We started in pursuit, after seeing Chisum who was still sick with the smallpox and could not be moved.

The Prairie Fire of 1906 As Told by Clyde Stanfield

from New Mexico Federal Writers' Project

The most interesting of these however had to do with a prairie fire that swept the prairies in the fall of 1906.

The fire originated at Taiban, New Mexico, and swept on to Hereford, Texas, destroying everything in its path.

As the rolling flames, bearing horror and death, approached the struggling and scattered settlement near Grady, the settlers prepared to fight the fire, but they were powerless in the face of so fierce an enemy, and on it swept, taking lives of men and animals, and leaving destruction and sorrow in its wake.

In the Grady community, the greatest damage was done near the place that we now call Cameron. John Turner, an early settler of the Llano Estacado, had filed on a claim in this region, had built a rude cabin, and was well on the way toward a prosperous farm. He had a number of horses and cattle roaming the prairies.

When the fire encountered his claim, it burned all his wood, stampeded his horses and cattle, burned those that could not escape, and wreaked havoc in general. His son's face was badly burned.

Another old settler, Ed Leach, had to take refuge in a lake to save his own life.

In combating the fire, cattle were killed and skinned, and their skins used to drag out the fire.

The fire reached this community November 16 and on November 18 a severe snow came, and found the settlers wholly unprepared for the blizzard. Most of the houses had been burned to the ground, and many of the people had barely escaped with their lives.

The first mentioned settler, John Turner, was forced to live in a tent and burn his corn and furniture (what little had been salvaged from the wreck) for fuel.

He found some of his horses later, but he suffered a great loss in cattle, both through stampeding and asphyxiation.

The Old Barber House: Former Residence of New Mexico's Cattle Queen

by W. L. Patterson

The Old Barber House, built by Mrs. Susan Barber, once called "The Cattle Queen of New Mexico," is situated about 8 miles east of Three Rivers station, on the Southern Pacific Railroad and U. S. Highway 54, in Otero county.

Mrs. Susan McSween, wife of A. A. McSween, one of the faction leaders of the Lincoln County War, killed in the fighting, was married about two years after her husband's death to Attorney George L. Barber, of Lincoln. Four years after the ending of the War in 1878, and the closing up of McSween's estate, a herd of cattle was turned over to Mrs. Barber by John Chisum, a prominent cattleman, in payment of a debt he owed McSween for legal services. She then moved over to Three Rivers and established her ranch, but retaining her home at Lincoln.

The first ranch houses, built of adobe and now in ruins, were up near the mountains, but later she moved further down upon the plain. It was a residence of fourteen rooms, a story and a half high, with porches back and front and a one story addition in the rear, set in a spacious yard in a commanding location. Mrs. Barber managed her own business and was very successful. She was divorced from Barber about two years after their marriage.

As related by Mrs. Barber herself to an interviewer (Walter Noble Burns), after she had retired to White Oaks to live, she prospered in her ranching enterprise. She said: "As my business expanded, I built a beautiful home back from the river in the foothills in the White Mountains. I set out more than four thousand apple, pear, peach and plum trees, which in time bore splendid crops of luscious fruit. I increased my land holdings and my ranch extended three miles along the river, and it filled me with joy to see my herds grazing on a thousand hills. My cattle numbered 8000 head when I finally sold out. Whenever I dropped into Albuquerque or Santa Fe for a visit, the public prints referred to me as the Cattle Queen of New Mexico. So far as I know, I owned more cattle than any woman in the Southwest."

Mrs. Barber sold out her ranch holdings in 1917 to Albert B. Fall, United States Senator and afterwards Secretary of the Interior, and retired to the little town of White Oaks, purchased a residence and spent the remainder of her life there. Her death occurred in that town January 3, 1931, at the age of 86 years.

Sources of Information: Walter Noble Burns, *Saga of Billy the Kid*, pages 164, 166; Mrs. O. J. Norton, Three Rivers, New Mexico.

Estancia Ranch, New Mexico, J. R. Riddle, ca. 1886, NMHM/DCA #076091

The Old R. M. Gilbert Ranch, Now the W. C. Marable Ranch

by Katherine Ragsdale

Located one and one-half miles southwest of Dayton is the old R. M. Gilbert ranch, the oldest living ranch in this part of the country.

In 1870 R. M. Gilbert squatted (called squatters rights) here, and in 1884 it was surveyed and Mr. Gilbert proved up on it. Prior to this time Bob Gilbert lived southeast of the Mart Fanning ranch on south Seven Rivers but the Indians attacked him and stole his cattle so he had to move. He located closed to the Peñasco river, built a house, planted fruit and shade trees and a garden. He had plenty of water from the Peñasco for his trees, farm, and for his cattle.

This was in the day of the notorious outlaw Billy the Kid, and as Gilbert was a sympathizer of the Seven Rivers Gang, Billy the Kid told him to leave the country. Gilbert remained for several months and Billy the Kid returned, shot six bullets through the door (still to be seen) and told Gilbert that his next bullet would be saved for him if he didn't leave. This time Bob Gilbert moved to the Jim Miller Ranch and worked for him for several years.

During this time the Gilbert place was used as a stage stand and hotel on the Pecos, Texas–Roswell, New Mexico stage line.

Later Miller bought this ranch from Gilbert and sold it to W. C. Marable, who is still residing there.

Source of Information: W. C. Marable.

Chisum-Hagerman Ranch

by Redfield and Cooke

A panorama of Western history, replete with intrepid pioneers, desperados, ladies of courage and downright he-men unfolds itself in the story of Chisum Ranch, known now as the Hagerman Ranch, seven miles south of Roswell, near the head of the South Spring River.

To parade the noted or notorious citizenry, from the fiery chronicles of New Mexico's vivid days of yester-year, one would surely list the names of all who had stopped to pay respects and share the hospitality of John Chisum, a Texas bachelor, for whom the ranch was named— whose turbulent life as a cattleman was woven deeply into the fabric of so many exciting events in the 70s and 80s. This John Chisum should not be confused with the Chisholm of Texas, another cattle-trail maker of later date.

The ranch itself now comprises 1,800 acres flanking the much-storied Pecos, yet its present area is but a vestige of its former greatness. True, its existing beauty—entwining vines, banks of roses, hollyhocks, encompassing verdure—a source of much delight to the tourist, brings many to its venerable doors, but its association with Billy the Kid; John, James and Pilcher Chisum; Tom Catron; Alexander McSween; John H. Tunstall; the Murphy-Dolan-Riley trio—not to forget Charles Goodnight and Oliver Loving—creates the allure for the lovers of true Western lore. One cannot escape the feel of the hallowed vistas of its large ranch house, the old bucket well, the corral stamped hard by the hoof-beats of the long-gone champing cow ponies, and the old buildings, so much a part of the story of Chisum Ranch.

Retracing decades, we find John Chisum in Texas—Paris, Texas, to be exact—employed as County Clerk. He had come from Tennessee with his family and, as things go in new-born communities, he was doing "right smart," but listening to the tales of returning Western nomads, he resolved to seek his fortunes in the new markets created by the need for beef.

Chisum drove no herds to the north but after the war took three small bunches of cattle to Little Rock and sold them to a packing-house owned partly by himself. Poor practice caused the ruin of this enterprise and all, save he, took refuge in bankruptcy. This later caused him much trouble and litigation as the creditors took judgment against him alone. But his only assets were wild Texas cattle, inaccessible for attachment and incontrovertible into cash, so Chisum turned his eyes and feet westward as the judgments went on file—to crop out again in his hectic career.

Charles Goodnight and Oliver Loving had already blazed the trail westward to New Mexico that took their name, and Chisum, seeking fortune again with cattle, started his drive over the same route with a motley crew of hands. He first established himself in the Bosque Grande, 30 miles south of Fort Sumner in the Pecos Valley on a ranch site previously established by Goodnight. His first herd of 600 beeves he sold to authorities at Fort Sumner, and what is relatively more important, obtained a contract to deliver 10,000 more.

Realizing the value of the Pecos Valley, he determined to make this locale the home of his further operations. On his second drive he made his permanent headquarters at what is now the Chisum Ranch, yet he maintained two other cow camps, one at the above-mentioned site and another near Carlsbad. On his second drive, besides filling his order to the government, he delivered thousands of beeves to Goodnight and others, who took them further north to Pueblo and Denver. Chisum was a shrewd trader and his financial dealings were unique in themselves, yet in the final reckoning they served to wreck his majestic empire.

Back in Texas he secured powers of attorney from the different ranchers to drive their cattle to the Western market and gave notes in return to be paid on subsequent drives. It is recounted by authoritative historians that many notes "reposed" permanently in Texas, as Chisum created his beef baronetcy in New Mexico.

Thereby, the Chisum Ranch came into being and from 1870 to 1881 he was credited with having the largest holdings of cattle in the world. The Chisum Ranch then extended from Ft. Sumner on the Pecos for 200 miles southward to the Texas line. In breadth, the Chisum grazing land was 100 miles. The might of a feudal lord was the law of the Chisum Ranch. Settlers were unwelcome there—this was Chisum's edict then and, to further substantiate his iron rule, he made petition to President Grant for a patent to the whole area. The outcome of this petition is obvious as these were public domains and the ruling thus made the lands free to all comers. But for some time no one dared dispute his rights and the cattle with the "long rail" brand and "jingle bob" ear mark (vertical split in both ears) multiplied.

The magnitude of his operations can be gleaned from his deliveries from 1873–1880. In 1875 he sold thirty thousand head to Hunter and Evans, commission men of Kansas City, and by 1800 his deliveries to them had totaled fifty thousand. During these seven years he annually sold approximately ten thousand head to Goodnight. He also delivered thousands to Patterson and others.

As early as 1876 he was the dominant interest in all the Pecos Valley, yet other factors—Indian raids, "rustlers" and small owners—were beginning to make themselves felt. The Chisum ranch, regardless, with more than a hundred thousand head of cattle, reached its zenith about 1878 and then, with the advent of the Lincoln County War and subsequent ramifications, political animosities and cutthroat competitors, Chisum's power and wealth lessened.

Chisum always played a lone hand. He never was allied with the powers that be at Santa Fe and this fact served to earn him many political enemies who lined up with his personal and business interests to curb his power. It is recorded, though, that Chisum was usually more than a match for the strongest, yet it was Tom Catron, a young and ambitious Territorial attorney who, playing with the opposition forces, brought about the opening wedge in the long-drawn legal fight to "get" Chisum. Catron brought suit against Chisum on account of stolen cattle. But "Uncle John," affectionately so-called, had the ace card in this affair. He presented at court his old power of attorney and therefore argued "I stole no cattle."

But Catron, backed by powerful interests antagonistic to Chisum, was no quitter and learning of the old packing house judgments, accepted them for collection and, in the course of this litigation, Chisum was thrown in jail. He was shortly released and the judgments were never collected during his lifetime, but a Court of Chancery at Roswell later held that they were valid and they were collected from Uncle John's estate.

Hunter, a trader from Kansas City, a shrewd businessman, heard of the old Chisum notes in Texas. He bought them for as little as two cents on the dollar and in the course of a big deal presented them for payment. Obviously Chisum suffered heavily from this transaction.

Such litigation, the cattle wars and new competition made serious inroads on the Chisum holdings. This, together with an impairment of health, made Uncle John's last days turbulent and fraught with trials and tribulations. Yet, it is said, to the last he never lost his sense of humor or his implacable desire to "rule the roost." He died in 1884.

Surprising as it may seem Chisum never carried a gun, yet he handled a battalion of hard-fighting men, and old ranchers of the West assure you that no better cowman ever lived.

His part in the Lincoln County War, the famed feud between two rival cattle interests, was that of field marshal. No record of him has been made as the initiator of the quarrel, but his deft undercover maneuvers filled in the stop-gaps in the bloody hostilities. In the instance of the Lincoln County trouble this characteristic of his led to an event which indirectly brought about the opening foray. The Murphy-Dolan-Riley trio—Chisum's most influential and powerful rival in business—hired McSween, a young attorney, to defend cattle rustlers who had been hauled into court, accused by Chisum of stealing his cattle. McSween refused to defend them on moral grounds and quit Murphy. Chisum immediately retained him and so for Chisum, McSween prosecuted the thieves Murphy had ordered him to defend. And on top of a conviction, McSween produced evidence that purported to show that Murphy was their backer and sponsor, and not only bought their stolen cattle but did a regular business in buying stolen cattle from thieves who lived by plundering Chisum's herds. The proved source of supply of Murphy's cattle was the explanation of his ability to underbid all competitors in securing government contracts, which was another matter that had been the cause of such friction between rival herd owners.

That was the state of affairs just previous to the beginning of actual warfare between the contending forces—the Murphy-Dolan outfit on one side and McSween and his adherents on the other, with Chisum as McSween's backer.

Soon after the break between McSween and Murphy, John H. Tunstall, a young Englishman, arrived in Lincoln and decided to make that part of the country his home. He bought a ranch on the Rio Felix, thirty miles southeast of Lincoln, stocked it with horses and cattle and settled down. He and McSween were drawn together by common sympathies, and soon were close friends. A little later he formed a partnership with McSween, and the two built a large adobe store building in Lincoln and opened a general merchandise store. With the financial assistance of John Chisum, and Tunstall's money, a bank was established and soon the new firm was making great inroads on the business of their competitors. In a little while the competition became bitter.

A crisis was brought about during January of 1878 over the payment of insurance money by Murphy to McSween and the outcome of this was the death of Tunstall at the hands of a Murphy crowd.

At that time Billy the Kid, now famed in Western song and story, was working for Tunstall and his pledge to "get" Tunstall's murderers and avenge his death brought him to the fore as a feared gun-fighter. Throughout the war he aligned himself with the McSween interests, and the fact that he was "without the law" because of several shootings made him the integral leader of the McSween forces. Of all, the Murphy gang were most anxious to get Billy the Kid.

The bloody encounters that ensued, lasting for three years, vendettas by far more fierce than recorded of the Italian Mafia, downright displays of "guts" and cruel killings make the Lincoln County war a saga of elemental man in all his fury. Billy's death at the hands of Pat Garrett in July, 1881 was the last singular event of the internal war, memorable for all its fierceness and notorious actors.

In all this Chisum, again the strategist, served as liaison officer. He supported the McSween crowd and his ranch was often the base and succor for the weary badmen. Chisum's part in the war as a power, was an initiatory factor; his active part relatively important and his association with all events leading up to and with it an assured fact.

It is the consensus of opinion that the Lincoln County War availed nothing, yet for the purposes of this recounting, it had much to do in the breaking down of Chisum's preponderant authority.

Yet withal these turbulent days were interspersed with many lighter times, the Chisum Ranch had much to do with the social life of the Pecos Valley. Naturally it was a meeting place for the itinerant businessmen of the era, a stop-over for the trail drivers, a resting place for the rover, and, being near the settlement of Roswell, it was a live spot in the sparsely settled West. Mention is made in many of the Western chronicles of

Chisum's Ranch. Trees and roses brought in a covered wagon from Texas by the Chisum family soon made a beautiful place and from miles around, at regular intervals came the residents of mountain and valley for the seasonal round-ups and holiday parties. Cattlemen and cow punchers mixed with patrician traders who dared the rigors of the new found country; gun-fighters "tossed off" conviviality with wide-eyed tenderfeet, as Uncle John, in good humor, basked in the glory of his cattle kingdom. His pride was the now famous Chisum orchard—first planted in 1872—indeed the first in the Pecos. To the present day it is said that this planting of fruit trees was the most favorable advertisement for the Pecos Valley.

After Chisum's death, the above mentioned legal battles, their attendant decisions and legal forces made definite inroads on the Chisum estate. Uncle John was not there to defend his own and his heirs and legatees evidently took the attitude that the residue itself would be more than sufficient. In their hands it remained until 1893 when J. J. Hagerman, an enterprising businessman from Colorado, invested heavily in the Pecos Valley, and among other purchases, bought the Chisum Ranch.

Hagerman was an empire builder of another sort, and with Charles B. Eddy and other forward-looking citizens of Roswell succeeded in developing the transportation facilities of the valley. Outside capital was interested and the Chisum Ranch in 1894 was the scene of a mammoth party celebrating the arrival of the first railroad train of Roswell.

In 1904, Hagerman remodeled the ranch house but the main structure was left intact and made the central part of the new abode. Again, the Chisum Ranch, now the Hagerman, was the locale of Pecos Valley's social highlights and has remained so today—still a part of the Hagerman estate.

Chisum-Hagerman Ranch breathes romance—aye! to the tourist it is the living symbol of the raw West of building days and no song or story of sunset land holds more vivid color than the everyday chronicle of this exciting locale.

Sources of Information: J. Evetts Haley, *Charles Goodnight, Cowman and Plainsman,* Boston, New York, London, Houghton Mifflin Co., 1936; Ex-Governor J. F. Hinkle; Miguel A. Otero, *The Real Billy the Kid,* New York, Press of the Pioneers, 1935.

Seven HL Ranch (Excerpt)

by Georgia B. Redfield

The old Seven HL Ranch was known after 1889 as the Bar V Ranch, but as the Seven HL it became known as one of the finest ranches in Southeast New Mexico.

During the winter of 1883 a group of men in Missouri organized the Cass County Missouri Land and Cattle Company. They planned dealing in land and raising cattle in New Mexico.

In January 1883, J. D. Cooley, W. G. Urton and a man by the name of Easley came to New Mexico, made arrangements for bringing cattle which they brought in 1884 and placed on the ranch called Seven HL 60 miles northeast of Roswell on the Pecos River. They drove 3,000 two-year old heifers to the ranch, which were branded with an H and turned loose on a range that extended 150 miles north to Las Vegas and to the Texas line on the south, near the present City of Carlsbad, only there was no Carlsbad there at that time, and there was no railroad closer than Las Vegas over a hundred and fifty miles distance to which place they traveled every two or three months for mail and provisions.

There were no wells or man-made watering places. The company bought about 1,600 acres of land along the Pecos for a distance of 80 or 90 miles. Each tract having a Pecos watering place, for the range was governed by watering places.

All ranchers worked together with range rights granted those on whose range the work was being done.

J. J. Cox owned a ranch on the west side of the Pecos, while the Seven H was on the east side, the Pecos being the dividing line between the two places.

Easley was at first the manager of the HL Ranch. Later J. D. Cooley was made manager in Easley's place. In 1886 Cooley moved back to Missouri and W. G. Urton was manager in Cooley's place.

Cox on the west side of the river and Mr. Urton became friends from the first, working together for the best interest of both cattle outfits, and looking after each others' stock.

The cattle "rustlers" became the worst problem on the open range. The Cass Land and Cattle Company suffered heavy losses from this source.

In 1887 two brothers by the name of White located on a ranch twenty miles from the Cox cattle outfit. Cox had claimed this range before the White brothers moved in. In the fall there was one small "dogie" in the outfit, the owner of which was to be settled. The owners of the two outfits met to attempt a decision as to who should have the dogie, and in controversy White killed the Cox foreman.

Such small matters as these were the cause of frequent range killings. The calf was branded for Cox, who became the owner. When a cattle "pool" was formed of cattle belonging to the Cass Land and Cattle Company, the Cox and several other ranches, "a tenderfoot" from the East was brought to be foreman. His name was Tom Baldwin. He had a hard time of it with those who considered themselves pioneer cattlemen, and finally gave up the work as too hard a job, and returned to the East.

In the spring of 1889 Cox died, the Cass Land Cattle Company bought the Cox Ranch and all holdings. It was then the name of the Seven HL Ranch became the Bar V. The price the Cox property and cattle interests were sold for was a hundred thousand dollars.

Two outfits were put on the range, running separate "chuck" wagons and trail "bosses." G. R. Urton, brother of W. G. Urton, was manager of one outfit and R. L. Moss was manager of the other. Three years after the Cox outfit was bought the entire amount of the hundred thousand dollars purchase price was paid from sales of steers and from that time on reaching 125 percent dividends.

In 1895 John Shaw, then of Roswell, joined with the company. He branded x-x and his interests were separate from the company's except for the range work. The x-x brand is the only brand that has continued to the present time on the Pecos River. R. L. Moss is the owner of this outfit and his headquarters is the old John Shaw Ranch.

In 1895 John Shaw constructed the first drift fence in that part of the country on the Pecos. This was a saving in expense of roundups as it prevented cattle from drifting far. The fence being on public domain, the Federal Government sent an inspector and had all drift fences on public land removed. Work became harder on the range and with new ranches and more cattle rustlers the profits were less.

Sources of Information: W. C. Urton; *Roswell Daily Record* Oct. 7-97.

De Baca County History: Billy the Kid at Fort Sumner

by J. Vernon Smithson

Billy The Kid At Fort Sumner: After the close of the Lincoln county war in 1877, Billy the Kid and some of his followers, Charlie Bowdre, Tom O'Folliard, Fred Wayte, John Middlestone, Hendry Brown, and Doc Scurlock, moved to Fort Sumner and made it their headquarters, from that time until the death of Billy the Kid.

Horse and cattle stealing and gambling were Billy the Kid's main activities and his support. Stealing cattle and horses in the south and driving them north as far as Tascosa on the Canadian river in Texas and selling them. Then, on his return trip, he would steal from the north country and bring them back south for sale to unscrupulous buyers.

Middleton, Wayte, and Brown soon quit the gang and went east to settle down, part of them to become respectable citizens in later life.

When General Lew Wallace was appointed Governor of New Mexico, President Rutherford B. Hayes issued a proclamation directing all men under arms that had engaged in the Lincoln County War to return to their homes.

Billy the Kid, having no home to call his own, went to work for Frank Coe on Coe's ranch in Lincoln county. Civil authorities did not long leave the Kid alone and there was a warrant charging him with the murder of some of the combatants of the Lincoln County War, issued for his arrest. He left the home of his friends and went into hiding in the mountains. After seemingly miraculous escapes from pursuing posses, he returned to Fort Sumner where he found his pals, O'Folliard, Bowdre, and Scurlock in the same position as he. The President's proclamation has been disregarded by the civil authorities and they were all being sought by the law. Rewards were offered for Billy the Kid, dead or alive. But with the aid of his many friends around Fort Sumner who were always willing to help him, he managed to evade the law.

The glamour and good manners of Billy the Kid made him very popular in Fort Sumner and he attended parties and dances while he was hiding from the law.

During the latter part of December, 1878, Billy the Kid and Tom

O'Folliard visited Lincoln and were captured and put in jail but managed to escape. Again in March, 1879, they were captured at Lincoln and jailed but again they escaped.

Returning to Fort Sumner, Billy the Kid and his friends renewed their stealing and selling of cattle. Billy the Kid had an occasional gunfight with someone who wanted the reward for his capture, or was desirous of killing him for the renown that would be gained, and they all fell victim to Billy the Kid's steady nerve and lightning-fast trigger finger.

The officers of the law, abetted by the irate cattle and horse owners whose stock had been stolen by Billy the Kid, pursued them, but for an occasional wound to some of his gang or the loss of their horses, they were able to defy all attempts of capture.

Patrick P. Garrett, former buffalo hunter and later a resident of Fort Sumner, who had at one time been a close friend of Billy the Kid, was elected Sheriff of Lincoln county in 1880. With Sheriff Garrett in office, Billy the Kid's life grew harder than ever, for the Sheriff put forth every effort to catch him. Azariah F. Wild, a Secret Service operative, and Frank Stewart, a cattleman's association man-hunter from Texas, with a posse of experienced man-hunters helping them, Billy the Kid grew very wary.

Escaping from posses who were hunting him near White Oaks in November, 1880, after he had spent the celebration of his twenty-first birthday in that town, he headed back toward Fort Sumner. On Christmas Eve night, 1880, he and his gang were surprised by Sheriff Garret and his deputies as they approached Fort Sumner, evidently intending to engage in the season's festivities. Tom O'Folliard was shot and killed in this affray and the rest of the gang escaped unhurt except for the loss of a horse or two. Later Billy the Kid was captured at Stinking Springs, after the posse had killed his friend, Charley Bowdre.

Sheriff Pat Garrett took Billy the Kid to Santa Fe for safekeeping and he was later taken to Mesilla for trial. Tried first for the killing of Joe Bernstein, Indian Agency clerk, he was acquitted. Next he was tried for the killing of Sheriff Brady during the Lincoln county war and sentenced to death on the gallows. He was taken to Lincoln and was to be kept there until the date set for his execution. He escaped by killing his two guards, Bob Ollinger, and J. W. Bell. After several days of hiding, Billy the Kid went to Fort Sumner, where, it is said, his sweetheart lived.

In the meantime, Sheriff Garrett and his deputies had spent days of fruitless searching for Billy the Kid, and had decided to go to Fort Sumner in an effort to get some track of Billy the Kid. Arriving in Fort Sumner he was unable to find out anything definite and was about to return to Roswell, which he made his headquarters.

He stopped after night at the home of Pete Maxwell, son of Lucien B. Maxwell, who had bought the old Fort Sumner and lived there with his family. Pete Maxwell was a friend of Billy the Kid and Garrett and his deputies thought that they might get some definite information as to the whereabouts of Billy the Kid.

Billy the Kid had ridden in from a sheep ranch that night, from south of town on the Pecos river. He had stopped at the house of Saval Gutierrez, Pat Garrett's brother-in-law. Hungry and tired, he learned from Saval Gutierrez' wife that Pete Maxwell had killed a beef that day and that it was hanging on the porch of the nearby Maxwell home. In his sock feet, bareheaded and coatless, the butcher knife in his hand, Billy the Kid started over to get himself a steak for Gutierrez' wife to cook.

Maxwell was asleep when Garrett and his deputies came by. Leaving his deputies outside on the porch to wait until he talked to Maxwell, Garrett went into the room where Pete Maxwell was sleeping. Garrett had only awakened Maxwell and started to question him about Billy the Kid's whereabouts, when Billy the Kid stepped on the porch.

Neither of the deputies recognized him as the desperado they were hunting and remained silent to his questions of who they were. Holding his gun on them, Billy the Kid backed into the darkness of the room in which Pete Maxwell was sleeping. He asked Maxwell who the men outside were, and Garrett, hidden by the darkness, recognized the voice of his former friend and shot him. He shot twice, and he and Maxwell bolted from the room and told his deputies what had happened.

The dark room was silent and the four men huddled together out on the porch, afraid to go see if Billy the Kid was dead. Finally Pete Maxwell took a candle and set it on the wide ledge outside of the window. Deluvina Maxwell, a Navajo servant of the Maxwell household and worshipful admirer of Billy the Kid, went in and discovered the body of the Kid lying there.

The news soon scattered and feeling was rife. Many of Billy the

Kid's friends were in favor of lynching the officers. But the next morning the inquest was held and it was found Pat Garrett had killed Billy the Kid in discharge of his official duty and the Sheriff returned to Roswell.

Billy the Kid was buried by the sides of his friends, Charley Bowdre and Tom O'Folliard, in the little military cemetery a short distance east of town. The entire population of Fort Sumner attended his funeral.

Sources of Information: *The Saga of Billy the Kid*, Walter Noble Burns, Doubleday, Page & Company, Garden City, N.Y., 1927; *The Real Billy the Kid*, Miguel Antonio Otero, Rufus Rockwell Wilson, Inc., New York City, N.Y., 1936; Charlie Foor, Mrs. Joe Stearns, Peter Abrea, Mrs. Lucero, Mrs. Adeline Welborn, Frank Lavata and J. P. Brooks.

History of Portales Springs

by Vernon Smithson

Located in Section 16, Township 2 south, Range 35 East, three miles east and two and one-half miles south of Portales is Portales Springs. A few caliche bluffs from which there is a seep of spring water, and a draw running to the southeast containing a little water and surrounded by grass flats, are all that remain of one of the most historic spots in Eastern New Mexico.

Water was very scarce on the Llano Estacado in the early days so it is very probable that the Indians made use of the Portales Springs, coming and going on their raids in the country below the breaks of the Llano Estacado into Texas. Later, Portales Springs must have been headquarters for numerous buffalo hunters camps and a watering place for the buffalo.

History gives us the first authentic mention of the Portales Springs in 1874, when the United States began its final campaign against the powerful Comanches of the plains. Colonel Nelson A. Miles from Fort Dodge, Kansas, and R. S. Mackenzie from Fort Sill, Oklahoma defeated the Comanches in a series of battles along the Canadian and Red Rivers, dislodged them from the Palo Duro Canyon, and the Comanches started out over the dry expanse of the Llano Estacado hoping to shake off their pursuers before they reached the Pecos river.

They traveled by way of the Running Water Draw in Texas, and by the Portales Springs in New Mexico. They succeeded in losing some of the army pursuing them; others gave up the chase because of thirst, but the bulk of Miles' men kept after the fleeing savages as they crossed the Plains. The Indians were overtaken and captured between Portales Spring and the Pecos river. Thus the Llano Estacado, long the possession of these fierce, proud Indians became available for ranching.

The first ranch on New Mexico's part of the Llano Estacado was established at Portales Springs in 1881. Doak Good and Ben Webb secured a contract to carry mail on a new route from Colorado, Texas to Fort Sumner, New Mexico. The route ran by way of the Yellow House springs in Texas and Portales Springs in New Mexico into Fort Sumner on the Pecos. Doak Good established headquarters at Portales Springs and began running a small herd of cattle in connection with his mail carrying.

Jim Newman had established a ranch at the Yellow House springs in 1882 but was forced to leave when the State of Texas sold that land to the Capitol Freehold Land Syndicate, who established the great XIT ranch in Texas. Newman moved to Salt Lake (sometimes called Portales Lake), fifteen miles southeast of Portales Springs, in 1886.

Newman's cattle, a much larger herd than that of Good's, drifted over to Portales Springs. Differences soon arose as to whom would use the water from the Portales Springs, although it is said that at that time the run-off from the Springs was enough to water 10,000 head of cattle. Their quarrel became bitter and it is said that they started shooting each other's stock.

Good, a bachelor, lived alone in a story-and-half adobe house near Portales Springs. Adjoining the springs was an abandoned rock house. One morning, while dressing, Good looked out of the window in the upper part of his house and saw a man peering around the corner of an old rock by the side of the Springs. Good finished dressing but stayed from in front of the window. He picked up his old Sharps buffalo gun and crept downstairs and out around the corner of his house with his gun ready for action. The next time the man showed his head around the corner, Good shot him.

Soon after this affair, Good sold out his stock and left the country. It was said that he only had 250 steers left to sell when he left, from an original herd of 1500 head.

Curtis and Davis soon bought out Newman and ran their DZ brand over all the country, their cattle ranging from the present site of Portales east to the Texas line, and as far south as the present sites of Dora, Inez, and Causey.

With the coming of the railroad in 1888 from the Pecos Valley into Amarillo, the country surrounding Portales Springs was fast settled up and the larger ranchers had to quit ranching or move into other regions. None of them owned much of the land that they had been using and it was soon taken up, farmers homesteading on the land.

Since that time the Portales Springs has not been used by any large ranchers. It is on state school land, and is open for leasing. The old buildings have been destroyed or have weathered away and there are no traces of where they once stood. A few troughs, built for cattle to drink from, are still there but not in use. The pumping from the shallow water district has lowered the flow of the Portales Springs to a bare seep, which would not furnish water for many cattle. The draw which the springs runs into furnishes a winter haven for many ducks and geese that come south during the winter months.

The Last Great Roundup of the Llano Estacado

by Vernon Smithson

In the spring of 1898, probably the biggest roundup that was ever held on the Llano Estacado of New Mexico took place in the country surrounding the present Tatum, New Mexico.

This roundup, which covered some four or five hundred sections, was held on the old LFD range, and lasted for forty days. All of the surrounding ranches were represented, the DZ's, the 9R's and other lesser ranchers.

Everyone knew when the roundup was to be held and they were arranged so that the men could go from one roundup to another and gather all the cattle that belonged to the ranch that they were representing. Roundups usually began in the southern part of the region and went north, as all the cattle drifted south during the winter months.

In the roundup of 1898 there were 125 men, and their horses totaled 2,700. A cowboy couldn't get by with less than 12 or 14 horses and the more one had the better. Horses were ridden hard in the early days and after a day's hard work a horse needed three or four days rest. Riders frequently changed horses four or five times daily.

The usual procedure of the day's work started at daylight. A body of men would strike out in the general direction of that day's work, running their horses as hard as they could go as far as 15 miles. When the horse began to tire, the riders would drop out of the bunch and round up the cattle and head them in the general direction of the camp. Rounding up the cattle worked much faster then than now; a whoop was all that was needed to make the cattle run for miles.

No estimate could be made of the number of cattle that were gathered in the big roundup of 1898. "There were cattle in every direction as far as you could see!" said my informant. Some size of the herd might be judged from the fact that they branded 1,000 head of strays that spring.

The chuck wagons of the different outfits were in keeping with the size of the outfits they represented and sometimes they were so large that eight mule teams were needed to pull them. On arising each morning the cowboys would throw their bedrolls on top of the wagon and seventy-five bedrolls would make a towering load for the wagons.

The barbed wire fences did away with the big roundups; although there are still roundups that seem enormous, in comparison with the early day roundups, they are very small.

Source of Information: George Anderson.

A Cattle Round Up in the Zuni Mountains, New Mexico, Ben Wittick, ca. 1880–90, NMHM/DCA #015545

Maxwell Ranch

by Thorp and Breit

(U. S. Highway 64, near the town of Cimarron).

Still standing on the banks of the Cimarron, Maxwell's Ranch is a dilapidated monument to an age forever gone. The dwelling, the finest in the country for its time, was of adobe and as large as a city block, with a huge verandah and patio. Old cronies and newcomers off the Barlow and Sanderson stage came to the Maxwell house with a regularity that only could mean one thing—Maxwell was a true host and all were welcome. His expansive nature reflected in the character of his ranch was in turn symbolized by the vast land grant bearing his name.

The Grant is one of the largest and most famous of the land grants in New Mexico. As Spanish land grants go in New Mexico, the majority dating back to the 17th and 18th centuries, its history is comparatively recent, having been made under the Republic of Mexico in 1841.

The size of the grant was tremendous. Three times that of Rhode Island, 1,714,764.94 acres of mountain and plain, farm and forest, pasture land and gold mine, it was a rich, self-sustaining feudal world. Its original domain includes the present towns of Springer, French, Maxwell, Schomberg, Hebron, Otero, Dillon, Raton, Van Houten, Vermejo Park, Dawson, Cimarron, Ute Park, Elizabethtown; and in Colorado, Vigil, Stonewall, Torres, Cuatro, Tercio, Primero and Segundo.

The history of the Maxwell grant is particularly interesting because, like Bent's Fort further north, it was the center of pioneer life and a meeting point on the old Santa Fe Trail for Indians, mountaineers, traders, and adventurers of all types. Great events took place during this time: the Mexican war, the cession of the Southwestern Territory to the United States, the Civil War, each affecting the persons connected with the grant. Lesser events, but no less spectacular and dramatic were occurring in the diurnal scheme of things: the Indian battles, the personal feuds, the hunt for gold, the bawdy, the cowardly, the courageous, all congregated on common ground—on the Maxwell territory. The most striking personalities of frontier life are connected with the history of the Grant; through it moved Carlos Beaubien, Charles Bent, Ceran St. Vrain, Jesus G. Abreu, Kit Carson and Lucien B. Maxwell. The life was history in the making, it was progress and, hence, necessary. Land had to be cultivated for the new people, land had to be made safe for the building and extension of the railroads. The excesses also were necessary—the personal affirmation or protest of the steady march westward. The life was wild, sudden and reversible: an ebullient life could be ended in the middle of the night; and overnight, a hardy frontiersman might appropriate a taste for luxury, elegance and finery. The Maxwell land was a cross-section of the entire southwest of the time; upon its soil, progress was stamping itself indelibly, and also, the personal life was expressing itself, rich, turbulent, with the face turned to the unknown.

The exciting and varied events that unfolded in this territory are seemingly a mirror of the legalistic war over property rights carried on incessantly throughout forty-one years, a war which is the tissue of the history of the Maxwell Grant.

From January 8, 1841 on, when Carlos Beaubien and Guadalupe Miranda requested the grant from Governor Armijo of New Mexico (then under the Mexican Government) it could be said its life consisted in court contest after court contest, suit after suit, litigation after litigation. Hardly a year's peace was enjoyed by any one of the owners of the Grant. The claim was contested by various individuals and by the United States Government. The suits pivoted around the question of ownership and the extent of the property. In August 1882, the Maxwell Land Grant and Railway Company received a favorable decision against the United States Government.

Carlos Beaubien, one of the original grantees, died in Taos in 1864; Lucien B. Maxwell, married to Luz Beaubien, a daughter, bought out the remaining heirs and on May 29, 1865, Maxwell and his wife became sole owners. Maxwell was a strong man, domineering, a man of courage and mighty single-handed feats. He had over 500 peons working for him. Both cattle and sheep were raised and on two occasions Maxwell drove herds of 100,000 each to California. Kit Carson, one of Maxwell's best friends, served as guide in both instances. Agriculture was carried on extensively by Maxwell with Fort Union, 60 miles south, a market for surplus crops.

Maxwell's other side was that of the sport, the dandy, the host; a lavish entertainer whose fame spread far. In the rainy season stage coaches were held up for days at the river ford and during these times Maxwell provided for the travelers and teamsters with a generous abandon, refusing all payment. He was a lover of horses, costly furniture, and extravagance of any sort. New settlers coming for land received livestock, seed and implements from Maxwell without scratch of pen or contract. Perhaps after three or four years, Maxwell, finding himself in need of produce, would request a thousand bushel of grain, a hundred head of stock. The requirements would be met without question—such was Maxwell's system of business.

Gold was his undoing. The metal was discovered in 1867 on Maxwell's property at the foot of Mount Baldy. The gold venture cost Maxwell a great fortune and yielded nothing. Many squatters drifted in and settled upon the grant, an omen of Maxwell's fate. On April 30, 1870, an English syndicate, the Maxwell Land Grant and Railway Company bought Maxwell's holdings for $1,250,000. For Maxwell, it could be said, everything he touched hereafter turned to dust rather than to gold. Investment after investment failed. He established in Santa Fe the first banking institution in New Mexico or Arizona which still exists; however, for Maxwell it meant still further losses. On July 25, 1875, Maxwell died in Fort Sumner, a poor man.

Today, the nearly two million acres have been partitioned out to individual investors. On the great Maxwell land there are numerous large and small ranches. Wade Phillips of the Phillips Petroleum Company has built, close to the old Maxwell house, one of the magnificent residences in the State.

Sources of Information: R. E. Twitchell, *Spanish Archives of New Mexico, Vol. 1 and 2, Leading Facts of New Mexico History, Vol. 5*; Manville Chapman, *Blazed Trails, A Series of Colfax County Historical Narratives.*

The Old Bar W Ranch, Lincoln County, New Mexico

by N. Howard Thorp

The Old Bar W Ranch, known as the Carrizozo Cattle Company, is situated seventy miles east of San Antonio, and ninety miles west of Roswell, on the Pecos River. This ranch was first owned by a Spanish-American family, who sold it to the Hon. Thomas B. Catron who, in turn, sold it to Captain Scott and his associates in England.

Their first foreman was an Englishman named Jim Alcock, a fine chap, but sadly out of place running a cattle ranch, and whose methods almost drove the company on the rocks.

Finally W. C. McDonald—who afterwards became Governor—bought out Alcock's interest, and from then on the ranch was a great success. Under Alcock's management, Jim Neibors was foreman.

When Mr. McDonald took charge, Pete Johnson—formerly from Halfs Ranch on the lower Pecos in Texas, was appointed. Johnson was one of the best cowmen that ever came out of Texas.

Succeeding Johnson, a nephew of Colonel Scott's from England was appointed. But he made a failure of it, finally killing himself in Tularosa.

The next and last foreman under Governor McDonald's management was Fred Crosby.

Some of the old hands whose names I remember were, Allen Hightower, Marion Hill, Randolph Reynolds, John Latham, Charlie Zelmer, and Skeeter Henley. For many years old John Patten was cook, and Jim Redman, windmill and tank man.

This cattle company could lay claim to some twenty-five thousand head of cattle in the Bar W brand.

From the headquarter ranch they owned practically all the waterings, as far north as the Gran Quivira, and Montezuma Springs. On the west of the ranch, all waterings, like Duck Lake, Indian Tanks, and south to Mound Springs, Salt Creek, Candelario Wells, and as far as the Alkali Flats, and all waterings on the east side of the Mal Pais, and tributary thereto. This controlled an enormous amount of range, but the Carrizozo Cattle Company only owned outright small blocks of land covering the waterings.

The following description of old ranches in New Mexico very well covers, with a few changes which will be noted later, the old Bar W Ranch.

Most of the old ranch houses of New Mexico were built after the pattern of those in old Mexico and were called Haciendas or Estancias, properly speaking; this included the home buildings, corrals, gardens, vineyards and ranch properties.

Numerous families were sometimes attached to these Estancias, the overflow of people at times forming towns. When the families of the owners of these ranches dwelt upon them they had numerous servants; these in the majority of cases were bought as Indian children, bought from the nomadic tribes, who in turn stole these children from the different Pueblos.

These large ranch houses were built in the form of a hollow square, and during Indian times, all windows in the different rooms faced the inside on the patio or plaza. Three sides of this square was composed of rooms; the remaining side had a high wall to the height of the main building. This wall had a large gate built of heavy plank, built wide enough so a coach and horses could enter. Directly opposite and across the plaza was another gate; this was the front entrance to the house.

Some of these old ranch houses were from one to two hundred feet square, making the inside court large enough to hold a band of horses or such gentle stock which might be close to the ranch in time of Indian raids.

A well was dug in the plaza for domestic purposes, and also for the use of livestock in times of Indian trouble.

These houses were almost invulnerable, as they could not be burned, and in case of attack a body of men laying on the roof, protected by the "pretils" or walls which surrounded the outer edges of the roof, could repel almost any body of Indians.

The corrals, which usually were not far distant from the main house, were entered through a high gateway, the sides of which were made of heavy ax-dressed timbers. The two side timbers being set in the ground to a depth of three or four feet, then extending above the ground ten or twelve feet. The upper ends of these side timbers were pointed, and entered holes bored into the cross timber which extended from one upright to the other. The gate or gates were made of hand-dressed timber, about four inches square, the gates being about eight feet high. One side of each gate—if two were used—extended up to the cross piece above, and the end being pointed, entered through a hole in this timber, the lower end being also sharpened, entered an old wagon hub, which had been set in the ground, exactly as the former wagon axle had rested. This constituted a gate hinge, a very strong one, and was called a "sambullo," a Spanish word for socket.

The corrals were made of various materials, adobe, rock, cedar or brush.

If cedar posts were abundant, a trench the size of the corral wanted was dug to a depth of some eighteen inches; the posts were then placed in it close together. When this was done, dirt was filled in around them and thoroughly tamped, leaving the posts extending some seven or eight feet above the ground.

Then long poles, quaking aspen, pine, or whatever was most convenient, were laced to the upright post with strips of green rawhide; the rawhide shrinking as it dried, pulled the poles up tight to the posts, and made a very strong corral. This main corral if on a large ranch would sometimes hold two thousand head of cattle. Adjoining this usually were two other corrals of about half the size of the main one, all three corrals connected by gates.

Connecting with one of them was a round horse corral, never over thirty-five to forty feet across, so a roper, when the horses circled in the corral, by standing in the middle would be close enough to four-foot a horse he passed. This corral, like most of the others, had a bramadero or snubbing post in the center to snub the broncs to, when caught. This horse corral had two gates, one opening into the adjoining corrals, the other to the outside range. Young horses, after being blind-folded, hackamored and saddled, were usually first ridden in this corral.

The material of which these ranch houses were made was of sun dried brick or adobe; a few were made of rock; while others of terrones: these were cut out of sod with a spade and left to dry before placing in the wall, and were generally a little smaller brick than those made of adobe.

To make the adobe brick the mud was mixed with the straw by tramping with the feet, then poured into molds and left on the ground a few days in order to dry, after which they are stacked on edges in rows, until hard and ready to be used in the building.

The early ranch buildings had walls of three feet or so in thickness;

this was partly as protection from roaming bands of Indians, and also so the rooms would be warm in winter and cool during the hot summer months, these thick walls being almost impervious to climatic changes. The inside walls were plastered with mud and given a finishing white coat of gesso, a form of lime.

The floors were of smoothed mud, and the ceilings of the rooms—some, ten to twelve feet high. These roofs were supported by vigas (logs), usually a foot in thickness, the big end being laid on the outer wall and the small end some six inches in thickness laying on top of the inner wall, which gave a slope to carry off the rain.

These vigas were covered with small poles, cleaned, as were the vigas, of all bark. These small poles of some two inches in diameter were called morillos, and usually were laid "herring-bone" fashion. On top of these morillos was placed several inches of hay, straw or leaf cactus; this was to keep the earth from falling through, and above all a foot or so of dirt carefully packed down.

This sort of roof would keep out any ordinary rain, but if there were a soaker of several days duration they would leak badly.

The above is—with a few changes—a fair picture of the old Bar W, or Carrizozo Ranch, as it was some fifty years ago.

After the Indian troubles were passed, the well in the patio was filled up, water being procured from the spring south of the building, the corrals also being moved to the south side.

Heroines of Pioneer Days (Excerpt)

by Clay W. Vaden

While living at the Y Ranch, Mr. Kiehne was in Texas to bring back a large herd of cattle over the trail and when he heard of the Indian outbreaks in this section of the Southwest he wrote his wife advising her to take the children and go to Socorro. However, their nearest Post Office at that time was at Magdalena, perhaps 100 or more miles from the Y Ranch and the letter was delayed and Mrs. Kiehne felt safer at the ranch because every night during the Indian scare the neighboring ranchmen and cowboys would take turns about standing guard as sentinels. Had Mrs. Kiehne become frightened and panicky and taken her husband's advice she and the children would have been on the St. Augustine Plains at the very time of greatest danger when a freighting outfit was ambushed and murdered near Durphy's well, 20 miles west of Magdalena.

In about three years the Kiehne family moved to Magdalena to give their children school advantages. In 1889 they moved to Negorite country about 16 miles Southeast of Reserve, now in Catron County. While living there, five of Geronimo's Indian braves came by their place on one of their raids. Mrs. Graham, who was with them at the time, had Mrs. Kiehne hide the children under feather beds, claiming that she knew from experience that bullets would not go through the thick feather beds. Mrs. Graham, a crack shot with either pistol or rifle, stood in the doorway with her Winchester, determined to protect the other women and children at the cost of her own life, if necessary. The night was a beautiful moonlit one, nearly as bright as day. The Indians in single file were creeping near the ranch house when a faithful Mexican laborer on the place threw a shell into his gun and the click frightened them away.

Hellroaring Mesa

by Clay W. Vaden

Some folk say "There is nothing in a name" but Hellroaring Mesa on the west side of Negrito, south of Reserve, Catron County, between August Kiehne's ranch and N-Bar Ranch, certainly seems to have been given the appropriate name for it is a rocky bit of wilderness only accessible on mule, burro, or horseback.

During a terrific snowstorm in 1886, Bob Lewis, now City Marshall at Magdalena, together with Captain Mansell and Major Troke, the latter a giant of an Irishman over six feet and two inches tall, from T Bar Ranch five miles East of the N-Bar Ranch, were riding through the blizzard and when they finally reached the said mesa (sometimes called Rainey Mesa) Captain Mansell, in a disgusted manner said, "Wal, boys, this must be Hellroaring Mesa from the way the wind and snow are blowing a gale," and from that day to this it is called by that expressive name, "Hellroaring Mesa," as so many things are often born in a storm.

Source of Information: a personal interview with Bob Lewis, Magdalena, New Mexico, April 18, 1936.

SHEEP

"Most of the sheep men—especially those who had moved their flocks to the mountains—managed to weather the drought, but Mac, sticking to the flats, and hoping for rain, lost most of his sheep, and his creditors took the rest, leaving him high and dry."

From "Fried Snakes" by N. Howard Thorp

Basílico Garduño, New Mexico Sheepherder

by Lorin W. Brown

It was late afternoon when I approached the campsite, in the shadow of El Cerro Redondo (Round Peak), near Jémez Hot Springs. The sheep were still grazing, although all had their heads turned toward the wooded base of the peak, which dominated this upland pasture. The meadow, stretching as far as I could see, encircled the peak. I knew enough of sheep habits to go in the direction in which they grazed, for there would be their *majada* (bedding ground), and close by would be the camp of the *pastor* (shepherd).

A curling blue column rising from a cluster of fir and spruce indicated the spot I sought, and three nondescript dogs gave warning of my approach. Then Basílico's squat, broad figure emerged from the patched and weather-beaten, one-pole tent. He was clad in bib overalls of denim, over which an old, ill-fitting jacket of the same material was worn. This was buttoned over his shirts (the weather determined the number worn). A battered black felt hat and homemade shoes completed his costume.

A low, muttered command to the dogs quieted them, and a circling motion of his arm sent them racing around the edge of the flock to urge on lagging members toward the *majada* and make the group more compact.

"Buenas tardes," I said, and added praise for the well trained dogs. My greeting was returned in a low tone, strange and hesitant, the reluctant, inhibited speech of one used to living alone. "*Llegue, amigo* (Come in, friend)," said Basílico, his wind-reddened, bloodshot eyes glaring into mine as if he were angry. Years of squatting over a campfire had given him this baleful look.

I seated myself on a block of pine, while he poured a cup of coffee, the *pastor's* first act of hospitality. A blackened coffee pot is always present on the edge of the campfire. Ground coffee and water are added as needed. Some of the essence of the first pot full made in each camp remains until the camp itself is removed.

The beat of many hooves accompanied by the throaty bleating of the sheep and the quicker blats of goats announced the arrival of the flock at the salt troughs scattered near the bedding ground. I looked up to see the sheep clustered in shoving, butting groups along the length of the slightly hollowed logs that held the coarse rock salt. This salt had been brought from the natural salt deposits of the Estancia valley, several miles south of the sheep camp.

A ten-pound lard pail huddled in the coals near the coffee pot, its nail-punctured lid emitting jets of vapor, which I hoped might come from beans and fat mutton cooked together. Without saying anything more, my host set an iron spider on a bed of coals and put in two spoonfuls of lard to melt. From the tent he took a sack of flour and rolled down the edges, until a mound was formed of the exposed flour. Into this he poured a cup of water, then added the melted grease. Stirring the mixture in the sack, he soon lifted out a ball of dough, which he placed in a small pan. All the flour that had come in contact with the water and grease had become incorporated in the ball of dough, the rest remaining dry. Evidently, baking powder and salt had been added beforehand, making the mixing of a batch of dough a quick and simple process.

Pinching off small portions of dough, Basílico rolled them quickly into small balls, then flattened them into round flat cakes, a little thicker than tortillas. These were *gordas* (fat ones), the bread commonly made by the New Mexican sheepherder. Soon six browned *gordas* were taken from the skillet and stacked on a cloth spread across a water keg. The pail of beans was dragged out of the fire and its lid pried off. Just as Basílico was about to seat himself on a log close to the bean pail, one of two goats that had approached quite familiarly to the fireside bleated softly. Taking down a small pail that hung from a tree branch overhead, Basílico approached the two goats, seized one of them by a hind leg, and milked her. The other was treated likewise. Tossing the two a piece of old bread, he set a cupful of milk down on the keg holding the *gordas*, first straining it through a piece of thin cloth, part of an old salt sack. The goats' milk was almost as thick as cream.

Basílico needed no spoon. Each mouthful was picked up with a split *gorda*, bent between thumb and forefinger. Meat was enfolded in a piece of the *gorda*, and eaten with it.

A muffled drum of hooves caused me to look away from the fire. The dim forms of burros loomed up, and I realized that it was growing late. Their feet were hobbled, and the two leaders were belled. One of the *almanaques* (almanacs), as Basílico called them, was obviously a pet. He asked for a tidbit in the intimate, demanding tone that pampered animals use. The herder rose and fed them the remnants, and while they ate he removed their hobbles.

"Aren't you afraid they will stray away, if you loose them?" I asked.

"No, not at night, and scarcely ever in the daytime, either. At night they stick very close to where I sleep, as you shall see." I realized that I was going to spend the night at the camp. It was just as well, since I had not yet even mentioned the purchase of the *cabrito* (kid) for which I had come.

I picked up the hobbles that were thrown in a heap close to where I sat. They were homemade, and I was curious about their construction. They were about three feet long and as many inches wide, the inner side lined with cowhide on which the hair had been left to give more protection from chafing. The wide straps fitted closely around a forefoot, just below the fetlock. After several twists, which took up slack and looseness between the two front feet, each end of one fitted into a slot cut into the end of the other. A neat and efficient fastening, which, since the leather was soft, would not be difficult to fasten or unfasten by benumbed fingers on a cold, damp morning. I appreciated this feature, because of my experience with store-bought hobbles of heavy, thick leather straps linked with chains and secured with heavy buckles. There is no agony equal to that of trying to unbuckle one of these manufactured hobbles, wet and stiff from snow. Awkward, unmanageable, and perverse, they inevitably produce torn finger nails and bad tempers. These seemingly crude hobbles of Basílico's were a vast improvement. Later on, I saw Basílico use them as a tie strap to secure a pack and for other purposes by linking five pairs together.

The burros did stay close to the fire, except when Basílico slaughtered a lamb and they moved over to the scene and looked on. The lamb had been seized and carried from the bedding ground to a convenient tree, then suspended by a hind leg from a lower branch that was just high enough to be within easy reach. Basílico's left hand held the lamb's muzzle and bore his head back and down against the bole of the tree, as his right drew a sharp butcher knife across the taut throat. This stroke was followed by a sharp cut down the under side from tail to severed throat. Incisions up the length of each leg connected with the central belly cut. From this point on, Basílico had no more use for the knife. He tossed it aside, and started ripping off the skin with his hands. One held the carcass away and against the pull of the other. In separating the pelt from the sides and back, he used his fist in a knuckling, rolling fashion, neatly separating the pelt from the carcass while rending the paper-thin tissue which held the two together.

The pelt, flesh side up, was stretched out on the ground, and the smaller portions were laid on it, the quarters being hung on limbs to cool. The dogs sat around with lolling tongues and cocked ears deftly catching each offering that Basílico tossed them. They did not fight over each other's share but gulped their own and resumed their eager, expectant attitude.

"Hey, don't throw them all of that," I called out excitedly, as I saw Basílico start to apportion the liver amongst the expectant circle. "I should like some of it for breakfast."

"Here's something else we will have for breakfast," said Basílico, as he held out the lamb's head for my inspection; and from the way he kept his eyes fixed on my face, I knew he was trying to get my reaction to this novel breakfast dish. He had not neglected to save a piece of liver as well.

"*La cabeza es del matador*," I said. My saying that the head belonged to him who killed the animal evoked a pleased smile. I had given him to understand that I knew a delicacy roast head was considered; especially that of a lamb or *cabrito*.

Digging a hole in the spot from which he had cleared the coals of the campfire, Basílico deposited the head therein, after first throwing a little water on it and on the sides and bottom of the hole itself to dampen them. He placed a tin lid directly over the head and covered the whole with hot ashes and glowing coals.

"In the morning it will be done to a hair," he said; "but for now I will make some *burrañiates*. Do you know what they are?" I pretended not to know, in order to allow him the pleasure of introducing a new dish. Taking a chunk of leaf lard from around the kidneys, he gave it the form of a wiener; around this he wrapped a good length of the milk intestines, which had first been stripped of their contents through thumb and forefinger. With greedy eyes I watched to see how many of these delectable bundles he would make.

Six—three apiece—I thought to myself, as he handed them to me saying, "You roast these while I make three or four more *gordas*, and don't forget to salt them when they are just about done."

"Leave them to me," I answered, pleased that he had thought I could be useful. Folding a *gorda* in the center, I placed my *burrañiates* inside, sandwich fashion. The filling had just the desired crispness, having body, yet no greasy taste as might be expected. The forest round about was quiet, its silence unbroken except for the occasional sound of the cowbells as the burros cropped the grass near by.

"And why do you call your burros *almanaques*?" I asked, as Basílico was fixing a pallet for me near the fire. "Oh, they are the almanac of the *pastor*. I can tell of sudden changes in the weather by watching their actions and hearing their braying at unusual hours of the day or night." That was new to me. I had heard them called many things, some of them unprintable, but never almanacs.

My bed consisted of three wooly sheepskins next to the ground, a blanket over these, and another with which to cover myself. Additional warmth, if needed, would have to be supplied by the "poor man's blanket," the fire, wood for which stood neatly stacked close enough so that I could throw an occasional stick on the fire without getting up.

My friend, as I thought of him after those *burrañiates*, lay on a pallet similar to mine on the opposite side of the fire. Both of us had lighted cigarettes, and I talked to him about the stars. He had interesting names for some of the more familiar constellations. The Pleiades, he called *Las Cabrillas* (herd of little goats), the Great Dipper was *La Carreta* (the cart), and he pointed out to me what seemed to be one star, but which were, he said, in reality two, if your eyesight was good enough. He said the Indians used the phenomenon to test the eyes of their young men. I took his word for this; all I could see was one star. *La Estrella del Pastor*, as the morning star was called, received its name, according to him, from the fact that the shepherd is supposed to be up when it appears. He added drily that all the stars might so be called, since a *pastor* sees them all nearly every night, sleeping as he does with one eye open, especially when on the summer range in the high mountains.

The moon appeared over the top of the El Cerro Redondo. He said it promised wet weather because its points were tilted so that it would not hold water. He told me he could figure in advance the different phases of the moon for months ahead. This knowledge he found very useful in caring for his flock. For instance, a full moon was of great advantage at lambing time. He therefore figured out the exact day to turn the rams (*carneros mesos*) in with the ewes so that the lambs would begin to drop while there was a full moon to light the *pastor's* labors. A full moon was also to be desired when the sheep were driven from summer to winter range or back again.

Basílico claimed, too, to have a method of predicting the weather for a year ahead, by means of *las cabañuelas*. "And how do you do that?" "It is very simple," he replied, then launched into a very complex account.

I was lost in a maze of *primeros, segundos* (firsts and seconds), and *cuarto días* (quarter days). Boiled down, the method was based on an average of the weather for the first twenty-four days of January, called *las cabañuelas*. These twenty-four days were paired to make twelve units, using the first and last together, each pair determining the weather for one month. For instance, the second and twenty-third days of January represent February; the third and twenty-second days, March, and so on. Then there are *los pastores*, the succeeding six days of January, which do not enter into the calculation of *las cabañuelas*. These are divided into quarter-day units, twenty-four in all, and, as in *las cabañuelas*, are paired, the second and twenty-third entering into the calculations for February, and so on.

"*Y el ultimo día de enero*" (and the last day of January)—I was very drowsy by this time, and gathered that the last day of January also entered into this complicated system. Vaguely I heard Basílico explaining that the twenty-four hours of the last day were paired in the same manner as had been the two-day units of *las cabañuelas* and the quarter-day units of *los pastores*, and that they entered into and figured in the calculations for the weather for the months of the year in the same sequence. I recall dreaming something about Einstein and pairs of sheep darting off in different directions, and the next I knew Basílico's voice was urging me to breakfast. The coffee pot was hissing and the table was laid, my cup and saucer on one keg, his on another. The baked head of lamb lay on a pie tin, skinned, and broken into convenient pieces. The brain pan has been opened, exposing its steaming contents. Basílico had baked several loaves of *pan de pastor* (shepherd's bread), round loaves made of the same dough as the *gordas*, but baked in a dutch oven. This bread keeps, and sheepherders bake supplies of it when time cannot be spared to prepare *gordas* at every meal. The dutch oven sat close to the fire with hot grease smoking inside. "I left that for you to fix your liver to your own taste; I know nothing about that," said Basílico, as he handed me the chunk of liver and a sharp knife. Like most of the rural people of New Mexico, he would not eat liver, professing not to know even how to prepare it. (Some think this prejudice is based on the fact sheep liver is susceptible to disease). I sliced the liver, which was soon fried, and heaping my saucer, joined Basílico. The meat of the jaw-bones of the sheep's head had a sweet, nutty flavor, and I also sampled the brains.

The sheep were beginning to move slowly out of the *majada*, the vigilant dogs posting themselves on the outskirts of the flock on higher points where they could catch the warmth of the sun. Basílico had already prepared his lunch. It was wrapped in a white flour sack, strapped to his waist with the long straps of the sling he carried, and fitted close to the small of his back.

"I am going to graze the sheep towards El Rito de San Antonio (St. Anthony's Creek), where they will water, and I can get water for the camp also. Do you want to come along?"

Two burros, already saddled and with water kegs hanging on each side, grazed close by. Basílico handed me a flour sack which bulged with a quarter of lamb. "Here is something for you." I could not refuse the gift, nor could I now say that I had originally come for a *cabrito*.

Since the small streams lay for a distance along my own route back to the springs, I followed the slowly moving flock. I noticed that the ewes were heavy, and mentioned the fact to Basílico. "Yes, we'll be lambing about San Domingo Day. Come and visit my camp at that time, if you wish to see us then. We will be on the north slope of El Rito de los Indios (Indians Creek), where there is better shelter."

The dogs kept the sheep moving in the desired direction. I commented on their training.

"Do you remember that *melada* (goat) I milked last night? Well she is the foster-mother of my two youngest dogs. I take young puppies, newly born—before their eyes are opened, and suckle them to a nanny goat. In this way I get dogs that think they are part goat, I guess, because they soon learn to love these animals and take care of them. They take care of the sheep also, but treat them with contempt, just like these *mocasas* (snivelers) deserve, for they are a very foolish animal."

We came to a saddle in the low ridge along which we had been walking. Here Basílico and his flock would cross and go down the left-hand slope, while I continued along its length for some miles more. As the dogs turned the flock, pressing in on its right flank, its leader, a patriarchal billy goat, swung the first of the woolly wave over and down the slope. We stood to the left and a little higher, like commanders of an army watching it pass in review. Basílico scanned the flock closely, seeming to take note of each individual mutton. "'*Sta bien*," he said to himself as the last sheep passed over. "You didn't count them, did you?" I asked. "*Sí y no* (yes and no)," he replied, "I counted my *marcadores* (markers); they were all there, so the rest must be." These *marcadores*, he explained, were the black sheep in the flock—about one of those for every hundred of the others. Any *corta* (stray bunch) would be almost certain to include one of the black sheep. So if all the black sheep were accounted for he assumed the whole flock would be intact.

Many *pastores* cannot count beyond the number of fingers on both hands and must use counters to overcome this handicap. The old Spanish saying, "*Carnero entregado, peso contado* (whether sold and handed over, a dollar counted out), applied to them as well as to others with the same disadvantage. This means that the price is paid for each animal as it is sold because of the seller's inability to reckon the total.

A full tally of the sheep is usually made by the owner or *patrón* on one of his periodical visits to the sheep camp. At that time the *pastor* may hand his *patrón* a tobacco sack full of pebbles. Some of these will be larger than the rest and are usually black in color. In this case the *pastor* has made a count of his *rebano* (flock) some time prior to his *patrón's* visit, and his count is recorded in these pebbles. The black pebbles show how many hundred there were; the white ones, how many tens; the remainder are either committed to memory or shown by notches cut into the shepherd's staff. To account for sheep killed by wild animals or dying from any other cause, the *pastor* skins and saves the pelt, ears and all, against the day when his *patron* comes to count his sheep, because he is responsible for every one.

Why don't you come over to the Springs to visit me?" I asked. "I shall be there for a week or ten days more."

"I will if the *patrón* sends me a *remuda* soon. But, *amiguito*, I have known those springs for many years. In fact, that was where I first started in to herd sheep. My father and I both worked for Don Mariano, who first owned those springs—that is, the grant on which they are located. He was *muy rico*, a man of many sheep and much land. We used to lamb in the grassy valley just above the springs and dip the sheep in troughs built just below the main sulphur spring; and we used nothing else except the very water from the spring to rid the sheep of scab and ticks. It was much better than this stuff we have to use nowadays. He was a great *patrón*, a great fighter and eater, but of good heart. When he came to visit our camp to count the sheep, my father would always kill the fattest lamb, then open it while it was still warm, even before skinning it, and remove the paunch. This he would place to roast on the *rescoldo*, a big bed of coals prepared beforehand. There was nothing Don Mariano liked better than paunch roasted thus; when it had roasted sufficiently, he would cut it open with his *daga*, empty the half-digested contents, and cut up the paunch and eat it. He said that besides liking it very much, it was very good for a stomach trouble from which he suffered. "*Quién sabe?*"

By *remuda*, Basílico meant a herder sent up to relieve him. On holidays, Basílico usually took all of his burros and stopped at his *patron's* house, where he left them. He then went about his own affairs. With many *pastores*, these leaves meant drinking sprees or women, until, funds exhausted, they were rounded up by the *patrón* and set upon the sobering trail which led back to camp. With the married ones, while it might also mean a spree, in most cases there was a re-union with wife and children.

As far as I knew, Basílico had never been married. He was very reticent about what he did on these leaves. His *patrón* confided that Basílico would go to Santa Fe and return on the appointed day, with never a word as to his activities.

I shook hands with Basílico, ensuring him I would return at lambing time if possible. He promised to have ready for me upon my return a pair of *teguas* (moccasins), which he had offered to make for me. I had seen *teguas* worn by other *pastores*, but they were hybrid affairs, with handmade soles but with uppers salvaged from some pair of store shoes or boots. Basílico's were his own handiwork throughout, being made of cowhide, with the neatest of stitching, close fitting, and undoubtedly very comfortable; he wore no other kind. He was a master in working leather. He could braid quirts, belts, hat bands, *reatas* (ropes), and those long braided, tapering whips known as blacksnakes. His neatest job, next to the *teguas*, was the *hondas* (slings) he made, like the one he now carried. They were shorter than those I had when a boy. The egg-shaped piece that carried the stone was larger also, and on the end of each swinging string was a lash, which cracked like a pistol shot after each throw. He was amazingly accurate with it; he never hit a sheep or goat, but would sling a stone to strike in the vicinity of a straggler, and thus startle it back to the flock.

Basílico's every day attire, varied on his rare Sundays in a settlement only by being newer and perhaps a little cleaner, was topped by a brand new black hat, brushed for the occasion. This hat was kept at his *patron's* home in town for just such rare outings, and was the *patron's* annual bonus to his faithful servitor, a gift added to his wages. Each year the holiday hat was taken over for work days, and soon became the battered affair that Basílico doffed as we parted there on the ridge.

I returned to Basílico's camp the day before San Domingo Day. True to his prediction, there was a full moon in the sky that night, and soon after its appearance, the thin blasts of newborn lambs sounded. Basílico, with three extra men who had been in camp since the first of the month, worked from the time I arrived until morning. He and his helpers would appear at the campfire, singly in most cases, to drink a cup of coffee, then return to their labors.

I wandered over to the corral that had been built a few days before for *el ganado preñado* (the pregnant ewes). The bobbing lanterns revealed the whereabouts of the men. Spotting Basílico, I drew close to him, and found him skinning a still-born lamb. Its mother stood close by baaing incessantly in that stupid manner so characteristic of sheep. I said, "Surely you don't have to save the skins of such as those for accounting to the *patrón?*"

"No, no, I am fixing it so this *tonta* (fool) may have a foster son, tomorrow perhaps. There will be some ewes that will die tonight, leaving *pencos* (orphan lambs), and others that will have twins. I will take either a *penco* or a twin lamb away from its mother, tie this skin to his back, and fool this *vieja* (old woman) into adopting him. The ewes recognize their lambs by scent at first, and through this trick we save many lambs that would die otherwise." Several diminutive pelts hung around the corral, separated from each other so the scents would not be mixed.

In the midst of confusion and noise and the constant blatting and bleating, the herder and his helpers moved from one birth to another. I asked one man how he could pair up the right ewe with each lamb pelt; they all looked exactly alike to me. He said there were differences of appearance, and besides, each ewe had a different note to her bleating, by which he could fix her in his mind. Listening to the bleat of one particular ewe, I was able, finally, to distinguish her baaing from the medley which arose from the corral. There were not many of these adoptions to be arranged. Basílico's flock had wintered well, and the ewes had reached the lambing season in very good condition.

It was close to four in the morning when I returned to the campfire. Above the commotion from the corral the shrill yapping of coyotes could be heard. They seemed to know what the sound issuing from the corral meant. I could imagine their slavering jaws and burning eyes as they pointed their slender noses to the sky.

In the morning, I accompanied Basílico in a round of inspections of the corral and the *chiceros* (small brush pens). At the corral, we picked up the carcasses of the lambs that had been skinned the night before, and tossed them over the side of a near-by bluff. At the *chiceros*, in which the lambs born the night before were kept while the flock grazed, Basílico paused to count again the lambs that huddled together for warmth. He chuckled with satisfaction as he commented on their number and general sturdiness. As we stood there, one of the extra men appeared with four more lambs. From time to time throughout the day more lambs were added to the *chiceros*.

One of the men drove a small group of nervously bleating ewes close to the *chicero* where the orphans and twins were segregated. With a lamb clothed in one of the pelts removed the night before, Basílico would head for one of the ewes. Sometimes a good deal of persuasion was necessary to induce the ewes to allow the lambs to suckle. They would be held and forced to smell this odd-looking lamb with the legs of its strange covering dangling from its sides. The lamb on its wobbling legs would be butted and shoved aside, but it persisted in satisfying its hunger, bringing its mouth again and again to the ewe's side, in spite of all rebuffs. When, after many attempts, accompanied by strong language on the part of Basílico and his helper, the lamb was accepted by the ewe; it would kneel to receive the milk, while its tail wriggled ecstatically just below the lifeless one of the lamb whose place he was taking. After the lamb had finished, the ewe would move off to graze, still eyeing dubiously this mysterious creature that had the scent of Esau but the voice of Jacob.

That evening I left the camp after negotiating for a kid, which I held on the saddle before me. Also tied to my saddle were the *teguas* that Basílico had promised me. Somehow during the busy days of preparation for the lambing rush, he had found time to make them. Basílico's helpers would depart in a few days, leaving him to the solitude that he seemed to prefer. I said I would try to get back again in a few days. "Yes, come back after these other ones have gone, then we can talk." As I rode away, my cargo awakened the echoes of hillside and canyon along my back trail.

The next time I saw him was by chance. I was out riding around the hills below the lambing camp and on the slopes of the mountain that led toward the settlement on the Río Grande. Entering an open park, I happened onto a flock of sheep, obviously on the move from one camp to another, for burros loaded with camp equipment grazed at the edge of the flock. I recognized the animals as Basílico's, and rode to the rear of the flock in search of him. I met him carrying a lamb in his arms; it had played out some time back. Its excited mother alternately grazed in erratic pauses close on Basílico's footsteps, then dashed towards him, baaing in a stupidly inquiring manner, evoking plaintive responses from the lamb.

"Where are you going with that *ganado*; is it that your *patrón* has sold it and you are taking it down for delivery?" I asked, for a movement of a flock from the summer range to winter range country at this time of year was unusual.

"No, *nada de eso* (no, nothing like that); the *patrón* has a shearing shed down here a little way, and I am driving the sheep there to be sheared."

As we crossed a small stream, Basílico stooped to pluck a green feathery plant which grew under the overhanging bank, close by some violets. "What is that?" I asked, as he thrust the fern-like wisps into his mouth. "It is *plumajillo*; very good for the stomach. Try some?" It was bitter to the taste, and should have rated very high in the locality, where the efficacy of any medicine is by the strength of its flavor. Basílico asked if I would bring him some *hediondilla* from the vicinity of Socorro the next time I was down there. I confessed that I did not know what that was, but from the name, which means "stinking," it could not be anything pleasant. I learned later that it was the creosote bush, popular remedy for kidney ailments, and that he had need of it.

"You know much about herbs, no?"

"Yes, every *pastor* knows about *yerbas del campo* (wild herbs); it is well that he does, he is so much alone. Knowing them, he can treat any disease that might strike him while out alone with his sheep. Only a broken leg holds any terror for a sheepherder. I can name you a great number of herbs, and the particular benefits of each, but that would take a long time. Some other time I will give you some of each and directions for what ailment to use them."

After the sheep had bedded down, as we sat smoking our after-supper cigarette, Basílico talked about herbs. He recited a list that would put an herbalist's catalogue to shame. The most prominent was *osha*, which is so highly regarded by native New Mexicans that it is considered virtually a cure-all. Others were *altamisa, chimajá, chamiso, orteguilla, poleo, yerba Buena, amole, canaigra*. The only way one could fix this list of names in mind would be, he suggested, to get a sample of each and record its properties in detail. While on the subject, Basílico also mentioned *pinque* (Colorado rubber plant) and loco weed, from which the *pastor* must guard his sheep. *Pinque* is most destructive in the month of October, or after the first frosts. It is more resistant to frost than grass, and stays green and tender after the latter has begun to dry up. For this reason the sheep turn to the *pinque*, and great losses result. The symptoms are salivation, nausea, depression, and weakness. The careful *pastor* will keep his *rebaño* away from a region infested with this weed during that critical period. Loco weed causes losses in the months of February and March. Stock that feed on it go "crazy"; sheep having tasted it once cannot leave it alone; it affects them like a drug. Eating nothing else, they stagger along, their actions extremely erratic, and finally they die from lack of nourishment.

In the morning the shearing crew arrived in a cloud of dust, in a small truck piled high with bedding rolls and other equipment. They were a noisy band of itinerants, shearing sheep on a commission basis all over the State and into Colorado. Basílico would have nothing to do with them, except for handling his sheep so as to keep them constantly supplied. To prepare the sheep properly for shearing, he would drive about a hundred of them at a time into a small adobe room, which had only one opening. Here, closely confined, the warmth of their bodies caused the "sweating" that made shearing easier. To get them into the room, he made use of the oldest and wisest billy goat, the patriarch of the small herd he kept with his sheep. It was amusing to see how well the bearded old rogue knew his business. He no sooner entered the door with the sheep close on his heels, than he stepped aside, close to the exit. He knew that he must get out again and be ready for the next bunch. His whole demeanor showed his supreme contempt for the victims of his guile and his wish to escape close confinement with such idiots.

The sheared sheep, looking more foolish than ever in their nakedness were held by the dogs in a corner of the hills, while Basílico took care of doling out the others to the shed, as required. I watched the shearers deftly turn their victims, the wool clip rolling off in a soft mat. As each was finished, a cry of "*Uno*" (one) brought the boss, who acted as inspector. His "*Bueno!*" (good) permitted the shearer to release the animal as properly sheared. A metal disk was handed the worker, to be used at the end of the day in computing his pay.

The crew of shearers would be in the neighborhood for several days, since other sheep owners had requested the use of the sheds for the shearing of their flocks. I knew Basílico hated to remain in their company any longer than was necessary. His temper was lost under the bantering of the shearers, who treated all *pastores* with contempt. The crowning insult was that they persisted in calling him Basil Loco (Crazy Basil, lit.). I left that evening, atop a load of the huge sacks into which the wool was packed after shearing.

Basílico and his flock were at the shearing sheds again when I next saw them. The flock now seemed much larger. I thought at first more sheep had been bought, but I soon discovered that it was the spring lambs that made the increase. They were large now, weighing seventy to seventy-five pounds, a good average for this type of sheep. I was surprised to see what sturdy, fat fellows they were.

Basílico's *patrón* had ridden in with a helper to aid in castrating and docking the lambs. In the first process the lamb was up-ended and held with his head away from his captor. Sometimes, in the case of a particularly vigorous lamb, the forefeet were tied. Both hind legs were held in encircling arms, with hooves caught in the sheepman's arm-pits. The right hand, holding an opened clasp-knife, severed the tip of the lamb's gag, held in the left hand. The tip of the testicles showing were seized in strong teeth and withdrawn with a jerk of the head, to be deposited in a pan or pail close by. The men worked singly, as a rule, scarcely making a sound—perhaps because of blood-smeared faces. The stain spread down the fronts of their overalls. An element of rivalry entered into this task, each worker trying to outdo the other in the number of lambs altered. At this time, too, the ears of the lambs were marked with the *patron's* distinctive crop or slit, or combination of both, and its tail was docked to within an inch of its base. The poor creatures, after undergoing this three-way treatment, stood dripping blood from many parts of their bodies, bleating disconsolately and shaking their heads vigorously, sending thin sprays of blood through the air.

At supper that evening I received my introduction to the so-called "Rocky Mountain oysters," a big dutch oven full, that had been fried, and a pile on a lard can lid that had been roasted over the coals. Both ways, I found, they deserved their fame as a seasonal delicacy.

"Yes, we had a very good *hijadero* (lambing season); about half and half ewes and males, and about ninety lambs for every hundred ewes, and very little loss. We will sell nearly eight hundred lambs, and the *patrón* has had me cut out very nearly three hundred old and toothless ewes. These he is going to pasture on his home meadows, selling them to Indians of the pueblos and his poorer neighbors. They are good for nothing else but meat now."

"I will stay here until time to turn the rams in with the sheep," Basílico went on. "This we will do the first of the month of the dead (November). I will winter with my sheep on the *chamiso*—covered flats between here and the Río Grande. During the month of December I have for many years taken the part of *El Diablo* in *Los Pastores*, that old play that deals with us shepherds, our life in camp, our language. It is directed by my *compadre*, Higinio Costales. I make a very good *Diablo*, wouldn't you think so?" "Wonderful," I said smiling, taking in his great dark head, wild hair, and angry-looking eyes under heavy brows. "Come down to see me do it in the month of *Noche Buena* (Christmas Eve)."

I resolved to do so. *Noche Buena* was the month of *luminarias*, those small fires still lighted in New Mexico on Christmas Eve in commemoration of the shepherd campfires long ago outside the town of Bethlehem. In *Los Pastores*, the Christmas play, with its scene laid near the town of Bethlehem, I would see this solitary Basílico, who lived all year with sheep, among his brothers.

Source of Information: K. W. Parker, Prevention of death losses in sheep on areas infested with pinque; bulletin 241; Agr. Exp. Station, State College, New Mexico, May, 1936.

Note on the *Partido* System

by Lorin W. Brown

The *partido* system played a part in the development of the sheep industry in New Mexico and was important to the economic welfare of the type of the population which might rightly be termed the subsistence class. It was this class that made possible the *partido* system. Their status prior to the American Occupation, that of legally recognized peonage, gave impetus to the system when their enslavement was terminated. Even though the *partido* system was followed in some instances from the very beginning of the Spanish entry into New Mexico, and was followed to some extent throughout the Spanish and Mexican régimes, its general use began with the American Occupation with the added impetus given the sheep industry by the demand for mutton in the gold fields of California.

The system did not prevail south of Albuquerque with the exception of parts of De Baca and Quay Counties, the San Francisco watershed of Catron County, most of Lincoln County, and down the Rio Grande to Garfield in Dona Ana County.

The hacienda system resulted when the sheep barons or *ricos* of the early American Territorial era saw the writing on the wall. Their former peons were free, and some method was necessary to hold them, to retain their services as sheepherders. Large numbers of sheep were held by a few wealthy families, and herders were essential. The system evolved from necessity was a paternalistic one.

"The patron was admired and respected by the partidario (share-herder). He financed the sheep operation at a reasonable charge, compensated the renter when the lambs averaged more than the specified weight, and paid the highest market price for both lambs and wool. He furnished a capable range man to advise on the operation of the range unit, this contributing to managerial ability essential to the enterprise. He secured supplies and ram replacements at cost and assisted the partidario in getting proper range and in meeting other administrative problems. The patron also looked out for the well-being of the partidario and his family. He encouraged frugality and good management, made advances for subsistence if necessary, attended at weddings and christenings, secured medical attention when needed and always had their interest and comfort at heart. The renter was given an opportunity to become established as a sheep owner, yet if he failed to accumulate sufficient property to live on at retirement, the patron cared for him in his old age." (*Development of the Partido System in the New Mexico Sheep Industry*, thesis of Ralph Charles, State College, New Mexico).

This arrangement between the renter and his erstwhile *patrón*, and in some cases his military chief as well, was one of expediency, seldom bound by any written contract. Ties of long standing between the families of both made for a just recompense for the renter for valuable service rendered his *patrón*. There were some instances, of course, in which an unscrupulous *patrón* took advantage of the renter's ignorance, violating the trust which years of almost entire dependence had fostered and robbing the renter of his just share in the increase of the flocks. These cases were in the minority, however, and on the whole these unrecorded *partidario* agreements operated for the economic benefit of both parties. They enabled many hitherto dependent peons to acquire the status of an independent owner—that is, those who had initiative and thorough knowledge of the business.

The usual arrangement in what might be called the hacienda system, a type of *partidario* contract, was an annual payment to the *patrón* of twenty fleeces and as many wethers for each one hundred ewes in the renter's *partida*, the feminine gender of the word *partido* being the term applied to the band of sheep which a *partidario* took on the share basis. Nearly all natural losses such as blizzards, a hard freeze, lightning, floods, and heavy snows, were termed acts of God; but in losses caused by negligence on the part of the renter he was held to the unwritten terms of the generally accepted practice in such cases, the return to his *patrón* of the same number of sheep, of the same age, the same sex and condition as the original band taken over by him at the outset. Losses incurred through acts of God were accepted philosophically as a mutual loss and a hope that the forthcoming year would be more favorable. Customary length of these arrangements was five years, but they could be continued indefinitely if satisfactory to both parties.

With the recognition of the *partido* system by the Territorial Legislature of 1883 by the passage of a law permitting the filing of contracts with county clerks and even before this, contracts have been as varied as the characters of the sheep owners and their *partidarios*. Those contracts studied show that most contracts gave the owner by far the greater advantage, affording the *partidario* little protection. By signing the contract, he must at the end of a specified period return to the owner a certain number of sheep of such ages and classes as he admitted receiving from him. While they were in his possession he agreed to feed and care for them properly, mating them with rams which met the owner's approval, paying an annual rental at a certain time and place, and agreeing to a certain penalty if the count was short at the end of the period. A very broad provision present in most *partidario* contracts provided for repossession of the sheep by the owner if the *partidario* failed to comply with the terms of the contract, a provision which allowed the former to break agreements almost at will. Furthermore, a mortgagee or co-signer secured the owner against loss of his sheep not caused by so-called acts of God.

As now practiced, many small operators, possessing a small band of sheep but unable to care for them, turn them over to a relative or other individual. The usual arrangement is for rental or the division of the product on the basis of the contribution of each. These agreements are usually on a share basis, but there is a lack of definite information on this phase. Mr. Charles, in his thesis—"Such arrangements commonly have been associated with subsistence populations throughout history. The share renter who must give the patron half of the returns from each application, the returns from which are less than twice enough to reward him. It is advantageous only when holdings are small, the renters poor, and the patron is willing to exercise minute supervision over the details of the operation. As operated among the Spanish-American people in northern New Mexico, the system not only is desirable but is beneficial in that it works for the convenience of both parties."

And summing up: "It is generally believed that the high level of well being of the flocks throughout northern New Mexico is the result of the partido system. The almost universal practice in late years of requiring mating with good quality Rambouillet bucks, of dipping for disease in accordance with sanitary regulations and of proper feeding, grazing and sheltering, has built the herds up to a high standard of quality."

Cattle and Sheep Grazing

Report of the Governor of New Mexico Made to the Secretary of the
Interior for the Year 1879 by Lew Wallace

from New Mexico Writers' Project

Off the Pecos and Rio Grande rivers there are vast tracts of tablelands called "mesas," which are to be distinguished from the mountains and valleys. They are too high for irrigation, yet they yield grasses of the richest kind for subsistence of cattle and sheep—grasses that cure themselves in the standing stalk.

The variety of these mesa tops, permitting, as on the mountain sides, the growth only of grass and cedar and piñon, the latter invaluable for shelter of animals, particularly in winter—will forever limit their use to grazing. The ranges they offer cannot be excelled for that purpose; adding to them the ranges on the mountain sides, and the vastness of accommodations for feeding cattle, sheep and horses can be appreciated. The inexpensiveness of the mode is well understood.

The old dispute as to which is most profitable, cattle-raising or sheep-raising, is yet unsettled, each having very intelligent and practical adherents.

That New Mexico has not her proper place in the meat and wool markets of the United States may be set down to causes now very soon to disappear. They are, first, difficulties with Indians; second, the inferior quality of the stock, no attention whatever at having been given by owners to importation of blooded animals; third, other localities, claiming original shipments, have been largely credited with the products due this territory.

I regret not having statistics to enable me to give the quantity of wool produced or the number of cattle and sheep in ownerships. The results in either case would be astonishing to those who know little or nothing about New Mexico—who are in the habit of regarding it as desirable chiefly on account of its climate. The increase of both sheep and cattle is constant, and the improvement of breeds is becoming more and more noticeable.

Lew Wallace
Governor of New Mexico

Sheep herd of M. Chaves Esq., Coyote Canyon, New Mexico, Cobb, July, 1891, NMHM/DCA #015139

Delivered at Fort Defiance Before August 15, 1869
by Command of Major General Getty

from New Mexico Federal Writers' Project

News Item
June 5, 1869

Mules Stolen—Information has been received in this city of the robbery of more than three hundred mules near Sheridan on the 26 ult., by the Indians. The mules belonged to the trains of Messrs. W. H. Moore & Co. of Fort Union and Mr. Daily of Las Cruces.

The Quakers have not had that portion of the Lo. family in hand yet.

July 31, 1869. The reports are that some Navajos were at the Placers and vicinity last week and stole some horses and a considerable number of sheep from the citizens. We learn that a portion of the (M) belonged to don Leandro Perea of Bernalillo.

News Item
Two men wounded by Indians—July 10, 1869

On the night of the 26th inst. a herd of 3,500 sheep belonging to Jose Pino y Baca of Lemitar was camped near this place the herders were attacked by Indians and two of them wounded, one of them supposed to be mortally. The Indians succeeded in driving off a small portion of the sheep, the greater portion of which was subsequently recaptured, the Indians escaping. From the arrows found where the attack was made they were judged to be Navajos as on the same night they ran off stock from the Alamosa and on Sunday on the road from Socorro to Fort Craig they ran off four mules and a valuable horse belonging to Juan Montoya of Lemitar. They had just stopped to graze when the Indians made their appearance with the above results.

(Letter from James Logan at Socorro)

Editorial, "Parties and Reservation," *Santa Fe Weekly Gazette*—May 20, 1865

from New Mexico Federal Writers' Project

There having been made some attempts to explain away the non-committalism of the so called administrationists in regard to the Indian policy that should be pursued in this Territory, we will ask the indulgence of our readers while we give the matter a brief review.

It is, and for many years has been, an admitted fact, that the manner in which the Indians of New Mexico were managed by the Government was the cause of the decline of the Territory. From being a country wealthy in all the various kinds of livestock, she came to be exceeding poor in that very stock which formerly constituted her wealth. The change of condition is indisputably attributed to the inefficient policy that was observed by the Government toward the Indians. For this there was no remedy. Campaigns against the robbers increased, rather than diminished, their plunderings, forays and murders. This was the condition of affairs in this Territory until about two years ago.

Whole flocks of sheep amounting to from one to ten thousand head were driven off. Herds of cattle and mules went the same way. By this method the property of our citizens was transferred to the Indians.

Governor's Report to the Secretary of the Interior, 1885
by Edmund G. Ross

from New Mexico Federal Writers' Project

A. Serious drawback to immigration is the impression that seems to have found lodgement in the public mind as to the insufficiency of our land titles.

B. Spanish and Mexican Land Grants page 4.

C. Fraudulent Land Entries.

1. If lands had been obtained for actual occupation and cultivation, the results would not have been so disastrous to the territory, but in many cases they have been thus absorbed into great cattle ranches, merely for the purpose of getting control of water courses and springs, and thus keep out settlers and small herds.

2. Connivance of public officials?

3. Recommends abrogation of all laws for disposal of public lands, except for bona fide homestead purposes.

4. Opposed to recommendations for modifications of the laws providing for the disposal of public lands in such a manner as to allow the purchase of large areas for grazing purposes.

5. Questions theory that the aridity of western plains and mountains condemns them to be devoted permanently to grazing purposes.

Cites the sinking of wells in the Jornada del Muerto, on the Llano Estacado, near Deming and elsewhere.

Sums up by saying "The absorption of large areas for stock ranges means the occupation of the country by dumb brutes to the exclusion of people, where there can be no society, no schools, no roads, no improvements, no development. Under such conditions the country would be condemned to perpetual semi-barbarism."

Reports 778,271 head of cattle, 36,153 horses, 1,470,824 sheep and 44,619 other domestic animals.

Governor's Report to the Secretary of the Interior, 1897
by Miguel A. Otero

from New Mexico Federal Writers' Project

Chapter leads: Page 15

"No country in the world is better adapted to sheep raising and wool growing than New Mexico."

"There are within her borders 122,000 sq. mi. of land—78,000,000 acres. Of these not more than 3,000,000 are cultivated leaving the balance for grazing."

"The original stock was of Spanish merino—"

"Sheep can pasture 20 miles from water—"

Page 9

"New Mexico is famed for its livestock industry—More recently a revolution in modes of cattle raising have ensued, due to the encroachment of agriculture—"

Page 10
Railway Facilities
A. Report of cattle shipments.

Santa Fe Weekly Gazette
March 18, 1865

Recapitulation of a Census of the Navaho Indians on the Reservation at Bosque Redondo, New Mexico, on the 31st day of December 1864, their stock etc. Taken by Captain Francis McCabe, 1st Cav., New Mexican Volunteers.

No. of males from 50 to 8 years of age							300
"	"	"	"	18 to 50	"	" "	2129
"	"	"	"	5 to 18	"	" "	1525
"	Infants						134
"	" Females	"	50 to 80	"	" "		373
"	"	"	"	18 to 50	"	" "	2187
"	"	"	"	5 to 18	"	" "	1418
"	Infants						288
Total population							8354
No. of Horses							3,038
"	"	Mules					143
"	"	Sheep					6,962
"	"	Goats					2,757
"	"	Looms					630
"	"	Lodges					2,276
"	"	Families					1,782

Average No. of persons to each family is near 5
" " " Horses " " " " " 2
" " " Sheep " " " " " 4

Santa Fe Weekly Gazette, March 18, 1865 from New Mexico Writers' Project

Santa Fe Weekly Gazette, August 12, 1865, News Notice

from New Mexico Federal Writers' Project

A party of fifty-two citizens started from Abiquiu on a scout to the Navajo country of the 19th of June, and after having passed over a greater part of the country encountered about two hundred Navajo and Apache warriors near the San Francisco Mountains on the 8th of July. Two fights ensued, one of which lasted three hours and the other an hour and a half. Nine Indians were killed by the citizens and one Mexican of some ten years of age was captured; eighty-five Indian horses, and about one thousand sheep were taken from the Indians. In the fight two of the citizens were wounded pretty severely. The third day after the second fight, when the citizens were divided, the Indians surprised the herders (twenty-two in number) and retook all of their stock excepting some fifty or sixty sheep which had been killed for subsistence of the party. The latter, after having lost their captured property, found their provisions growing short, and thinking it useless to campaign without a force sufficiently strong to protect whatever property they might capture, returned home.

These occurrences took place about 250 miles from Fort Wingate and west of the Moqui villages.

The citizens of Cubero and Sebolleta intend to start on a campaign with a force of about one hundred strong.

We gather the above facts from a report made by Colonel J. C. Shaw dated at Fort Wingate July 24, 1865.

It is to be inferred from the great distance which this combination of Apaches and Navajos had removed themselves from the settlements and Fort Wingate that they had no confidence in their ability to defend themselves, and that they intended to seek safety in the seclusion of their retreat. But the perseverance of the citizens of Abiquiu enabled them to find their hiding place and administer to them a sound drubbing, but they were not strong enough to secure the advantages they had obtained and which should have awarded their exertions.

The New Mexican, Santa Fe, New Mexico, November 10, 1865

from New Mexico Federal Writers' Project

New Item

The New Mexico Press says while the District Court was in session at Lemitar, in the county of Socorro, the Indians said to be Navajos, stole two thousand head of sheep from within a mile and a half of the courthouse. They were pursued by the citizens and the sheep were recovered with the exception of about two hundred and fifty. Indians also attacked the wood train of José Jaramillo and Antonio José Chaves, in Valencia county near the Puerco, drove off thirty two head of oxen and killed two men.

The same paper states that four Indians from the pueblo of Isleta were killed by Navajos near the Puerco, on the 30th ult.

Dec. 22. Navajos stole about fifteen thousand head of sheep at Galisteo on Wednesday last week, and killed five herders. These are only a few of the outrages that are constantly being committed by this tribe, falsely represented to the government as subdued. (note) Undoubtedly this is a gross exaggeration. Fifteen thousand sheep would have been divided into six or seven bands and would have been scattered over a large area.

**Flock of Sheep, near Romeroville, New Mexico,
Unattributed, undated, NMHM/DCA #184842**

Cattle and Sheep Industry and Early Day Ranch Life

by Georgia B. Redfield

Life on the first cattle and sheep ranch headquarters, during the early days, was not an idle life or as easy as one would think. However, as judged by colorful stories of ranch life in the west, there were highlights in experiences and phases, even of hard work, enjoyed by old time cattlemen and ranch women, which they remember with great pleasure.

With the discovery of the artesian water basin, in 1890, the days of long cattle and sheep drives to the water holes or river watering places were practically over. Reservoirs for storage of water appeared around the Artesian Belt section of Chaves County soon after the first artesian well was brought in, and dozens of small ranches, supplied with either artesian water or equipped with windmills, pumping water for stock day and night, appeared in every direction from Roswell, during the early nineties.

Numerous cattle and sheep men who live in Roswell or Chaves County at the present time—prosperous bankers, merchants, lawyers, and real estate men—came to Southeast New Mexico as cowboys, driving cattle for large ranching outfits, the first herds coming from Texas, and later ones from Colorado.

These old time "cow-punchers," as they were called, once spent long hours, from daylight until long past night, driving herds sometimes over a hundred miles a day; then they slept in the open, often with only a saddle blanket for a bed, and their saddle for a pillow. Those who later watched herds of sheep were scorned by the cowboy, who believed the job more suited to old men or young boys than to red-blooded cowhands, when in reality the stronger and more hardy ones should have been picked for the sheepherding work. For, while fortunes were made in a very short while, during the early years of sheep raising in Chaves County, the grim side of the sheep industry was the frequent loss of part or entire flocks, during seasons of blizzards or hail or when bobcats or coyotes, not so numerous at the present time, played havoc with the herds or flocks, when they were guarded by feeble or simple-minded herders.

Until the late eighties or early nineties there were no fences in any part of Lincoln County, a part of which became Chaves County in 1889, and herds of cattle and flocks of sheep drifted with the icy winds, and often were never found, or they died from freezing.

The first make-shift enclosures were only drift fences between ranch grazing lands, which helped considerably in holding cattle on ranch lands of each cattle outfit.

Ranch life during the early years was especially hard on the women who had practically no conveniences with which to make work lighter or life more enjoyable.

Before completion of the railroad into Roswell and the Pecos Valley in 1894, outside of one or two trips a year to the nearest post office or railroad town, in many cases by mule or ox-wagon for supplies, and to get mail from homes in the east, there was no break in the everyday routine of ranch life on the plains.

Horseback riding was a pleasure enjoyed by almost all of the ranchmen and their wives and children. Roping and branding contests were put on at frequent intervals by the cowboys and barbecues and chuck-wagon meals at "round-up-time" were occasions for social contact with all the ranch settlers on the different outfits.

Entire families packed in wagons or buckboards, the men usually riding horseback, would travel long distances to attend a barbecue or "baile" at a new ranch building or school house where the young children and babies would be put to bed on "pallets" on the floor, while their parents and older sisters and brothers danced until it would be light enough to see to travel over new rough wagon trails.

The spirit of helpfulness of the pioneer ranch women, and encouragement of their husbands in their new hard life, and particularly contentment (which is very seldom shown at the present time of ease and pleasure) helped to make ranch life the great adventure one often reads about those first dangerous years of outlawry and raiding Indians. All honor is due those women who did their share in the pioneer work, of building the great cattle industry of Southeast New Mexico and the beautiful city of Roswell that was only a cattle trading point on a cow trail, seventy years ago.

Sallie Wildy Lea, wife of Captain Joseph C. Lea, came with her husband and "entourage" of cattle, sheep and cowhands, and lived at first in a small adobe shack on the Hondo and later climbed upon soap boxes to white-wash the rough walls of the first adobe residence built in Roswell by Van C. Smith, which became the home of the Lea family.

Then there were the brave wives of Joseph and John Rhea, who had no electric lighted air conditioned houses on the treeless plains, where they first made their home.

Mrs. Joseph Rhea—who kept house for her husband and his brother John before his marriage, lived in a dug-out home with a dug-out barn for their horses and cow. In this home Billy the Kid was entertained overnight, as hospitality was always extended any cattleman or cowboy that might happen to be passing. Until long afterwards she had believed him to be a cowboy in need of shelter, when what he needed most was—a place of hiding on this last journey to his death which occurred a few days later in old Fort Sumner.

Also this proverbial hospitality of western people, no matter how meager the larder might be, was shown by J. M. Miller, and Martin V. Corn whose first home on his ranch for himself, his wife and seven children was a dugout and one tent. All of these first sheep raisers, the Lea family, the Rheas, the J. M. Millers and Martin V. Corns became the first important sheep raisers, and their families at the present time enjoy all the luxuries of modern homes in Roswell, equipped with every convenience and comfort that the pioneers would never have believed could be developed through their first hard years' work in the cattle and sheep industry of Southeast New Mexico.

Drift Fences: History of Cattle and Sheep Industry in Chaves County, New Mexico

by Georgia B. Redfield

When fencing public lands for private cattle grazing pasturage was prohibited by law, long drift fences appeared on the plains, which were used as a protection of cattle from drifting before blizzards and from herd stampedes. Also they served to separate cattle of the different ranching outfits that settled on the plains east of the Pecos River.

During the year 1890 a train of freighters with six horse wagons were continually busy hauling in ranch supplies, mostly fencing material, for drift fences.

A drift fence was built by the late J. P. White of Roswell, manager of the L F D Cattle Company, that stretched across the entire distance of the Eddy (now Carlsbad) and Chaves County line, which became widely known as the "L F D Drift Fence." Another erected by the L F D outfit swung along the Cap-Rock north, about thirty-five miles, to Mescalero Spring.

Another long drift fence ran between the L F D cattle range and the D Z outfit, maintaining large ranch headquarters, north of the L F D's, which was established by Jim Newman at Salt Lake, or Portales Lake as it is sometimes called.

Still another one known as the "Rat Drift Fence" separated the Rat Range and the San Simon's Ranching outfit, southeast of the old Jingle-Bob Ranch operated until the early eighties by John Simpson Chisum, or some member of the Chisum family.

The moving in of the small cattle outfits during the early nineties, which brought about the cutting up of the large free cattle ranges, was foreseen by John Chisum, who began in 1878 to make arrangements to leave the country which he complained of as having become "a hotbed of cattle rustlers and Indians and other out-law-element which was rapidly coming in, and would soon fence the entire open range," which prophecy came to pass even sooner than Chisum expected.

Several skirmishes between the Chisum cowhands and the outlaw bunch at Seven Rivers resulted in a controversy over cattle stealing during which Jim Highsaw, a Chisum man, killed Dick Smith. Highsaw claimed Smith was a confederate of the Seven River thieves, of whom it was said,

"They did nothing for a livelihood but cattle rustling from the Chisum range."

While there was considerable loss of stock from Indian raids, especially horses of the Chisum outfit, the loss through white cattle thieves was the greater, as they made a business of cattle stealing and paid the Indians for stampeding herds or stealing, especially from John Chisum, whom the rustlers knew the Indians hated for having been the cause of killing many of their raiders.

There were losses of many thousands of head of cattle and sheep during seasons of drouth as well as blizzards and from lack of water or cattle becoming stuck in quicksands or bog holes. Bleached bones, the remains of large herds, strewn over some sections of the plains speak of the slim years when the cattle men could do nothing to bring the rain so needed for famished and starved cattle, and even drift fences could not save the dumb animals who stood in their tracks and slowly froze to death during blizzards.

During the big blizzard of 1933, the most severe ever known to have come to southeast New Mexico, many thousands of both cattle and sheep that did not perish from freezing, were shot when they became helpless from freezing of their legs.

Former Governor of New Mexico, J. F. Hinkle, while driving two thousand head of cattle in 1885, lost over five hundred head that stuck in quicksands of the Pecos River at Hagerman Crossing, which was dreaded and always avoided by the early cattlemen, if possible.

During the last few years, outside of an occasional cow, calf or sheep being stolen for immediate use for eating, there has been practically no cattle thieving in Chaves County. Whether this is true because of a better class of people living on the ranches and plains or because the chance of detection is greater in the thickly populated county, and severe punishment is too certain for one to dare run the risk of wholesale cattle stealing.

In spite of every precaution taken to protect stock in the county, there are still heavy losses of both cattle and sheep. However, cattle and sheep raising has remained, and is likely to always be, the most important and best paying industries of the Pecos Valley.

Sources of Information: J. F. Hinkle, Pioneer Cattleman, and Mrs. B. Mosley on "Drift Fences" Manuscript 1936.

History of Sheep Industry in Chaves County

by Georgia B. Redfield

While the cattlemen driving the first herds of cattle to the Pecos Valley in Chaves County came in the middle seventies, and the covered wagons, with pioneer settlers, came in the eighties, the sheepmen didn't arrive until the early nineties.

It is said by all old cattlemen of Southeast New Mexico, that "the cattlemen stood for the covered wagon fellows pretty well, but it took them a long time to get even on speaking terms with the sheepmen." The reason for this was that the sheepmen at that time "were mostly trespassers, not land owners, who drifted about grazing their sheep over Government land, and watering them on privately owned water rights land."

The legislature finally passed a law that sheep herds traveling must move six miles a day, which helped the situation some, for the range was not completely spoiled by constant or continual grazing of sheep.

As told by J. F. Hinkle in his book, *Early Days of a Cowboy on the Pecos*:

"Sheep men who gave trouble mostly would go in on the Peñasco River, on the CA Bar Ranch grazing land, where they watered large herds, then graze out three miles on one side of the river, then would go back the next day and water and graze out three miles on the opposite side, making the six miles a day."

Another case as related in the same article by Mr. Hinkle was even more brazen than the first.

"A party from Texas drifted in with a large number of sheep, grazing first on one range and then another, until he found a pretty good place on which he decided to stay. He was ordered off by the Cowboys of the ranch. The man explained that he couldn't move because his wagon was 'broke down,' and showed the cowboys the wagon with a wheel gone. As it was fifty miles or more to a place where the wheel could be repaired, the "punchers" were very lenient, but on looking around they found the wheel hidden in some mesquite bush. Of course the party then moved, pretty P. D. Q."

"The first sheepmen, like the cattlemen, had a hard time getting along during the years of low prices and adverse conditions.

"During a political campaign one fall, the cattlemen went after a sheep man, one John Martin, to get out and get active for the Democratic ticket. Martin said, 'No, I am a Democrat, but voted for free wool and came within four cents of getting it.' With four-cent wool and sheep at seventy-five cents to one dollar a head, it was indeed hard times for the sheepmen."

J. M. Miller who came in March, 1878 to make Roswell and Chaves County his home, settled on a ranch eleven miles southeast of Roswell. He talked with Captain Joseph C. Lea who owned a small bunch of sheep, and was advised by Captain Lea that there was a promising future here for sheep raising, if it was handled on a large scale where the sheep could range on hundreds of acres of fine, open pasture land. Mr. Miller then bought his first bunch of sheep in 1880, and, as he had long desired to be, was at last launched in the sheep business for practically the remainder of his life. He knew that the best blooded stock would pay better in the end, so he paid a very large amount for one of the best rams that could be bought, for his own use as well as for the use of smaller sheep owners.

After continuing in the sheep business for about eighteen years, Mr. Miller sold about twenty-one thousand head in 1897, and practically retired from the sheep business retaining only a few head. Two years later, in 1899, he again entered the sheep business, on a still larger scale, in partnership with two sons, Fred and Sherman Miller.

Small sheep owners as well as cattlemen were assisted in getting a start by Mr. Miller, on land already pastured by large cattle owners.

It was in this way that sheep raising—one of the best paying industries of the Pecos Valley in Southeast New Mexico—was started.

Sources of Information: *Early Days of a Cowboy on the Pecos*, J. F. Hinkle, 1937; Jim Miller, pioneer sheepman, now deceased.

Fried Snakes

by N. Howard Thorp

Some forty odd years ago, there were many Scotch, some Irish and a few Englishmen ranching in the Estancia valley of New Mexico. These men were working under ideal conditions. Grass was abundant, labor cheap, and supplies in proportion. Though a few of these ranches had cattle, for the most part they ran sheep.

Albuquerque was their base of supplies, and the market to which their lambs and wool was taken. For the most part these ranchers were young men under thirty years of age, fresh from the old country, from where they brought a generous supply of brogue. They were a thrifty and canny lot, liked their liquor, but with the exception of one—whom I shall call McKinney, though that was not his name—did not let drinking interfere with their business. None of them—at the time I speak of—were married, and when the wool and lambs was taken to market they were all given to holding a day or twos celebration. Those were carefree days, and youth rampant.

After a celebration, on horseback or buck-board, all would return to their ranches, their four-horse wagons loaded with provisions accompanying them. From now on they stuck pretty well to their flocks until spring. Usually McKinney, "or Mac as we called him" on one excuse or another would linger behind, promising to show up in a day or so, which he rarely did. He had a "braw of a thirst." A better companion than Mac didn't exist, but his love of the bottle kept him in constant trouble. This continued, until it was a question of attending to his sheep interest, or his drinking, and as he expressed, why let business interfere with pleasure. On several occasions—while off on a celebration—sheep camps would run out of grub; his herders would turn his flocks loose, and go to town to hunt him up. The flocks without a herder would either get mixed up with other sheep, or scatter far and wide, and many of them be killed by Coyotes and Lobo wolves. When the other ranchmen would hear of the "scatter" they all would try and round the sheep up, but never without a considerable loss.

In the days I speak of, there were but few roads in the Valley, and the greater part of the flats were either great "Mots" of Chamiso brush, or bunches of grass, the wind having blown away the earth between this bunch or salt grass made it very rough going.

The sheep camps would be a mile or so apart, and whenever a buckboard drawn by a small pair of galloping mules were seen, with a man standing up encouraging their speed, with whip and song—he never sang but the one Scotch ditty—one might know it was Mac, on his weekly visits bringing supplies to his herders. This was usually a sign Mac had gotten off the straight, narrow, and unpleasant path.

As time went by settlers began coming into the valley, and in consequence, the range was gradually eaten off. To make things worse there came a two years' drought. In consequence, all the ranchers moved their sheep, most of them going to the mountains, where—even though the grass was short—there was enough forage to tide the flocks over. All moved but Mac, and no amount of persuasion could induce him to leave.

"Ah, byes," he would say, "the more of yees moves out the more grass I'll have, good luck to yees, but I'll stay."

Unfortunately the drought did not break, and conditions got worse; all got discouraged, and Mac drank more and more, and continually complaining about his hay fever, from which for years he had suffered.

Christmas arrived, and all the ranchmen met in Albuquerque to celebrate that day. They found seated in a comfortable chair on the hotel porch—all dressed up and feeling well primed—Mac. "Byes, byes," he said, "I am going back to the old country, yee've seen the last of me."

"What is the matter Mac?" we asked in chorus. "Byes, I've been grievously insulted." "How so?" asked Angus—who usually was spokesman for our little group—"Weel," replied Mac, "you weel know byes, that for years I've suffered much during the summer from hay fever, until it became so bad I decided to go to the Doctor for relief. I climbed the stairs, and opened the door to his office, and I was so blind with the trouble I could scarcely see him. 'Doctor,' says I, 'you've got to do something for this hay fever, it's driving me crazy.' 'Get out! Get out!' says he, 'I've got it Meself.' I'll not stand for such gross insults."

This insult—as Mac considered it—rankled in his mind all during the holidays, but eventually we got him to go back to his ranch, so temporarily, at least, the visit to the old country was postponed.

Most of the sheep-men—especially those who had moved their flocks to the mountains—managed to weather the drought, but Mac, sticking to the flats, and hoping for rain, lost most of his sheep, and his creditors took the rest, leaving him high and dry. He was now left sitting on the veranda of an Albuquerque hotel with his weekly bill coming due. Unfortunately his credit was good, so he could procure all the whiskey he wanted. In the fall when the lambs are sold, the last creditor took over Mac's bucks and ranches, so now he was completely stranded.

That winter he stayed in town, and when lambing started in the spring it commenced to rain. As usually happens in New Mexico after a severe drought, the elements seem to try and make up for their omission, and in consequence, for days it poured. The little flimsy sheep-herders' tents were small protection, so the herders sort out old adobe houses on abandoned ranches, and moved in them, for if the rain does not continue until the thick dirt roofs become soaked through, those old houses are warm and dry. In each room there is a large open fire-place, and although in many instances these were in bad repair they could still be used.

As lambing began, the crews commenced to arrive, and an old neighbor of Mac's, finding him in Albuquerque, brought him out and gave him a job as a cook for his lambing crew.

In the previous six months Mac had done nothing but drink, and when brought to the ranch was in pretty bad shape. He went to work, however, cooking over one of the open fire-places of an old adobe house for a crew of some dozen men.

In the shaky condition Mac was in, he was having a hard time of it, talking to himself, and occasionally "seeing things."

Rain continued to pour down, and outside of the necessary work around the dropping bunch, and in the chiqueros, the men kept as much as possible inside of the old adobe house. As the sheep were still thin, and even the goats too poor to use as meat, the outfit was living on beans, potatoes, chile and coffee; with for breakfast a pan of bacon and corn syrup, or "Lick." Crowded in as they were during the rain, there was lots of idle banter, a good portion of it being directed towards Mac and his cooking. All sorts of suggestions were made, as to the best way to prepare fancy dishes, none of the ingredients of which Mac had. The chaffing continued in a friendly manner, with Mac patiently waiting his turn. Mac had an enormous frying pan—one of those long-handled ones—used on camp fires, which at the time was filled with sliced bacon and frying away in preparation for breakfast. The hot grease from the bacon sent out a pleasant odor, and everyone was anticipating sopping his hot biscuits in the savory bacon grease.

Now there was no doubt that Mac—as a result of his hard drinking—had been seeing things, but when a big house snake fell out of the chimney, and into the frying pan, everybody yelled at the squirming animal. Not Mac! who thought that the boys were guying him, and that in reality there was no snake there. With a very sober face he advised them, one and all, to in the future avoid the use of hard liquor.

Ojo de Nuestra Señora Ranch
Owned by Don Mariano Sabino Otero

by N. Howard Thorp

In order to obtain an insight into the ranches of fifty or more years ago, it is well that one may know something of the class of men who had the ambition, determination and skill to fight the numerous obstacles presented in those times, and overcome them.

Not only roving bands of Indians, but out-laws of many nationalities, desperate discontented men from every walk of life, had taken to banditry, as much to retaliate for some fancied wrong dealt them in the game of life, as for any material gain.

As individual ranchers had to depend upon themselves and their retainers for protection from these bands of thieves, it took a man of courage to remain in the ranching business.

Such a man was Don Mariano Sabino Otero.

Born at Peralta, Valencia County, New Mexico, in 1844, by 1878 he was a delegate to Congress, then a member of the Territorial Legislature, which office he filled with great credit. Married to Filomena, daughter of Don José Leandro Perea, after an eventful life, died in Albuquerque in February, 1904.

At one time owner of the Baca Location Number one, a hundred thousand acres of fine pine timber and grazing lands, and through which runs San Antonio Creek, he also owned Sulphur Springs, and the Cañón Diego grant which included the Jemez Springs.

These lands and properties mentioned all lie practically east of the headquarter Ojo De Nuestra Señora ranch, which was on Government land and was subsequently acquired by Don Otero.

Some sixty years ago, he ran fifty thousand sheep; these were divided up into bands or flocks of twenty five hundred each, making twenty flocks in all.

It was not customary to run these sheep around the ranches but to send the Caporal in charge to graze the flocks on the public domain, and reserve the range adjacent to the ranches for lambing and shearing purposes.

The winter of 1876 found Don Otero's flocks in the mountains near Nacimiento, or as afterwards called by the Americans, Cuba. One of the many canons near this point was afterwards named Cañada de Navajo, on account of Don Otero's herders having been run away from their flocks at this point by the Navajo Indians.

It seems the herders and the Navajos had been gambling, and after the Navies had won the saddle horses, arms, and everything the herders had, threatened to take all the sheep as well. The herders, by this time un-armed, became thoroughly frightened, abandoned their sheep and started afoot down the Puerco River, to Bernalillo and help.

At that time the region along the Puerco River was practically uninhabited. They arrived in Bernalillo, a distance of one hundred and twenty-five miles, in a foot-sore and starved condition. Upon their arrival they reported their loss to their Patrón, who was thoroughly disgusted with their behavior and discharged the lot.

Don Otero immediately assembled a strong posse of fifty well mounted and armed men, and with new herders, plenty of provisions and ammunition, started back to try and find the abandoned flocks of sheep, and if necessary punish the band of Navies.

Arriving at the point—where from their description—the herders had lost the sheep, the posse began to find a few strays. Continuing down the canon and sending men out to comb the mountain sides, they soon began to throw different bunches together, who appreciating their freedom were contentedly grazing.

A week of this work. With the exception of a few the Navajos had eaten, and those the coyotes had killed, Don Otero had practically the whole fifty thousand together in one mixed herd.

Now the hard work of separating the sheep and forming flocks of the same class of sheep began, as there were bucks, ewes, yearlings and big muttons all mixed together.

Brush corrals had to be built, and each head of sheep had to be individually—by its hind leg—pulled out of the main bunch and placed in a separate corral, to form a new herd. This was trying work, and continued for over a week.

After forming twenty flocks, with two men to a flock, Otero—after sending most of the armed posse back to Bernalillo—moved his flock out for fresh range. In some twenty miles he came to a fine spring, where he found a man running a large flock of goats.

Making arrangements with the goat men, so his flocks could water for the next thirty days, Don Otero left his flocks in charge of his Caporal and returned to his home in Bernalillo where he was then living.

A busy month now ensued, arranging for families of workers, material for the new ranch house, wagon and harnesses, saddles and horses, and in fact getting together all paraphernalia needed on the ranch.

A few wagon tracks constituted in those days the only roads, but Don Otero within the prescribed thirty days returned to his flocks.

Arranging with the goat man for his relinquishment of the Springs, Don Otero commenced at once the erection of his ranch house which to this day still stands. The workers who with their families were to take up their permanent abodes there, also built their little houses, making in all quite a colony.

'Tis a beautiful country, looking towards the mountains covered with pine and pinon, many of the later having to be hauled for roof logs or "vigas," corral posts and other uses, large pines also cut for watering troughs, and smaller ones for salt.

The building of a ranch in those days, except for the windows, which were purchased, was all from material found upon the ground. It was an undertaking: fence walls and house walls being made of adobe or rock; then the ceiling logs all of a size, and peeled from bark; window frames and doors hued out of logs, as were the benches and tables used in the house. That they were made is proven by the fact that some of the furniture is still in use on isolated ranches, such as the Ojo De Nuestra Señora, where the present owner, Mariano Otero, son of the founder, runs his cattle.

CATTLE TRAILS

"Travel-worn, hungry and thirsty the caravan arrived at Hope, about sixty miles southwest of Roswell, on December the twenty-third, and camped at Y. O. Crossing. On awakening the morning of the twenty-fourth (Christmas Eve) a four-foot snow covered the camping ground. The caravan members, suffering intensely from the blizzard, were disbanded. All of the cattle that had not drifted away in the wind and snow lay dead on the camping grounds. Only four head of drifters were found."

—From "Some First Herds of Cattle Brought to the Pecos Valley in Chaves County, New Mexico" by Georgia B. Redfield

Memoirs of Early Days in New Mexico: On the Trail to New Mexico in 1869 (Excerpt)

by Manville Chapman

Although the Santa Fe Trail has long been celebrated and written of, little is said of another trail which also brought many settlers and much wealth in cattle to New Mexico in the early days. After the Civil War there were great herds of cattle in Texas for which there was no market. These herds could often be brought to New Mexico and Colorado and sold at a profit. The cattle were as a rule rounded up at Ft. Worth and started West up the Brazos River, out across the Staked Plains to the Pecos River at about the present site of the city of Roswell. They were then taken up the Pecos and Canadian river and into Colorado, if necessary, before being sold. Cattle were not as plentiful here as in Texas and there was a demand for beef to supply the army camps as well as for breeding stock.

In the particular drive which we shall follow there were about two thousand head of cattle with ten or fifteen cow-punchers. Besides the chuck wagon following the herd there were four other wagons belonging to people going to New Mexico to settle. The company contained some forty people in all with at least twenty able-bodied men. It would not have been safe to start with less, since there was constant danger of Indian attack through the entire journey. Some of the wagons were pulled by horses and others by oxen. Most of the men as well as many of the women and girls rode on horseback all the way, this being much easier than riding in the rough and tiresome wagons.

Settlements were passes on the Brazos River where food could be bought, but after leaving these, a few staple groceries had to be relied upon, chief among these being pork, beans, flour, coffee, and of course beef. The beans and bread were cooked in the evening for supper and were made to serve for the next day at dinner as well. Dutch ovens were used for baking bread.

At night the wagons would be drawn up in a circle, where the horses could be kept, in case of Indian danger. Each family had a tent as well as the wagons to sleep in. The cattle had to be herded throughout the night, the men dividing into shifts to do this. These herders would ride round and round the bunch of cattle singing as they went. The singing of the watch seems to have a great soothing effect on wild cattle. Small stampedes, that took all the men to check and quiet the cattle, were common although few cattle were lost from this cause. Thunderstorms and heavy rains were often witnessed at night and it was not uncommon for the occupants of the tents to be forced to pile their beds on chairs and stand ankle-deep in water striving to hold their tent from being blown over by the strong winds. At times tents were entirely blown down and the occupants had to seize what valuables they could and hurry to the wagons.

Another peril of the Western plains, which was experienced on this trip, was a buffalo stampede. The roaring of many hoofs was the first warning of the coming buffalo and it was great difficulty, for those riding at a distance, to reach the wagons before being overtaken by the rolling herd.

Fortunately the main herd split on reaching the wagons, one part going on each side, thereby saving the destruction and often loss of life which came to many wagon trains that were run down by stampeding buffalo. The prime concern of the men present was then to prevent the buffalo from stampeding the cattle. They managed to keep the cattle at a distance, however, so that they did not mingle with the buffalo. Several, who were skilled in the dangerous art of buffalo hunting, then followed the herd and brought back several days supply of fresh meat.

The Indians menaced the party through the entire trip but they did not attack since there were sufficient men to ward off any but a very large band. From Fort Concho at the eastern side of the Staked Plains almost to the Pecos River the Government supplied soldiers for protection. This was a very dangerous section, many cattlemen having lost their entire herds of cattle, and horses as well, to the Indians here in prior years.

There is one stretch of these plains where there isn't any water for several days drive. There it was necessary to travel day and night in order to reach the other side before people and stock should suffer. On reaching the Pecos after a drive of this kind it was with utmost effort that the cattle were kept from stampeding ahead and trampling one another to death when they scented the water. They would rush into the river so fast that only a skilled cattlemen could keep them from crawling into the quicksands.

This herd reached the Horse-head Crossing, on the Pecos, in the fall of '69 over two months after leaving Ft. Worth. From here they were driven North up the Pecos and sold to Lucien B. Maxwell, one time owner of the Maxwell Land Grant, who was then engaged in moving from Cimarron to Fort Sumner. Besides his family, livestock, and baggage he had several hundred Spanish and Indian followers, a nuisance common to all wealthy New Mexican families.

From Fort Summer the party traveled less encumbered on up the Pecos and Canadian rivers and arrived at Clifton and Trinidad in the winter of '70 after being on the road about 100 days. To the young folks on this trip the journey seemed no more perilous and tiresome than a young person's first long trip would seem today. They enjoyed themselves most of the time, not understanding the anxiety which their elders must have held for the success of the enterprise, although even the older members did not see the danger and adventure which we now see in such an undertaking.

**Unidentified Group in Front of Wagon Mound, New Mexico,
F. E. Evans, undated, NMHM/DCA #122156**

History of Cattle in the Southwest

by Kenneth Fordyce

The cattle business in New Mexico is as old as its first settlers, the Spaniards. Previous to the Spanish occupation, New Mexico had no cattle or horses. These animals were foreign to North America.

In the year of 1521, the Spaniards landed the first cattle at Vera Cruz. In the year of 1598, Juan de Oñate trailed 7,000 head of cattle to New Mexico. Just what disposition was made of these is not known. No doubt a great many of the cattle brought in by the Spaniards went wild, as by 1718 great numbers of Spanish stock roamed over Texas and were undoubtedly the foundation stock of the Texas Longhorns.

There must have been a distinction in type of the Spanish cattle in Texas and the type that prevailed in New Mexico. Jack M. Potter, president of the Trail Drivers Association of the Southwest says, that he believes that the first Spanish cattle imported into New Mexico by Juan de Oñate were of a milk breed and altogether a different breed from the Texas Longhorn that originated in Spain and Spanish Islands. He also says that the native New Mexico cattle, before any new bulls were shipped in, showed milk breed colors and were small boned. When Mr. Potter first saw those cattle around such plazas as Anton Chico, and others, he thought that they were starved into being small. But when he visited such large ranches as the Roberos and the Lopez on the Los Conchas, he still found those open range cattle that had an abundance of grass still much undersized. The fine maturing country along the foothills of the Rockies should have raised a bigger animal than the Longhorn that was raised in the Texas coast region. However, the Longhorn Texas breed was far superior to the New Mexico breed; they were a big boned type and after spending two winters in the north developed into a heavy beef steer often weighing 1,400 pounds.

Undoubtedly the Spanish types were the first cattle in America and prevailed throughout the Southwest until well after the Civil War.

Fremont found cattle at Fort Lupton, Colorado as early as 1843. Then during the summer of 1848, 50,000 head of cattle crossed the Arkansas River on the Santa Fe Trail. In 1853, Gunnison found cattle near Raton

Pass, and in 1859, John Dawson and Oliver Loving trailed cattle to Cherry Creek in Colorado.

By the year 1860, New Mexico had 89,000 cattle—mostly Spanish types, probably a sprinkling of Shorthorns. The cattle business really began after the Civil War. By that time, Texas was flooded with Longhorn cattle. Because of the Union blockade on the Mississippi River they had no market and cattle were practically worthless. With the closing of the war, and the western trend of home seekers, the northern plains country needed cattle badly.

The buffalo was being rapidly exterminated and the railroads were pushing west of the Missouri River. With the utilization of the open range and the opening of the famous trails northward, cattle soon became king.

During the period after the Civil War and until well through the '80s the trail-drivers from Texas commercialized the cattle business on a large scale.

Because of the Indian problem in north and west Texas most cattle were trailed north on the Chisum Trail in east Texas and on the Goodnight-Loving Trail, which entered New Mexico in the Pecos Valley, came north to Fort Sumner, New Mexico, then branched three ways: the first trail led by Fort Union, Springer, and over Raton Pass; the second, by Mosquero, Gladstone, Capulin, and Trinchera Pass; and a third trail, probably the least used, was by Tucumcari, Clayton, and it crossed the Dry Cimarron near Kenton, Oklahoma. The terminus of the two western branches was usually Pueblo, Colorado; while the trail farther east extended on into Wyoming.

Another major reason for the cattle trails coming through New Mexico was an attractive market in the fancy beef prices which were being paid at the Army Posts, especially at Fort Sumner, with its 11,000 Indians to ration at Bosque Redondo and at Cimarron.

The first cattle to come into New Mexico from the north came in on the Santa Fe Trail. Mr. M. M. Chase and a man by the name of Si Huff trailed cattle from northwest Texas in 1876. Loving delivered cattle to Cimarron, New Mexico in 1860 and Lucien Maxwell at Cimarron had his range well stocked at that early time.

Colonel Charles Goodnight was the trail-maker to the Pecos Valley in 1866. He associated first with Oliver Loving and later with John Chisum.

Chisum trailed out of Texas to Fort Sumner, New Mexico and Goodnight from Fort Sumner on northward.

Here is how the two men are characterized. Chisum always genial and hospitable to a fault, but shrewd and at times unscrupulous in his dealings, won recognition as the cattle king of the Pecos country, but as an example of a square-dealing, straight-shooting cattleman of territorial days it would be hard to find the equal of Charles Goodnight.

The year after the establishing of the Goodnight Trail saw 37,400 head of cattle—Texas Longhorns—driven north and shipped over the Kansas and Pacific Railroad to eastern markets. This same year—1867— Goodnight and Loving trailed cattle through Raton Pass. These cattle were sold to John W. Iliff, who became the cattle king of Colorado on the Platte river, and who furnished beef to the mining trade in the Rockies.

The same year saw great activity in gold mining at Elizabethtown, New Mexico and Goodnight furnished beef indirectly to this trade.

In trailing over Raton Pass, Uncle Dick Wooton, builder of the famous toll road over the mountain charged Goodnight a toll of 10¢ per head. This Goodnight paid under protest and promised Wooton he would suffer for such a hold-up. From then on Goodnight drove his cattle through Trinchera Pass some fifty miles to the east. This trail passed just west of Capulin (then Deadman), dropped down to the Cimarron Seco, and turned up the south Trinchera to cross Raton Range full two-days drive east of Wooton's. Goodnight discovered, in passing through, the Welcome Spring that broke from the very crest of Trinchera Pass.

By the year of 1870, the west was fairly well settled by cattlemen from Texas and from Missouri River states. No doubt bulls from the east were being crossed with the longhorn cattle from Texas then.

The desire for better cattle was not noticeable in the crossing of the Texas cattle with the Shorthorns. However, the shorthorns were poor rustlers and were outstanding only where feed was abundant. Consequently they were not suitable for the short-grass country west of the Arkansas. However, the shorthorns predominated throughout the west well through the '90s.

A great many outstanding herds were established in New Mexico and some still exist today. One very good example of this shorthorn breed can be found on the ranch of Henry Brown on the Dry Cimarron. This herd was established by the late Mike Devoy and by Henry Brown, and won honors at the American Royal in Kansas City.

Since the shorthorn was a hard keeper and late in maturing, most stockmen, after the advent of barbed wire in 1880, began to look for a type earlier in maturity and a type that would rustle for feed. This they found in the Herefords, and with the cattle industry on a more scientific basis, pure bred sires were bought to head the range herds.

Goodnight, who had gone broke in Colorado in the panic of 1873, had reestablished himself in the Palo Duro Canyon Country of the Texas panhandle, and introduced Hereford bulls in the year of 1871, which he crossed on Texas longhorn cows, thereby gaining 300 pounds in mature weight.

Some seem to think that since Goodnight did not leave the Picketwire east of Trinidad, Colorado until 1873, that his crossing of the longhorns with the Herefords took place in Colorado.

The importation of shorthorns into America preceded that of the Hereford, likewise the shorthorns were first to come into the west. However, the Herefords gained in favor rapidly and since 1900 have virtually replaced the shorthorn on the range.

Dr. Owen trailed cattle from Texas to the Dry Cimarron in 1869 and there established a ranch the same year. In 1878, he established a ranch above Folsom, New Mexico along the route of the Goodnight Trail. In 1881, Dr. Owen purchased from Gudgel & Simpson, of Missouri, five cows and one bull—all Herefords—which are believed to be the first Herefords brought into New Mexico. Incidentally, his ranch has been known as the Hereford Park Ranch ever since. Tom and Ben Owen, sons of the late Dr. Owen, are still outstanding breeders of Herefords on their Hereford Park Ranch.

Jack M. Potter, old-time trail-driver and previously quoted, says that he believes that the first Herefords were shipped into New Mexico in 1880, the year after the Santa Fe laid first tracks into the territory over the Raton mountains, and that Colfax county received the first Herefords. Claims were also made that H. M. Porter shipped in the first imported registered bulls and also Dr. Owen was the first according to other claims. However, Francis Clutton was the first man to start a registered herd. Jack Potter actually saw the first Herefords in 1882 at the

Goodnight and Adair ranch on the staked plains, and saw Herefords and calves on the LX Ranch.

Judge O. H. Nelson later shipped some Hereford bulls into northeastern New Mexico. Lee and Reynolds had brought in a herd of Herefords from Fort Camp Supply and ranched at Endee, New Mexico for a time before moving back to Rito Blanco, Texas. Other Herefords were to be found by that time in the Dorsey Triangle Dot herd and in the Fork Owen herd. After a very few years of experimentation it was found that Herefords were next to Longhorns when it came to successful breeding and general endurance. After 1885, the Herefords were very popular.

The first Hereford bulls to reach the Pecos river were shipped to Las Vegas in 1884. These 200 head were owned by D. L. Taylor and Sam Doss of Trinidad, Colorado, who together started a new ranch at old Fort Sumner. Lucien Maxwell had a fine herd of shorthorns at Cimarron which he later moved to Fort Sumner—1871. Chisum bought bulls from Maxwell. The Big Bell Company on the Canadian River stayed with the raising of shorthorns throughout the 1880s. The Herefords, however, gradually began to predominate.

The cattle business boomed during the early '80s and large amounts of English capital were attracted to this country forming large cattle syndicates. Their practice was to gain control of land adjacent to streams and water holes and thereby control the use of government lands for grazing purposes.

The Prairie Cattle Company was perhaps the largest of these syndicates in northeastern New Mexico. It extended from the Arkansas River on the north to the Dry Cimarron and to the Canadian. The Arkansas division comprised 3,500 square miles; the Cimarron division 4,000 square miles; and the Canadian division 400 square miles. They branded JJ on the Arkansas, Cross L on the Cimarron, and LIT on the Canadian. Their herds combined, totaled 140,000 cattle.

The Prairie Company first headquartered at Kansas City but in 1885, they moved their headquarters to Trinidad and placed in charge Murdo McKenzie, who had been bookkeeper up to that time. McKenzie was a manager and a good one. He was never a cowhand and knew it and always stayed within his limitations. McKenzie is still active and connected with the Matador Land and Cattle Company. He has been with this firm since the forced liquidation of the Prairie Company was made necessary because of the settling up of the government land by homesteaders.

Cowboys in camp, New Mexico, Dana B. Chase, ca. 1885, NMHM/DCA #056993

Pioneer: A Hard Trail into New Mexico

by Kenneth Fordyce

Many settlers came to New Mexico and great wealth in cattle was brought into the territory from Texas immediately after the Civil War of the United States. After the war there were great herds of cattle in Texas and practically no market for them. In New Mexico, cattle were scarce; and in the territory were stationed large numbers of soldiers. It took beef for these soldiers. At one time about two thirds of the Union Army was stationed at Ft. Union in New Mexico. Then there were the cattlemen who had unlimited prairie-land with plenty of grass and they were willing to buy cattle to stock their large ranches.

These settlers and their stock came into the territory over a trail which was hazardous and replete with hardships. Many of the old cattle-trails were used extensively but of course none of them can compare, as a trail, with the Old Santa Fe Trail for color and background.

These people usually brought their cattle over a trail which started in the neighborhood of Ft. Worth, Texas and started west up the Brazos River. They crossed the Staked Plains making for the Pecos River. They usually entered the territory at the southeastern boundary and found the Pecos or Canadian Rivers, up which they would proceed to the central and northern parts of New Mexico. They usually found buyers in New Mexico but if they failed they could always continue into Colorado which was a good market place too.

These drives were made by groups, usually forty or more people in a wagon-train. This afforded better protection from the hostile Indians which they were in danger of encountering. There were the cowpunchers to 'tend the cattle, the women and children who were brought along for it was generally the intention to remain and make their homes in New Mexico and the other men to drive the wagons which were pulled by horses or mules.

As many as could, including the women and girls, rode horseback to avoid the discomfort of the rough-riding wagons. At night the wagons were drawn up in a circle to shelter the horses and furnish protection from Indian raids. Then there was the danger of stampeding buffalo. However, the buffalo usually divided on reaching a wagon-train and ran on either side of the group. The cattle had to be tended during the nights to keep them from stampeding. The cowboys, in shifts, literally lulled them to calmness many times by singing to them. Music, even poor singing, seemed to make them content to mill around and stay together until the morning when the drive started again.

The first part of the drive, just out of Ft. Worth and along the Brazos River, was in a section of Texas where the group could buy food at the different settlements. But soon they found themselves depending on their stock of pork, beans, flour, coffee, beef, and whatever else they stocked their wagons with. Occasionally they would have fresh buffalo meat when a herd was encountered.

From Fort Concho, at the eastern side of the Staked Plains, almost to the Pecos River, the Government would supply soldiers for protection along this route. The Indians would not attack if a group was sufficiently large to offer any sort of resistance. In the early days, however, many a group lost their cattle and all of their worldly possessions to the roving Indian bands.

In crossing one section of the route there was a stretch where there was no water for several days march. In crossing this, it was necessary to continue on day and night so that water could be reached before the members of the party and the cattle suffered. Clever work on the part of the cowboys was necessary upon reaching the water, for when the cattle would scent the water they would stampede ahead and trample each other to death.

It took over three months to cover the distance from Ft. Worth to Northern New Mexico. True, it was a hazardous trip which these people took to reach their new homes in New Mexico, but the daily anxiety and dread of danger was much greater than the actual danger which they encountered.

Many of the first homes of New Mexico were built by folk who came into the territory just like this. Many of them stayed and their children and children's children are living in the Sunshine State today.

Source of Information: Alvin Stockton, Stockton Ranch, Raton, New Mexico, January 1937. (Mr. Stockton's grandmother aided him in preserving this and other information before her death in 1933.)

Early Character Isom Like, Pioneer by Colonel Jack Potter

by Carrie L. Hodges

In the very late sixties, likely '69, a caravan of immigrants were camped on the banks of the Middle Concho, just out of Fort Concho, Texas.

It was customary in those days to hold up at this certain watering place, until there was congregated enough fighting men to combat the Apache Indians, whom you were sure to meet at the Horse Head Crossing of the Pecos, ninety miles away.

In this colony heading north to Pueblo were twenty families and their livestock consisting of cattle and range horses all in one herd, driven by men and children, both boys and girls on the immigrant colony.

Leaving the Conchos they started southwest to Horse Head Crossing, thence would go north up the Pecos River 400 miles, their object being to find a watered route.

Our character, Isom Like, who had a family of several children and a nice bunch of range horses and cattle, was appointed captain of the caravan and livestock.

On this ninety mile drive without water, Captain Like saw that every barrel was filled and good wooden plugs put in, and asked every person to abide by several rules regarding the using of water.

It pleased the kids to know they were forbidden to wash their faces until they reached the Pecos—whoever heard of a kid who enjoyed washing his face anyhow?

After every animal in the outfit had been watered at noon, the colony started out on the long stretch, many of them feeling blue. All the news that came in the west was adverse to their expectations.

Just the year before, Oliver Loving's corpse had been brought back over the Loving Goodnight Trail to Texas. He had died from wounds inflicted by the Apaches.

And now, the latest messenger coming in from the west stated that there were three more fresh graves at Horse Head.

What would you expect to find at Horse Head? A city with bubbling fresh water and shady lanes and all kinds of refreshments? No, this was what they found: not merely one horse head but a dozen more, where the Apaches met the Butterfield and killed the driver and horses and set fire to the stage.

What would you expect to find in the way of water? A swollen stream with four varieties of mineral contents and always rowelled up; the banks straight up and down, with an occasional trail beaten out that led down to the water.

When other cattle pushed their way down, the first ones would swim to the opposite bank, and not finding a going out place would swim back to where they had started, only to find the trail blocked with thirsty cattle and then the only chance for the cattle would be to mill around until they were trampled under to drown.

Well, after cutting the banks down and getting the caravan across, maybe after a week or so of waiting for the stream to run down, the wagons would be forded across. What then did they find?

The Apache behind every sand dune, looking for his chance to cut off someone from the caravan, determined to kill, steal, and protest every step of the way traversed by their hated enemy the Tejano (Texans).

The Apache way of fighting an enemy was not to take much risk in massacring, but to steal livestock, which would be beneficial to the Apache in a financial way and at the same time leave his enemy afoot.

However, everything went well until the caravan reached the Guadalupe Mountains, near the present site of Carlsbad. Then one night, when most of the colony was asleep, the Apache warriors slipped down out of their rendezvous in the mountains, overpowering the men on night herd, and drove off more than half of the livestock.

It was now getting late in the summer, and the immigrants knew that winter would overtake them before they could get to their journey's end at Pueblo, Colorado.

After much counsel they decided to winter at the Hondo. They prepared a barricade and corrals for the livestock, loose-herding them by day and corralling them by night. Finally it was decided someone should go in to Fort Sumner and try and get enough flour, tobacco, and coffee to last through the winter, and in the meantime to make a complaint to the military officer in charge of that territory for the purpose of getting their stock back or the equivalent.

These plans were carried out under the courageous leadership of Captain Like, who led a party of five men to Fort Sumner. They rode horses and took along the running gear or front wheels of an ox-wagon, and brought back provisions.

Later, a delegation went to Fort Stanton, about an equal distance to the west, to put in a complaint for lost stock. A quarter of a century or so afterwards, the claim was paid.

It was in the beautiful spring month of April when the work oxen were again yoked up and a general loading up took place, and the little colony moved on northward towards its destination. Pueblo, via Fort Sumner, thence north over the Goodnight trail via La Cinta Cañón, Don Carlos Mesa, and thence to Capulin Mountain, Trinchera Pass, then to the crossing of the Picketwire below Trinidad, and on to the Rattlesnake Butte and to Pueblo.

The colony scattered out, and Captain Like settled near Rocky Ford. His horse herd increased rapidly and in about ten years he moved to the south end of Las Animas County, Colorado, and established what is known as the IL Rancho on the Carriza.

This noted rancho is only about sixty-five miles north of Clayton, New Mexico, in an isolated place in the Mesa de Mayo country.

Mr. Potter adds a note on the margin:

This old pioneer died at La Junta, at the age of 102. He married the second time when 98.

Tales of Old Timers: The Staked Plains
by Colonel Jack Potter

by Carrie L. Hodges

I have been asked many time for a description of the staked plains and how much country they covered.

They are an elevated plateau country with the Pecos river paralleling them on the west side for 350 miles, commencing 40 miles north of Fort Sumner at the Mingus Rincon Mesa and the Cu-ne-va, (pronounced Coo-na-vah), a noted spring, which is called the head of the plains.

The plains are elevated about 700 feet above the prairie below.

The south end of the plains ends east of Pecos, Texas.

It is a peculiar thing on the east side of the Pecos, for the full length of the plains there is not a creek or river that affords running water at its mouth. On the west side many live streams empty into the Pecos.

Goodnight and Loving, in making their first drive to Fort Sumner with beef cattle to feed the starving Indians, and blazing the trail that bears their name, tried to come up on the east side of the Pecos but had to cross over to the west side because the Pecos river banks were so steep and they could not water their cattle even if there was an abundant supply of water.

The Pecos in the early days was just like a canal running down through that prairie country with perpendicular banks on each side. Sometimes you could find narrow trails where buffalo or mustang horses went down to water one at a time.

The Goodnight and Loving trail was later changed and the cattle routed from Horsehead Crossing, in Texas, all the way up the west side to Fort Sumner.

Every trail driver tried to avoid letting his cattle into the Pecos. Besides the bad banks and four kinds of poisonous ingredients in the water, the Pecos was noted for the worst quicksand in the world.

There is a chain of shallow lakes on the plains which extend clear down to Monnihan's wells, which are more than 300 miles distant. The great irrigation district at Los Portales, where hundreds of centrifugal pumps are used, is included in this stretch of country.

The Indians crossed these plains from east to west and then back for years before the Americans knew there was water there. These and many other fine watering places were not found until the buffalo hunter discovered them by hunting for buffalo. Wherever you found large drives of buffalo you might guess they would have to drink somewhere and the buffalo hunters soon had such noted watering places on the plains as Spring Lakes, Agua Negro, Casa Amarillo, Tierra Blanco, Tules on the New Mexico side and Los Portales Spring, which had enough run-off water to form a lake which would water 10,000 head of stock.

Fifty years ago old Vicente Otera, an old buffalo hunter who died last spring at the age of 105 years, told me that when he was a boy he went from the mountain country to Los Portales with other people to kill buffalo and antelope for their meats. It seems as if both the buffalo and the antelope ranged mostly on the staked plains in that part of the country.

On the east side the plains seem to be cut in two by the Palo Duro canyon. Yet on the east side, in climbing the plains near the old J. A. headquarters, it is several hundred feet to caprock, which caprock extends to close to Clarendon.

One night when I was with a floating outfit (an outfit with a cook and several cowhands that traveled around over the open range country in the winter time looking after the range cattle in a general way and branding what calves had been missed in the fall roundup) we were all sitting around the campfire, each man telling the story of some tragedy that had happened in the staked plains country.

The first one to lead out was old Jack Lewis, who told us about a negro who froze to death down south of Los Portales when the weather was not freezing. I happened to know this was a fact. The negro came to the Pecos river in the early 80s with Dr. Wimfrey and his family and was called the Wimfrey negro.

After the doctor had ranged cattle on the Pecos for awhile he changed locations to a shallow water district out between the Portales and Tierra Blanco and rode herd on his herd of cattle. One cold winter his cattle drifted south in a snowstorm. After the storm had let up several cowboys and the negro went south to round up and drift their cattle back. Late in the afternoon when they were riding along the negro complained of being cold. They tried to laugh him out of it, but failed. Finally he got off his horse. They put him back on and a cowboy rode on each side of him, holding him on. In a short while he died and was taken to the Wimfrey ranch on a pack horse and turned over to Dr. Wimfrey and buried at that ranch. Wimfrey made a thorough investigation of the matter and was convinced that the cowboys did not murder him because he was a negro. Every once-in-a-while in reading of some old landmark or an old story, I read of Dead Negro Draw, which was named for this negro.

Then old Sid Doykin butted in and told of the time when the relationship was strained between Doak Good and Jim Newman.

When the XIT people made Jim Newman leave the Yellow House ranch they took possession of it and had it fenced. Jim Newman moved across the line and put in a few troughs at some small springs around Salt Lake and turned a large herd loose and the cattle drifted a few miles over to Los Portales Springs, which was owned by Pioneer Good.

Good was a bachelor and lived alone. He lived in an adobe house, which had a loft in it with a half-window to the east. He and Newman became bitter enemies over who should use the water available. One day, while Good was dressing, he looked out of the window toward the spring, which was near an old abandoned rock house. He saw a fellow poke his head around the corner of the well looking for a chance to shoot. Doak Good stayed out from in front of the window, finished dressing and went down an inside stairway with his old Sharps buffalo gun and crept around the corner of the house with a draw gun and in a minute's time the fellow poked his head around again and Good shot half of it off.

After that incident Good, who was not a coward, made the remark that the country was "not big enough to hold Newman and myself, so I'm selling out and turning it over to Newman."

Well, then old Caleb Giles spit out his chew of tobacco and said, "I guess I am next."

He said, "I expect I have witnessed the most unique tragedy ever pulled off on the great staked plains.

"I was holding down a job with the DZ outfit and it was back when hundreds of Texans were droughted out in Texas and a colony of immigrants passed by an old immigrant and cattle trail going west every few days.

(This old trail began at Fort Concho, Texas, went to Fort Sumner, New Mexico and then on to Arizona. It crossed the staked plains coming from the east to the west and ran across the plains for some 300 miles lengthways with the Pecos river to the south.)

"I remember one afternoon one of the colony asked me about the grass and water ahead and I told them of a rainwater hole ahead several miles in a hard pan basin. It was in one of those fine loco valleys with loco big enough to mow.

"I thought then that I should have warned them not to let their stock have access to the loco; but I didn't. Well, what do you think? The second day after that a fellow came into my camp on a run and said, 'Get the boys together or there will be hell to pay over yonder.'

"I said, 'What is the matter?'

"He replied, 'Why that whole damn immigrant family is drunk on loco and rambling around on the prairie. You know why, without being told. You know in Texas the people are wild about their wild greens such as polk and lambs quarter. They thought this loco was lambs quarter and you can see the results.'

"We rushed off down there and commenced rounding them in. Some of them had become outlaws. We roped and tied them down and left them until we could get the milder ones."

Someone asked the question, "How long were they sobering up?"

"Oh," he said, "I think the second day we had all of them rounded up and the teams hitched up and our boss sent me along as one of the escorts to pilot them to the west side of the Pecos where it was too dry for loco."

Then someone asked, "Did you have any more trouble with them?"

"Yes," he replied "when passing the Tierra Blanco we went through another one of those loco valleys. It was hard to ride herd on them and keep them from breaking out."

We asked him if he was sure the immigrants were from Texas and he replied they might have been from Arkansas.

Then one of the boys wound up by asking Giles if he was through and saying: "We were telling facts, but can't help but think that you have taken advantage of us by having the last shot. We are not going to call you a liar, but believe you have handled the truth in a very careless manner."

Llano Estacado

by W. M. Jones

"The old chuckwagon-top gleams white!
The campfire smoke I see,
As in the early morning light
The 'grubpile' call rings free!
And from their tarps the punchers creep,
As morning stars grow pale,
And toss aside their dreams and sleep,
Upon the Chisholm Trail!"
—Cowboy Ballad

The cattle drive is a nightmare—insects, mud, dust, heat, drought, marauding Redskins, murderous Mexican bandits; pests of every description, human, animal, and vegetable. The cattle are losing weight and John Chisum is losing money. But the beetle-browed Emperor of the trail herds orders the drive to go on because he knows that in the Staked Plains (El Llano Estacado) the cattle thrive. Northward and onward the milling dogies trample their toilsome trail through the treeless, mountainless and almost waterless plains that have echoed adventurous feet before the coming of Coronado.

The level monotony of the grass-covered expanse offered no natural guide for the Indians so they put up stakes to mark their trails and indicate the hidden water holes. Because of these posts, the Spaniards named the area El Llano Estacado, or the Staked Plain.

With an elevation of 700 feet, this grassy plateau extends from the Pecos River eastward to the Caprock of Texas. The Pecos made the watering of cattle difficult because of its perpendicular banks.

For centuries the buffalo and the Indians claimed the Staked Plains for their own until 1874 when Colonel Nelson A. Miles, then in the adolescent stage of his Indian fighting career, cornered them, and drove them under the yoke on the Reservation at Fort Sill, Okla.

But poisonous water, quicksand, fire, flood, or famine could not stay Chisum, Goodnight, Loving, and the hundred other lusty trailblazers who cursed and clawed their way to survival in the Southwest.

Six flags have waved over the Staked Plains—France, Spain, and Mexico have held their temporal sway, the Lone Star of the Texas Republic and the Stars and Bars of the Southern Confederacy had their day. Last but greatest of all is the present glorious emblem—The Stars and Stripes.

Down the dusty trails of the Staked Plains comes the intrepid Coronado in 1541. Forty-one years later Espejo tramps along. Then come the Franciscans, the Indians, the buffalo hunters, the cattle kings and their rowdy retinue, ranchers, rustlers, outlaws—Good men, bad men, white men, red men, brown men, black men . . . they have left their footprints and their bones on the Staked Plains.

Cattle Roundup, Dana B. Chase, undated, NMHM/DCA #056989

"Lead Steers" of the Trail Days by Jack Potter

by Mrs. Belle Kilgore

"**M**y pet hobby has always been Lead Steers," said Jack Potter to the reporter.

"After driving on the trails for more than fifteen years, sometimes two herds a year, I can look back over the past and appreciate the service I got out of them and their peculiar habits.

"I believe the most noted lead steer I named Randao for the ranch he was raised on in southwest Texas. He had a fighting record and always came out victorious in his fights and could not be beaten as a leader.

"The next outlaw lead steer was only three years old. He had such a terrible record I named him Buck Shot Roberts. His record is mentioned elsewhere.

"All my other lead steers I named for the best men in the west. When Dodge City was at its best as a buffalo hide and cattle shipping point, Bob Wright was manager of Wright Beverly and Co., outfitters for trail herds. When I started on the trail with a herd from the coast of Texas, and a large long horn steer took the lead, I could think of nothing else but naming this steer for my popular friend, Bob Wright.

"And later, on one of my drives north, from Ft. Sumner, I named my old wise lead steer for John Chisum. Then on a later drive, I had a middle-aged gentle steer that was smart enough almost to talk. I always had great respect and admiration for Governor Lew Wallace, who quelled the Lincoln County war. I named this fine leader Lew Wallace and I never regretted it.

"Now I'm going to tell you about another steer that could smell water at a distance of seven miles or farther and I will tell you why I named him for our late Sid Boykins, of Clovis.

"It was back in the late eighties; I had gathered a herd of steers contracted to Bloom Cattle Co., and was supposed to deliver them at Thatcher, Colorado. While cleaning up the herd to cut back a certain percentage for Franc Bloom, manager, the boys brought in an aged steer, with his left side pretty nearly covered with brands, including Diamond A, Rafter T. and Boot Bar.

"Bloom says, 'We now own the Diamond A's and this steer seemed to have evaded the roundup, and is past the age to make merchantable beef, and about the best we can do is to get you to take him along and chances are we can get him in an Indian contract at Red Cloud agency, or else get him off as a canner.'

"When our herd was ready to start from the Bosque Redondo, the river Pecos had a little flood on and the water was boiled up so our herd did not drink well. Nevertheless, we had to start out on that eighty-mile stretch to Blue Holes on the Pajarita.

"When we pushed the cattle out from the water and started on the trail, this old Diamond A steer mentioned worked right up to the lead and showed that he was a trained leader.

"That night around the campfire an argument commenced among the boys and we began tracing up his record. I have heard Sid Boykin talk about him. He was the lead steer in the herd that Sid came to the country with. Can't you remember that Boot Bar Brand? Well, from this time on he was called Sid Boykin.

"The second day out, late in the afternoon, we were trailing along on the Plains between Agua Caballo and Cu-ne-va spring after making a night drive the night before. The afternoon was hot and the cattle had refused to graze. One of the boys made the remark that there would be hell to pay as these darn cattle are already taking on about a drink and we are not even halfway over the dry stretch. I was working up in the lead with the two pointers when all at once the light breeze switched around to the east and I noticed 'Sid Boykin,' our lead steer, stop suddenly and face the breeze and commence sniffing the air. Then he started off in that direction with other leaders following. I rode up in front and checked them and then the two pointers rode up and they asked what do you reckon is ailing that old scallawag?

"I said, 'He smells water.' Well, what if he does, said the boys. It might be a lake drying up and he smells the mud. As they started to push them back into the trail I said, 'Wait! Let's study this proposition over. It would be great to run on to some surface water and let this herd fill up. They are going to look like greyhounds if we have to go on to Blue Holes without water.' The two boys were kind of mule-headed. One of them said to me, 'I thought you were an old trained trail boss and now letting that old lead steer dictate to you.'

"Well, I can't help remembering a few years ago when that terrible blizzard that come on us at Clayton. My lead steer 'John Chisum' was piloting the herd fifteen miles facing the storm getting to shelter. We finally came into a big trail going angling to the northeast. I started to follow it when 'John Chisum' turned away from behind me and started on in the same direction we had been traveling. I turned and rode around in front of him and was bawling him out when all at once I had a hunch and said 'John Chisum, under the present conditions we can't stand but another hour of this storm. We've had nothing to eat and it's getting colder. If you know more than I do, you can take the lead and I'll follow.'

"In half hour we went off the high land divide down into a valley where there was all kinds of accommodation and were saved. I told one of the boys to start off to the east and ride like a drunk Indian and keep on high ground and look for a lake.

"'When you find it, get back on higher ground and wave your six shooter for a sight,' I instructed. 'The herd will be following up.'

"In one hour we could see him waving his gun and Sid Boykin, the lead steer, had won out. By dark we had arrived at a big surface lake fully seven miles from the place that he smelled water.

"It was a comforting thing to have rainwater to drink. The cook was taking advantage of having soft water and was cooking the first mess of beans we had seen in weeks. You could hear the cattle on the bed ground grunting and puffing they were so full of water.

"Sitting around the campfire that night one of the boys spoke up with 'We shore got some lead steer.' Another added 'And if I know myself we have got some trail boss.'

"All of us who have ridden the trails and know the cow country know that cattle have certain instincts. Horses likewise. If a puncher was lost in a storm, he would give his horse a slack rein and the horse would take him straight to camp.

"So the trail bosses learned to know that his horse and the lead steer were wise aids in troublous times such as those I have recounted."

Source of Information: Clovis *Evening News Journal*, June 1, 1937.

An All But Forgotten Cattle Trail by Albert W. Thompson

from New Mexico Federal Writers' Project

It wasn't such a long trail when compared with the John Chisum or Loving-Goodnight treks, but it was nevertheless for a number of years an important and well patronized avenue in unburdening the Pecos River district of its Southern New Mexico longhorns and verily these Pecos River longhorns were as radiant fifty years ago, in their coats of many colors, as was the famed garment of the Biblical Joseph. The cattle had long horns indeed. Their horns protruding generously and picturesquely from narrow heads and faces, tossing fantastically as they shuffled along the trail, noses close to the short grass which they nipped as they moved sedately northward, they formed odd looking spectacles.

Drives Began in '89

The spring of 1889 may have seen the first great drives of livestock from the Pecos Valley up the Clayton Trail. Usually forty days were consumed in making the trip. The roundup in the Pecos Valley began the last of April. On May 15th they met near Roswell, the herd cleanup point. Roswell was then an inland town of a few shacks. Here trail herd wagons loaded up with provisions with slickers, chewing tobacco, and a flask or two of rotgut. Rattlesnakes were numerous and angry between Roswell and Clayton, angry if disturbed. A man stepping off his horse to tighten his saddle girth might tread on one of them. Then the rotgut, if there was any left at the wagon, came in handy. . . .

The glory of the Pecos River-Clayton trail faded with the building of the railroad from Amarillo to Roswell. The thousands and thousands of cattle that plodded along its windblown path, and the riders who lined the longhorn's advance by day and at night, under a crescent moon and a slow revolving Great Dipper, rode around and around the bed ground on which contentedly lay their charges and lulled them to sleep with falsetto pitched sloughing, in their stirrups now and then to pull up their mounts, cross their legs over saddle horns while they rolled yellow cigarettes, are visions now of a brightly illuminated past. They had their day and it was a picturesque one.

John Hittson, Cattle King by Edgar C. McMechen

from New Mexico Federal Writers' Project

Western fiction writers have made promiscuous and unrestrained use of the term "cattle king" that many people today regard it as a hyperbole. True, if one applies the words to John W. Iliff, long reputed to have been the greatest individual cattleman of Colorado during the days of the open range or to Colonel Charles Goodnight, few will question the right of these famous cattlemen to the designation. Yet, if we may accept the word of several historians of fifty years ago, who write much about the open range, John Hittson, on the headwaters of Bijou Creek, operated on a grander scale than either of those mentioned.

Chief among the stock-raisers of this state is John Hittson, wrote one Colorado historian in 1880, while another writer of the same period mentioned as the recognized cattle kings of that day O'Connor, King, Kennedy, Hitton, and Chisholm in referring to the epic characters of the open range.

The same writer tells of Hittson's first trip into New Mexico to supply beef to the United States government for feeding the 17,000 Navajo Indians that had been rounded up by the federal troops and were being held at Fort Sumner. The trip started in August, 1867, and the herd followed the old John Chisholm Trail via Fort Chadbourne to North Concho River, thence along the river to its source; thence due west across the Staked Plains to Horsehead Crossing on the Pecos. The Hittson herd was one day behind that of John Chisholm and Hittson overtook the latter where Black River empties into the Pecos. The Navajos had robbed Chisholm of 800 cattle, but Hittson and his men safely delivered their animals to the government. On the return trip the Kiowas surprised Hittson's camp two hundred miles from home and took from the men their wagon and team of oxen.

This robbery rankled in Hittson's breast and, after reaching his ranch, he called for volunteers to return and secure the wagon. Chester Wentworth, Frank McLaura, James and John Hart, M. L. Johnson, Newt Kirksey and a negro named Andy joined Hittson in this dangerous venture. Good fortune attended them, for the party found the wagon in January, 1868, and discovered the oxen nearby.

Source of Information: The Colorado Magazine, Vol. XI, Sept. 1934, Number 5, "Cattle Trails of New Mexico and Trade," pp. 164–170.

Comanche Indians on Chisum Cattle-Trail

by Georgia B. Redfield

"In 1867 John S. Chisum brought his first herd of 'Jingle Bob' cattle across the plains and through the buffalo hunting territory of the hostile nomadic Comanche Indians.

"Scout riders were sent ahead by the trail-blazers to protect the herd from the Indians who were numerous in the lower Pecos Valley until after the extermination of the buffalo during the years 1877–78. The 'Jingle Bobs' were brought over safely and placed on grazing lands around headquarters established at Bosque Grande thirty-five miles northeast of Roswell, on the Pecos River. A younger brother Pitser M. Chisum was placed in charge."

In 1932 the writer of this article was one of the "Old Timers" who rode in the Old Timers parade in Roswell. Mrs. Sallie Chisum Roberts, riding a side-saddle and wearing her long old- fashioned riding habit, was an interesting and outstanding figure of that parade.

On this day, at the end of "The Trail," Mrs. Roberts told again the story we all loved to hear, of her experiences on the journey and after arrival in the Pecos Valley, and the first night spent on the Chisum Ranch.

"It was fifty-five years ago, this next December 24th, 1932, since I arrived in the Pecos Valley," said Mrs. Roberts. "We went to Uncle John Chisum's ranch five miles south of here. Uncle John was known as the 'Cattle King' of the west but that had no effect on our equilibrium.

"My Uncle John never married. My father (James Chisum), my two brothers (Walter and William) and I, left home in Texas and traveled through the open country expecting Indian attacks at any time. We had three wagons, a hack and our saddle horses. We spent one month on the road. We had packed all the fruit trees, flowers and shrubbery we could in the wagons, and they were the beginning of the first Pecos Valley orchards and flowers." Some of the plants from those old-fashioned roses brought over the plains by Sallie Chisum still flourish and bloom on the Redfield place, 705 E. College Boulevard in Roswell.

"Our last night on the trail we spent at the R. M. Gilbert ranch on the Peñasco River," said Mrs. Roberts.

"Six cowboys had been sent by Uncle John to meet us at Horsehead Crossing to act as bodyguards, and protect our stock from Indian attack at night. The first night we spent at the Chisum ranch, we were all tired out. We put our stock in the fenced in lot, locked the gate and all hands went to bed and slept soundly. The next morning we were amazed to find the stock all gone, and the gate still locked. The Indians (Comanches) had lifted the gate from its iron pivots, removed all our stock, replaced the gate very carefully and had completely disappeared, leaving only their tracks to tell the tale. We could not tell how many Indians were in the raiding. They got twenty-five horses and mules. I was heartsick for we had left our home at Denton, Texas to get away from Indians. 'Cheer up, Sallie, the worst is yet to come,' said my father.

"I knew he was right when I first saw Roswell. There was only one residence called a 'hotel' and one store which contained the Post Office. These two buildings had been built in 1869 by Van C. Smith and Aaron O. Wilburn on the block west of where the Court House stands at the present time. In 1873 the post office was stationed here with Van Smith appointed as postmaster. He named the town Roswell for his father Roswell Smith of Omaha, Nebraska. There were six little trees trying to grow on the west side of the main road. On the east side there were a few houses, some made of adobe and some of just mud, sticks, and gunny sacks. It was a cheerless looking layout and I said to Brother Walter, 'This is the jumping off place, I want to go back home.'"

The request of his sister to return to her home in Denton, Texas was repeated to this writer in 1905 by Walter Chisum as we walked through his beautiful orchard near the old Chisum Ranch at South Spring. It is needless to say the Chisums stayed in the Pecos Valley, and they are responsible for many of the beauty spots in and around Roswell which have caused this district to be called, "The Oasis In The Desert."

Source of Information: In own words of Sallie Chisum Roberts and Lucius Dills, Roswell Historian.

Old Trails Crossing the Pecos

by Georgia B. Redfield

That Alvar Nuñez Cabeza de Vaca, the other Spaniards and a negro slave passed through New Mexico in 1535, on their journey Westward from where they were shipwrecked on the coast of Texas to Mexico, is a much disputed question, remaining unanswered.

Some historians who know the topography and conditions of the country and wild life of New Mexico are convinced, after years of research work, that these Spanish explorers did penetrate into Southeast New Mexico. This section of the country seems accurately described by de Vaca in his "Relacion" first published in Zamora, Spain in 1542, translated by Fannie Bandelier in 1905, which is practically the same route given by J. F. Hinkle in "A Cowboy on the Pecos," published in 1937.

A very fine article: "Pilgrims of Conquest," by Tom Charles and a map presenting the probable route taken by the Spaniards, is given in September 1938 number of "New Mexico" magazine. The probable route taken by the Spaniards, as given by Mr. Charles, is across the plains, west from the Middle Concho River to Horsehead Crossing on the Pecos River, south of the present City of Carlsbad, up the Pecos to Rio Peñasco, about six miles south of Artesia, and west—a little north to the Sacramento Mountains, which also corresponds with the probable route given by J. F. Hinkle.

This route across Horsehead Crossing on the Pecos is the same traveled by John S. Chisum on the old Chisum Trail across which he brought the first herds to the Pecos Valley in 1867. Chisum crossed the Peñasco, leaving de Vaca's trail at this point, and traveled north up the Pecos to Bosque Grande (Big Forests) about thirty-five miles northeast of Roswell.

The districts traveled by Coronado's men after their first winter's camp at Tiguex, where they had listened to the tales of great riches told by a Pawnee Indian, called "The Turk," will be of especial interest during the Coronado Cuarto Centennial, celebration of the coming four hundred years ago of these Spanish conquistadores.

After breaking camp at Tiguex, April 23, 1541, in search of Quivira they followed "The Turk" across the mountains of Apache Canyon, then down the Pecos River to Puerto de Luna, where they made a bridge and crossed to the Llano Estacado (Staked Plains) of the buffalo grazing lands. Suffering from want of food and water, they soon came to the conclusion that they must turn back, for by this time they realized that the Turk's stories of finding great riches were all fabrications. They returned by a more direct route through districts near where Roswell is at the present time.

The ill-advised party, on their return journey, crossed the Pecos River at what is now known as Hagerman Crossing near Roswell and traveled up the Hondo River Valley camping between North Spring River and the Hondo.

An old legendary report says that Ruidoso (Spanish for noisy) was first applied to this River by Coronado's men who camped beside the stream that leapt with noisy vigor.

The ruins of the old Butterfield Overland Mail and stage station may still be seen sixty miles southeast of Carlsbad. The Butterfield line established in the '50s continued until 1869, operating from Missouri, through Fort Smith Arkansas over the Guadalupe Mountains to El Paso, Texas and Yuma, Arizona then to Los Angeles, Fresno, and San Francisco, California.

Old wagon irons and stage coach trappings often found not far north of Highway 62 near Carlsbad Caverns, tell the story of Indian raids and massacres that occurred in the early stage coach days in New Mexico.

In 1873 Pitser Chisum, younger brother of John Chisum, while taking cattle over the Chisum Trail lost the entire herd in an Indian Raid at Loving Bend. Bones afterwards found at Guadalupe Point showed the cattle had been held in this district and butchered by the hundreds.

On the sixth of June, 1866, Charles Goodnight left the frontier of Texas to blaze a new trail through the Indian infested country of New Mexico up the Pecos to Colorado.

Battles were fought during the journey with Indians, cattle thieves, and against dry waterless plains where his cattle died in great numbers from heat and lack of water. They fought to keep the cattle away from alkali water holes to which many escaped and drinking of the brackish water died an agonizing death.

"The Pecos—called the 'graveyard of the cowman's hopes'—is as treacherous as the Indian," was Goodnight's description of the River in those early days.

They traveled up the east side of the River because of there being no tributaries to cross and also because the west side was alive with hostile Indians. Traveling north and a little west they finally crossed at what is now known as Pope's Crossing. Then to escape deep sands they traveled on the west side of the river until the country around Carlsbad was reached; here a crossing was made to the east side of the river again. The cattle by this time, blear-eyed and half crazed from thirst and traveling night and day, were carried straight north through the Lake McMillan and Avalon country, until the fine grazing lands of the Bosque Grande were reached. Here the herd was rested, and the cattle fattened were sold to the Government soldiers at Fort Sumner instead of pushing on to Colorado as planned.

Other herds were again brought into New Mexico by Goodnight, in 1867–1868 and 1869. Ten, twelve and fifteen thousand dollars were paid to him for the different herds. But the money was well earned. There was a loss of nerve, strength and even life. Loving (Goodnight's partner in the cattle business) came to his death from wounds made by Indians in 1867 at Loving Bend (named for the brave cattleman) who, surrounded by Indians, was wounded and afterwards died of blood poisoning from an arm that had to be amputated, after he had crawled to about where Carlsbad is now and was picked up five days later beside the old trail.

Chisum's herd, brought to Bosque Grande in 1867, was the beginning of the great cattle industry of Southeast New Mexico. He was followed by Littlefield and J. P. White in 1882, and J. F. Hinkle in 1885.

The great cattle drives and stocking of the ranges on the Pecos wore down the banks and floods and erosion widened the stream. In driving 2,000 head of cattle across the Hagerman Crossing on the Pecos, former Governor Hinkle on one drive lost 500 that bogged down, and were lost, and at Horsehead Crossing thousands met a similar fate on different drives of other cattlemen.

There are no buffalo now on the Staked Plains to stampede the herds, no Indians to drive them away in the night, no cattle thieves, no rattlesnakes, and while there is more water, or watering places are known, the cattlemen and cowboys lead a less adventurous life. The old colorful cattle driving days are gone.

Vast fields of grain, beautiful trees, fences, gardens, and fine highways, with luxurious automobiles, are now seen by the thousands on the old "Cattle Trails" blazed by the pioneer cattlemen who have built up the fine country of Southeast New Mexico.

Sources of Information: James F. Hinkle, pioneer Cowboy on the Pecos; Tom Charles, writer, and custodian of White Sands; Vaughn's *History and Government of New Mexico,* 1929; *Land of Enchantment* folder, New Mexico Tourist Bureau 1935. Francis Tracey, Eddy Co. pioneer; Noel L. Johnson, Eddy Co. pioneer.

Ranchers' camp, D. B. Chase, undated, NMHM/DCA #056994

Some First Herds of Cattle Brought to the Pecos Valley in Chaves County, New Mexico

by Georgia B. Redfield

In 1867 John Simpson Chisum brought the first herd of cattle to Chaves County, which remained and was the beginning of the great cattle industry of Southeast New Mexico. There were several other herds brought by Chisum before 1880, but as far as can be ascertained, no other cattle were brought and turned loose on the free grazing lands of what is now Chaves County until 1884 when W. G. Urton as manager of the Cass Land and Cattle brought 3,000 head of two year old heifers, from Fort Griffin Texas which, after branding, they turned loose on the range in the Cedar Canyon Country. These were the first cattle brought to this section of Chaves County which is sixty miles northeast of Roswell. The Anderson Cattle Co. brought cattle from the east during the Autumn of 1884 which were placed on the Diamond A Ranch 25 miles west of Roswell and James F. Hinkle in October 1885 brought the first large herd to the southwestern section of Chaves County. This herd was from the C A Bar outfit from Texas, brought for their Peñasco River ranch.

Strange to say an ill-fated herd brought to Chaves County, of which only four remained after a long hard four-months drive from Johnson City, Texas, during a severe drouth season, was the beginning of one of the best cattle ranches on the Peñasco River, near the C A Bar Cattle ranch. This herd was headed toward New Mexico in September of 1887. The caravan with which the cattle came was made up of five families, twenty-five people in all counting Mr. George Hendrix, the leader of the caravan, his wife Sarah Hendrix and seven children. There were five covered wagons, one being the typical cattle "chuck" wagon, though this one was drawn by oxen instead of the mules or horses used by Chisum, Hinkle and other pioneer cattle men.

Very little water was found on the long hard drive or at camping places, as one of the severest drouth seasons ever known in that part of the desert country caused all watering places to become dry.

The cattle as well as the people of the caravan suffered acutely from alkali water they were obliged to drink. It was used once for making coffee, which, even when boiled, acted as a poison, though no one died. The starved and famished cattle became poor and weak, some gave out entirely and died, and many escaped from the herd and were lost.

The sick-looking stock was held up for inspection at the state line near Black River, which caused a delay, but no diseases were discovered other than sickness caused from starvation.

Travel-worn, hungry and thirsty the caravan arrived at Hope, about sixty miles southwest of Roswell, on December the twenty-third, and camped at Y. O. Crossing. On awakening the morning of the twenty-fourth (Christmas Eve) a four-foot snow covered the camping ground. The caravan members, suffering intensely from the blizzard, were disbanded. All of the cattle that had not drifted away in the wind and snow lay dead on the camping grounds. Only four head of drifters were found.

The Hendrix family, seeking shelter from the storm, were taken into the dirt-roofed adobe house of John Paul, who was the first man who came to that district, and settled the town of Hope.

Mr. George Hendrix never fully recovered from the hardships of the memorable journey to New Mexico. With his family he settled on a place rented from the A C Bar Cattle Company of which J. F. Hinkle of Roswell was manager. Because of the poor state of health of Mr. Hendrix, the girls as well as the boys of the family labored in the field, harder and longer hours than any pioneers of Chaves County ever were known to labor, raising cattle, as well as cultivating and improving the place.

The livestock of the Hendrix family, which fed on the fine grazing land of the Peñasco River Valley, grew fat and increased and the Hendrix place, while being rented, became one of the finest ranches of Chaves County, and afterwards became, and is now the property of, Angie Hendrix Cleve, April 22, 1894. Bernard Cleve was a cousin and partner of J. F. Hinkle in a store and cattle business. Mr. Cleve bought out Mr. Hinkle's cattle interests and built a fine home on the old Hendrix place, now the Cleve estate, where the five Cleve children were born.

At the time of establishing a post office on the Cleve ranch for the town or settlement of "Elk," mail, now delivered daily, was then brought in only once a week.

Mrs. Cleve, besides being postmistress since the death of her husband, March 26, 1913, has looked after her cattle and other ranching interests and conducts a "dude ranch" where the best ranch accommodations may be secured for any number of regular boarders or tourists.

While there is a prosperous agricultural industry and sawmill and lumber at Elk, cattle and sheep raising have remained the most important industries of this section of Chaves County.

Sources of Information: Mrs. Dorothy Cleve Norton, Roswell, New Mexico, and W. C. Urton, Roswell, New Mexico.

The Goodnight Cattle Trail

by Georgia B. Redfield

Many valiant cattlemen, though strong and resourceful, and with high hopes of being a successful trail-blazer, traveled to meet suffering and defeat on the first cattle trails through New Mexico.

In 1865 Charles Goodnight began to gather cattle in Belknap, Texas. He planned to drive them over a new trail blazed through New Mexico to Colorado. In September, he had rounded up two thousand head of fine steers and dry cattle, when Indians stampeded the herd, frightened off the cattle workers, and drove the cattle away.

Goodnight, who was away from camp at the time of the disastrous loss of his herd, was more than ever determined to make the cattle trail he had planned. Now he was resolved never to return to this country of cattle-thieving Indians and neighbors.

Goodnight was only thirty years of age when he started on his first cattle trail. He was strong and fearless, and had the experience and training of a plainsman, so he succeeded as a trail-blazer where many others had failed.

He planned, to the very smallest detail, to meet the requirements for a combat, as for war, and unusual hardships of a new trail across the desert.

He had a stout wagon entirely rebuilt, with the toughest wood available—"seasoned bois d'arc"—had axles replaced with others of iron, and took a can of tallow instead of the usual tar for wagon greasing. He carried twelve yoke of oxen for relief of the six they used at a time.

The first chuck-box of its kind ever seen was built by Goodnight for the back of his wagon. The hinged door let down on a swinging post to form a table. Those used at the present time are built on this same plan. Inside this chuckbox he placed the first round-up sour dough jar, which will always be linked with the chuck-wagon meals on the cow trails in the west. Goodnight learned the magic of sour dough for biscuit from his mother, who always kept a jar brewing in their home.

Goodnight himself selected his horses for this first drive. They were an important necessity for use on the perilous trail.

One big blue horse—brought by a boy with a drove—was cut-out and rejected for reason of overweight. The boy cried from fear of the big brute which he felt forced to ride to his home. "Never mind son," said Goodnight, "I'll ride him." He stepped lightly into the saddle. Immediately the powerful blue doubled, as if in convulsions, and literally rode the skies. Goodnight kept his saddle. The horse stopped as if surprised, headed for a steep bluff over the creek, and went into a high dive over the top. Goodnight was still all there in the saddle. The horse bogged in the creek's soft mud to the saddle girths; with all his mighty strength he heaved out and bolted to the barns. Goodnight calmly dismounted and said—"I'll take him, he's good enough for me." Of just such fearlessness and power was this trailblazer made. The very start on the trail was the battle with that horse, and this was synonymous with all the experiences on those first cattle trails during the sixties and early seventies in New Mexico.

Battles were fought with horses, Indians, cattle thieves, Mexican traders—to whom the Indians traded cattle, horses, mules and buffalo robes, for only a keg of liquor. There were battles with waterless plains and with the deceptive mirage, with its clear pools in the shade of many trees, giving promise of life to men dying of thirst, which, when reached, proved to be only shimmering, blistering sun on dry parched desert land.

On the sixth day of June, 1866, young Goodnight left the frontier of Texas to blaze a new trail through this hazardous country to New Mexico.

Oliver Loving, fifty-four years of age, but as sturdy as a young man, took charge of the drive. He threw in his own cattle, joining herds at Belknap, making two thousand head in all; these were the first of the famous long-horns located on ranches in southeast New Mexico. There was an outfit of eighteen strong, fearless men, who started those long-horns westward over the untried trail with vast stretches of desert without water for the herd.

Goodnight planned his trails with long detours to escape as many perils as possible. The drive from Belknap to Fort Concho was comparatively easy. From here running west along the Concho River the Staked Plains were crossed, and for three days—until Horse Head Crossing between Carlsbad and Pecos on the Pecos River was reached—the cattle had no water. At this dreaded place (named for the many skulls of horses that had perished in the treacherous river and bog-holes of alkaline water) the hardest battle of all was waged with the perishing stock that in a frenzy of suffering for water, stampeded. In spite of heroic efforts to guide the cattle from the alkali water holes, many escaped, drank the brackish water which brought instant agonizing death, which ended days of suffering. The riders were forced to push on, the herd refused to be turned. After battling two whole days with the herd, a hundred head was left to perish hopelessly bogged in the quicksands, beneath the unscalable Pecos Bluffs.

"The Pecos—the graveyard of the cow-man's hopes—is as treacherous as the Indian," said Goodnight.

Remaining on the east side of the river, because of there being no tributaries to cross, and also because the west side was always alive with hostile Indians, Goodnight continued north and a little west until crossing the river at Pope's Crossing; then, to escape deep sands, they traveled on the west side of the river until the Carlsbad country was reached, where a crossing was made to the east side again. From this point the herd was driven through the bleak barren river valley, where there were no living things in sight save rattlesnakes and the fish swimming in the Pecos. The cattle, by this time blear-eyed, half-crazed from thirst and traveling night and day, were pushed straight north through the Lake McMillan and Avalon Lake Country and east of the Bottomless Lakes area, until the fine grazing lands and waters of the Bosque Grande country was reached. Here a headquarters for the cattle was established. They were rested, fattened, and instead of pushing on the trail to Colorado as planned, the herd was sold to the Government at Fort Sumner for meat.

Forgetting the hardships undergone on this journey, the following year, 1867, Goodnight returned over the same trail with another herd, and with Oliver Loving taken on as a partner, the trail was extended north from Fort Sumner to Raton Pass into Colorado. Ten cents a head was charged for the entire herd going through the mountain pass to Denver.

The next year, 1868, in order to avoid this outlay of money in going over the pass, Goodnight drove his herd to Mosquero, going from this point northeast to the Mt. Dora area northwest to Des Moines, and on from this point to Denver.

Still another trail was made by Goodnight in 1869, when he brought a herd through by the same route to Fort Sumner, and traveled from here northwest, to Romeroville, then on through rough hard trails to Santa Fe.

Ten, twelve, and fifteen thousands of dollars were paid Goodnight for herds brought over these trails, but the money was earned, by loss of nerve, and strength, and by loss of life for Loving in the end, who came to his death from wounds made by Indians in 1867 at Loving Bend south of Carlsbad.

Goodnight lived to a ripe old age and his stories of adventure on the trails he blazed were the same as those others who came later—John Chisum in 1867, followed by Littlefield, J. P. White and others.

There are no buffalo now on the Staked Plains to thrill, or stampede the herds, no bog holes on river crossings to destroy the cattle and horses, there are fewer rattlesnakes and with building up of the country, fewer fish, no Indians, no cattle thieves. The cattlemen and cowboys lead a less adventurous life. The old colorful cattle-driving days are gone. Vast fields of grain, beautiful trees, fences, gardens, fine highways and luxurious automobiles are now seen on the old cattle trails, blazed by those cattlemen who have really made this great southwest country we enjoy today.

Source of Information: J. Evetts Haley, *Charles Goodnight, Cowman and Plainsman,* Houghton Mifflin Company, 1936.

Maxwell's Ranch: The "Closest Call" of Maxwell's Life by Colonel Henry Inman

by Helen Speaker

One night Kit Carson, Maxwell and I were up in the Raton Mountains above the Old Trail, and having lingered too long, were caught above the clouds against our will, darkness having overtaken us before we were ready to descend into the valley. It was dangerous to undertake the trip over such a precipitous and rocky trail, so we were compelled to make the best of our situation. It was awfully cold, and as we had brought no blankets, we dared not go to sleep for fear our fire might go out, and we should freeze. We therefore determined to make a night of it by telling yarns, smoking our pipes, and walking around at times.

After sitting awhile, Maxwell pointed toward the Spanish Peaks, whose snow-white tops cast a diffused light in the heavens above them, and remarked that in the deep cañón which separates them, he had one of the "closest calls" of his life, willingly complying when I asked him to tell us the story.

"It was in 1847. I came down from Taos with a party to go to the Cimarron crossing of the Santa Fe Trail to pick up a large herd of horses for the United States Quartermaster's Department. We succeeded in gathering about a hundred and started back with them, letting them graze slowly along, as we were in no hurry. When we arrived at the foothills north of Bent's Fort, we came suddenly upon the trail of a large war-band of Utes, none of whom we saw, but from subsequent developments the savages must have discovered us days before we reached the mountains. I knew we were not strong enough to cope with the whole Ute nation, and concluded the best thing for us to do under the ticklish circumstances was to make a detour, and put them off our trail. So we turned abruptly down the Arkansas, intending to try and get to Taos in that direction, more than one hundred and fifty miles around. It appeared afterward that the Indians had been following us all the way. When we found this out, some of the men believed they were another party, and not the same whose trail we came upon when we turned down the river, but I always insisted they were. When we arrived within a few days drive of Taos, we were ambushed in one of the narrow passes of the range, and had the bloodiest fight with the Utes on record. There were thirteen of us, all told, and two little children who we were escorting to their friends at Taos, having received them at the Cimarron crossing.

"While we were quietly taking our breakfast one morning, and getting ready to pull out for the day's march, perfectly unsuspicious of the proximity of any Indians, they dashed in upon us, and in less than a minute stampeded all our stock-loose animals as well as those we were riding. While part of the savages were employed in running off the animals, fifty of their most noted warriors, splendidly mounted and horribly painted, rushed into the camp around the fire of which the men and the little children were peacefully sitting, and, discharging their guns as they rode up, killed one man and wounded another.

"Terribly surprised as we were, it did not turn the heads of the old mountaineers, and I immediately told them to make a break for a clump of timber near by, and that we would fight them as long as one of us could stand up. There we fought and fought against fearful odds, until all were wounded except two. The little children were captured at the beginning of the trouble and carried off at once. After a while the savages got tired of the hard work, and, as is frequently the case, went away of their own free will; but they left us in a terrible plight. All were sore, stiff, and weak from their many wounds; on foot, and without any food or ammunition to procure game with, having exhausted our supply in the awfully unequal battle; besides, we were miles from home, with every prospect of starving to death.

"We could not remain where we were, so as soon as darkness came on, we started out to walk to some settlement. We dared not show ourselves by daylight, and all through the long hours when the sun was up, we were obliged to hide in the brush and ravines until night overtook us again, and we could start on the painful march.

"We had absolutely nothing to eat, and our wounds began to fester, so that we could hardly move at all. We should undoubtedly have perished, if, on the third day, a band of friendly Indians of another tribe had not gone to Taos and reported the fight to the commanding officer of the troops there. These Indians had heard of our trouble with the Utes, and knowing how strong they were, and our weakness, surmised our condition, and so hastened to convey the bad news.

"A company of dragoons was immediately sent to our rescue, under the guidance of Dick Wooton, who was and has ever been a warm personal friend of mine. They came upon us about forty miles from Taos, and never were we more surprised; we had become so starved and emaciated that we had abandoned all hope of escaping what seemed to be our inevitable fate.

"When the troops found us, we had only a few rags, our clothes having been completely stripped from our bodies while struggling through the heavy underbrush on our trail, and we were so exhausted that we could not stand on our feet. One more day, and we would have been laid out.

"The little children were, fortunately, saved from the horror of that terrible march after the fight, as the Indians carried them to their winter camp, where, if not absolutely happy, they were under shelter and fed, escaping the starvation which would certainly have been their fate if they had remained with us. They were eventually ransomed for a cash payment by the government, and altogether had not been very harshly treated."

Ranchers' Camp, D. B. Chase, undated, NMHM/DCA #056992

Condensed Version of "The Story of Early Clayton, New Mexico" by A. W. Thompson

by D. D. Sharp

The first person to be employed as teacher in the public school at Clayton was Miss Ida Cavanaugh of Las Vegas, New Mexico. Miss Cavanaugh had filed a homestead just west of the town on which she resided while she taught. In 1889 she married Colonel John Love and the school was taught by Ward W. Slavery who had filed a homestead in Apache Canyon. Mr. Slavery was a graduate from Yale College in 1883.

The growth of Clayton was slow, but it proved to be an excellent spring and fall cattle and wool shipping point. Great herds of steers and cows were trailed into Clayton from the south from May until October to be shipped north. During the winter months, when no trail herds were on the move, trade was slow.

The following is a quotation from a newspaper article published in 1891:

"And now at the age of two and a half years, thirty months after the first stone was laid in the town with not very imposing service, the founders of the village may well be proud. Eight business houses, including general merchandise, dry and fancy goods, drug store, two hotels, two restaurants, a shoe shop employing three men, and a repair shop with the same number of hands, are among the institutions of the town which supplies a district in which are located both cattle and sheep ranches by the score, dependent on Clayton. The new town, in fact, is a veritable 'hub.' The shipping of wool and livestock has become an important asset and it is gratifying to be able to state that more wool was shipped from Clayton than any other town or city in the Territory, and more sold here than in any place but one other, Albuquerque." Mr. Thompson notes that the number of saloons then existing, about half a dozen, were excluded from the report, of which he was the author.

Mike Beals, a cowboy, was killed in a barber shop by an officer from Texas in 1891. A feud had formerly existed between the two men, and on meeting, the officer got his gun out first. Beals dropped dead at the first shot of the Texan and as usual in such occurrences at that time, no arrests were made.

Among the better homes constructed in Clayton was a two story frame building situated across the street and south of the present (1932) Big Jo Lumber Company. It was erected in 1889. In 1890, and for some years after, it was tenanted by George A. Bushnell and family. With the Bushnells at this time resided Josefeta Carson, daughter of Kit Carson. "Feta" as she was called, was the youngest child of the famous scout. She was born in Boggsville, opposite Las Animas, Colorado in the spring of 1886. Her mother was Mrs. Bushnell's great aunt. In 1891 "Feta" married Bill Squires, a cowboy, who died sometime later.

Agriculture at this time was unpracticed in the portions of Texas, New Mexico, and Arizona, except along streams which supplied water for irrigation. The homesteader who attempted to raise a few acres of corn, maize or beans, was regarded with contempt and suspicion by his neighbors, who branded him as an interloper with whom no friendly relations were maintained. Frequently his life and the lives of his family were threatened if he persisted in plowing the sod. He was often subjected to indignities by cowmen and ranchmen. If he owned a few milk cows, these were more likely to be driven from his homestead during the night and never recovered. His horses, unless he carefully guarded them, would some morning be missing. He was accused of branding calves belonging to stockmen, which ranged the prairies near his homestead. These calves, it was claimed, after being weaned from their mothers and fed on milk from his cows, bore the grangers' brand and mark. The farmer was considered a menace to the community.

"One thing might mitigate in his favor. If he had a comely daughter or two daughters, indeed, whose ages were perhaps 18 or 20 years, his life was more agreeable. Cowboys found time to visit the young women, took them to dances, occasionally dropped in to partake of a meal and in winter brought beef to the family which they had rustled from some cattle owner. If the young daughter was of more than ordinary beauty or unusual attractions, cowboys started a brand for her, in which mavericks and 'long' calves formed the foundation. I knew a settler of northern New Mexico in the 80s whose worldly possessions consisted of a wife, several children (among whom was a comely daughter) half a dozen poor horses, a rickety wagon, and a few pieces of cheap furniture. He soon acquired a fine bunch of cattle. His 'cornfed' girl eventually married a neighboring ranchman and lived happily ever afterwards.

"In the fall of 1888 the merchants of Clayton sent word to the Pecos valley, to Roswell, White Oaks, and Fort Sumner, New Mexico, that Clayton was prepared to ship livestock to Montana and Wyoming Points, and to the market at Kansas City. Fat cattle could be shipped to the Missouri River by rail either by way of Trinidad, Colorado and from thence over the Santa Fe, or by the then just completed Southern Kansas Railway, now the Santa Fe, through Woodward, Indian Territory. The route from the Pecos Valley to Clayton could be more expeditiously negotiated than by any other then-established highway. Water for the herds would be available, except in one or two localities, every few miles, and on reaching Clayton, the Perico could supply this necessity for thousands of head of livestock. Ranch men south of Clayton living on Ute Creek and the Canadian River were urged to come to Clayton rather than to make the drive to Las Vegas, Springer, or other railway points.

"The invitation met with instant response from Southern cattlemen. By the fall of 1888 a trail had been laid out from the Pecos River, by the way of Fort Sumner and Puerto de Luna to Clayton, and several heads of cattle came in from these districts. Ranchmen were well treated and cordially received by the town. Stores and saloons catered to their trade and incited them to come again. The ranchmen responded in chivalrous fashion. The trail men even invited the denizens of the dance hall to dine at their chuck wagons, which were camped both on the Perico and Prairie Lake, which then extended south on Main Street between Railway Avenue and First Street, Clayton. The invitations were accepted with becoming acknowledgement. On these festive occasions the honor of waiting on the visitors and passing them tin plates filled with meat, sour dough bread, stewed fruit, and cups of coffee, devolved on the camp cook or wagon boss. Rough and insinuating remarks were not indulged in. The guests were treated with as much consideration and respect as if they had been the wives or daughters of Clayton's leading citizens.

"The spring of 1889 found thousands of cattle on this slow journey from the Lower Pecos River about Roswell then Peñasco, White Oaks, and old Lincoln, as well as from the Fort Sumner country; headed for Clayton.

Within the Pecos Valley at that time, were maintained many large cattle companies: The Jingle Bobs, successors to John Chisholm; the Bloom Cattle Company, the Bar V's, the LFD's or Littlefield Cattle Company, the herds of Captain Day, and Colonel Milne; the Richardson Cattle Company; Segrist's Cross S outfit; cattle belonging to John W. Poe, Carlisle Brothers, Jonny Riley, and others. From White Oaks came the herd of the Carrizo Cattle Company, of which W. C. McDonald (the first elected governor of New Mexico after the Territory had joined statehood in 1912) was manager. Pat Garrett was a smaller cattle owner and ranchman, Rhea Brothers from Stinking Springs, Brazel, and James F. Hinkle, the last, like McDonald, to fill the gubernatorial chair of New Mexico, were substantial herdsmen. Near Fort Sumner was located the ranch of the New England Cattle Company, successors to the L. B. Maxwell estate, of which Jack M. Potter, later of Clayton, was manager. On Black River, in those days, dwelt Clay Ellison, the noted gunman. (I do not recall ever seeing Ellison in Clayton.)

"The longhorns of southern New Mexico forty-five years ago (from 1932) which came up the trail of 300 or more miles to Clayton, were strikingly different from the large, white face, red cows and steers which stock the western ranches today. The former were of many colors and hues, whites, yellows, white and black, and brindles. Lanky in form and of light frame, the Pecos River herds had inordinately long horns which protruded almost straight out from their heads. Their flanks were drawn and their long tails often touched the ground as they walked. These cattle were descendants of the earlier Texas bovine. I have a pair of mounted horns of a Pecos River steer which measure on their mounting over four feet from tip to tip.

"The southern New Mexico trail men of 1890s who drove their herds to Clayton, were patterns of the genuine old time cowboy. Everyone was armed and each man knew how to draw his gun. Some of these trail men had been through the Lincoln County war and once brushed up against Billy the Kid. They were, for the most part, tall, angular, bow-legged Texans. Used to frontier environments and experts in the art of riding, roping, and handling of cattle, they spurred their horses to the lead of stampeding herds on dark and stormy nights uncomplainingly, and were afraid of neither man nor the elements. Their race is extinct, though it is absurdly portrayed in moving pictures of today.

"The cattle outfits which headed, both spring and fall, toward Clayton, the end of the trail, consisted of a dignified wagon boss, horse rustler (who took care of the remuda), cook, and five or six men. To each man, except the cook, were assigned eight or nine saddle horses. Starting from some point near Roswell, the daily order of march was simple. The Clayton trail followed close to the Pecos River until Fort Sumner was reached. Herds numbered from 1,200 to 1,500 head of mixed cattle, cows, cows and calves, and steers of various ages.

"After breakfast each morning the cook, who drove the chuck wagon containing camp bed and provisions, moved to some directed point assigned by the wagon boss. Ten or twelve miles constituted a day's drive. Stock was expected to gain flesh on the journey to Clayton and were slowly grazed rather than driven. Dinner was served at the chuck wagon about ten o'clock A. M., when, for two hours or more each day the cattle were allowed to rest. At sunset the herd was slowly bunched up, perhaps half a mile from the chuck wagon, and bedded down. Two men constituted the guard which rode around the cattle for two or three hours each night, the last guard starting the herd off on the trail the next morning. This work, on the whole, was tedious and uninteresting. The sun glared down fiercely throughout the day from a cloudless sky. The parched lips and tongues of the cowboys were moistened by occasional draughts of alkali water drawn from the water barrel fastened on one side of the chuck wagon. Finally night came with its quiet and perhaps a moon to light the lonely surroundings. Passing Fort Sumner the Clayton cattle trail followed the Pecos River for a few miles and then turned toward the east for its forty mile trek which was to consume two nights and two days, during which the longhorns and saddle horses were to do without water and the North star their guide across the unmarked stretch of prairie which lay between the Pecos River and the Blue waterholes on Parajito just west of the present Tucumcari. As night appeared the cook was instructed to keep the chuck wagon close to the rear of the herd, which the men were to push along as fast as possible.

"The shouts of the cowboys, as they urged on the lagging animals, intermingled with the rumbling wheels of the chuck wagon; darkness settled, owls hoo-hooed, occasionally a star from the clear heavens darted earthward to be lost on the horizon. About midnight the herd rested for an hour and then moved on. The cowboy started one of his prairie lyrics, 'Oh you wild and wooly punchers listen to my doleful tale, I'll tell you of my troubles on the old Clayton trail,' in which others joined. It relieved the monotony.

"Breakfast next morning at a dry camp, then the herd moved on again. An all day wind blew dust in the faces of the riders, heat became oppressive.

"'We're half way across, boys,' encouragingly called the wagon boss, 'from yonder range we can see the breaks of the Canadian and the Montoyo Grant. Pound 'em on the back and push 'em along.'

"At sunset the herd came to a halt. The cattle stood with outstretched tongues and panting sides. About the chuck wagon, with dropping heads, gathered the saddle horses. One or two of these, pets of their riders, were given short draughts of water from the camp's supply. Then into the second night's darkness moved the contingent. The next few hours work was a repetition of the night before.

"Toward morning a wind sprang up. The jaded, tired cattle raised their heads, sniffed the air, bellowed and started forward. They had scented water. When a few miles from it, the leaders broke into a trot. No attempt was made to hold them back, and by noon the last of the herd had reached the Parajito. Here the wagon was camped; cattle and horses, their thirst appeased, quietly lay down. The animals were too exhausted to graze. The long *jornado* was past."

The Indian Fight at Loving by Noel L. Johnson

Collected by W. E. Wheeler

Along about 1867, immediately after the Civil War, Texas was full of cattle, and was the feeding ground for the open ranges over the middle west that were waiting for men that loved adventure to bring these cows and stock to the open country.

There was a good market at Denver and in Kansas, so these Texas cowboys gathered cattle, and drove them to market.

My father with his wife and three children, in an ox wagon behind a herd of longhorns that were cared for and driven by eighteen picked men, left Palo Pinto, Texas, and with these men, armed with every kind of gun from a squirrel gun to a flintlock. There were pistols of the same kind. The sort that we used to see. You pushed the ball down on top of a charge of powder with a ramrod, or lever, then put a cap on the tube; sometimes when one shot was fired, the whole six shots would go off at once.

There were Indians all along the way, but these sturdy men were pointed for the big open west, and meant to get there in the end if they didn't all get killed before they made the grade because there was a demand for cows out there somewhere, and they were not worth branding in Texas.

He took the Goodnight Trail which ran from old Fort Chadbourne via Fort Concho (now San Angelo) on through the Castle Gap over the "ninety mile" drive without water to Horsehead Crossing on the Pecos, then up the Pecos to Fort Sumner.

From all the information that I can gather, Goodnight drove a herd over this trail the year before or in 1866, the first herd of Texas cattle that ever came over that trail.

Then in 1867, Charley Goodnight and Oliver Loving drove another herd as partners over this same trail, the year that my father came with his first herd. We wintered at the old Missouri Plaza on the Hondo some miles above Roswell, then next year meandered on up into Colorado and settled on the old Santa Fe Trail 60 miles north of Trinidad.

The story I am going to tell you about was told by old trail men like the Hitsons, Dawson, (of the famous Dawson mines), Sam Doss, the

Hudsons, Porters, Fine Earnest, Hall Brothers, Taylor Maulding, Charley Goodnight and the Chisums with others who often put their feet under our table at mealtime at our house on this old National Highway of the days when the west was in its youth.

Our family didn't see any Indians so we will never know whether it was best for the Indians or us, that we didn't meet them.

I am going to tell the story in Charley Goodnight's way, as he probably knew it better than any other man alive, except Wilson, who didn't talk (Charley or J. W. Wilson was the man that was with Loving during the Indian fight).

I've heard it told by many men that were very familiar with the details, including my father, and they all agree very closely as to just what happened, I am sure the story is true.

Goodnight said that the herd was sixty miles from Loving bend on the Pecos, drifting along up the river, with men that had been picked and were under contract to fight until the last man was killed in case of an Indian scrap. Also they agreed in the contract that if any of them should lose his temper on the trail and kill a companion, that the rest of the crowd would hang him to the first tree they could find. This little clause was calculated to bind these boys together for better or worse. It meant until death do us part.

Goodnight and Loving were partners in this herd, and they agreed that Loving should take a man and go on ahead to Fort Sumner and arrange for selling the herd. So J. W. Wilson, a one-armed man, cool, slow of action, but a buzz saw when he got started with a gun, was selected to accompany Loving. They rode on up the river, and on the second day after they had crossed Blackriver some distance, probably about where Loving, New Mexico, is now, which was said to be several miles west of the river, they saw a band of Indians coming in a hurry from the southwest. I've often wondered what they said to each other. It might have been nothing, but it was more like Wilson to say "Waspnest!" They rode as fast as they could to the river, sliding down a high bank into the mesquite brush and high grass and other growth on the river where they tied the horses and hid in the tall cane breaks or rushes that used to grow on the river in places.

The Indians came helter-skelter down the bank, and took their horses, then began to scream and dance around, looking here and there, but not venturing very far out into the weeds after the Tejanos, for they knew that business would pick up if they ever started anything.

Wilson was an Indian fighter and took command. He placed Loving back in the weeds and then watched himself in front, but Loving failed to hide altogether and was shot in the arm and then in the body. Wilson crawled to him and dragged him away farther back into the weeds out of sight. The sun was still shining and they expected every minute that the Comanches would attack them, but as time rolled on it became dark, and the Indians howled and danced around but did not advance.

Finally Loving told Wilson that he wanted him to try and get back to his family and tell them what had become of him. Wilson protested, and declared that he would not leave him until all was over, but after sometime Loving convinced Wilson that there was no chance for himself and if Wilson would try, he might escape, so without any other words, unless it might have been that Wilson took him by the hand and said, "So long, old boy! If I do not return, the mule is yours!" That was about as soft language as Wilson could utter, and about as sympathetic, for his was a rough and rugged life, and he looked on death as a practical joke, but like all others, just didn't like practical jokes.

He carried a boot full of water to Loving, straightened him around and made him as comfortable as he could under the circumstances, then took his gun, and crawled to the river's brink, took off all his clothes except his underwear and hat, hid them in some brush beside the river, and tried to swim but found that he could not with his gun, with one arm, so he wiggled back to the bank. It was dark now, and he stuck the muzzle of the gun in the sand under the water hidden. He then floated down the river under the tall grass and weeds that hung out over the river's bank so the Indians couldn't see him. After drifting down the river for some time, he finally waded and swam across. By this time the moon was up, and the only thing was to get away as fast as possible, barefooted through thorns and cactus. He traveled all night, all the next day and the next night, until about two o'clock the next day, when he was found by the men that were pointing the herd, standing on a rick close by where there was a small cave. They thought he was an Indian, for his clothing was red from being soaked with the red sand while crossing the Pecos. He was almost starved, sore footed and worn, but he made it and told the story.

After Wilson had refreshed himself, and rested for an hour or so, Goodnight picked several men, left the herd in care of men that he knew would handle it, and proceeded up the river to where Loving had been left by Wilson. It was nearly two days before they arrived, and after searching up and down the river, they finally gave him up and thought that the Indians had scalped him and thrown him in the river.

They didn't look very far up the river as Loving told Wilson that if he left the place where they parted, he would be down the river somewhere.

They returned thinking that Loving was dead, and one day after about two weeks had passed a man by the name of Burleson came along and told them that Loving was at Fort Sumner. On hearing this news Goodnight took two men and started for Fort Sumner, where he found Loving walking around but not doing well, as his arm was bothering him considerable.

The cattle came on, and were sold to the Indian agent there to feed Apaches at a good price except that some of the cattle were too poor to kill, and were started up into Colorado to market, while Goodnight with one or two men stayed at Fort Sumner with Loving, who took blood poisoning in his arm and died. He was buried in the same graveyard that Billy the Kid was planted in some thirteen or fourteen years later.

Loving said that after Wilson left him the Indians whistled, grunted, howled and hooted like owls. It was the most nerve-racking night that he had ever spent, and he thought they had captured Wilson and had killed him. The night wore on and finally day came. After some time, the Indians rounded up their horses, packed and moved on.

He lay there for some time, then sun came out and after he had stood it as long as he could, he dragged himself to the river bank and drank. He was hungry but there was no chance that he knew of to get anything to eat, so he forgot that for the time being, and crawled further up the river, traveled up the valley, keeping under cover as much as possible. He probably traveled over the ground where Carlsbad is now located, and was found five days later beside the old trail in the narrows on the Pecos, probably about where the present cement flume crosses the Pecos above Carlsbad, by a Mexican freighter's outfit, who were coming from some point down the river, possibly San Antonio, on their way to Fort Sumner. When they found him, he was chewing on a bootleg that he had broiled, thinking he might get some relief from hunger in that way. He gave the Mexicans $150.00 in gold to take him to Fort Sumner, where he could get some medical aid.

After they buried Loving at Fort Sumner, Goodnight went up into Colorado, sold the balance of the cattle at Pueblo, returned late in the fall, and preparing a wagon took the body of Loving up and hauled it back to his people at Weatherford, where it was buried.

This was one of the most outstanding true tales of the earliest of the cowmen that took the chance over that Indian-infested and dry, winding trail. Cynthia Parker's story and this, will probably be told in Texas history as long as the San Jacinto episode and the Black Bean will remain in the minds of the people of Texas.

There was an understanding between Loving and Goodnight, that Goodnight should continue the partner business until it showed a profit and provide something for Loving's family, and several herds were driven in the years that followed. Goodnight handed a small fortune to Loving's family one day, and took over the business himself.

He made a contract with John Chisum to deliver cattle above Roswell at $1.00 a head above the purchase price in Texas, thus avoiding the long dangerous drive, which also enabled him to keep in closer touch with the market on cattle.

Our family returned to Texas in 1877, accumulated all the chills and fever there was down there, and returned to New Mexico in 1880. We crossed the Pecos in a wagon bed at Loving crossing; we wrapped wagon sheets around the wagon bed, tied a heavy rope across the river to a mesquite tree on either side, then pulled the wagon box or crude boat across by hand. It took all day to cross the four wagons and their contents. Finally about night, the livestock were driven into the river and swam across. There was no sign of anyone living at Carlsbad at that time; a few settlers had stopped at Seven Rivers. The Jones of Rocky Arroyo lived at Seven Rivers. Also there was an old lady, Mrs. Stafford, mother of Bob Olinger, who was killed by Billy the Kid at Lincoln, when Billy got away. She lived in a half dugout in the south bank of Seven Rivers just above the present crossing on the old road, and there was a small store just south of where Lakewood stands, which was called the Beckwith ranch. The Fannings had just moved in, probably a few other families, but the country was not settled at all.

Roswell had three houses in it. We wandered on up to Las Vegas and after two or three years the family returned to Roswell, and I began my career as a cowboy, working here and there over the state.

The last Indian raids were made in southeastern New Mexico in 1880 by "Victorio" while we were traveling up the Pecos. We always put our wagons at night in a square, and slept inside, just as a precaution against a surprise, but I never saw an Indian fight myself.

If I should be called on to suggest a "pantomime" of the men and women that broke the trails out into the open west, I would draw a picture, suggested by the man that made the talk before the cattlemen of Texas some years ago, and suggested that the monument to old trail drivers should be a herd of cattle being scientifically pointed and driven into a swollen stream. This picture will trail any old-time cowman, for it takes practice to pull a stunt like that and unless a man knows what he is doing, it cannot be done.

I would say, that the picture should have a covered wagon drawn by a yoke of longhorns, a black and a spotted steer. Beside the wagon walking through the sand and cactus, a woman with a Bible under her left arm, and a six-shooter in her right, with a face plainly indicating that she is determined to go on. Just ahead of this woman there should be a boy about ten years old and a girl by his side, of approximately the same age, who were eager in their desire to go ahead. Then looking across the river out in the sand hills and sagebrush, one could see the father, brothers, and sons of this trio, driving back the redman, renegade and lawless element, with buffalo, antelope, deer and wild horses scurrying out of the path that was being cleared for the coming van. And beyond, on the horizon, a halo of light, with the words, distinctly readable, "Chaos is Giving Way to Law."

I wonder if Loving ever had a thought during those trying five days without food, wounded, with no prospects for being found, in a country where everything was against his ever being relieved of his desperate condition, that some day there would be a city built there, where first aid could be found at any door, where hospitals and doctors could have relieved his suffering, where broad fields of every kind of farm products were growing, with tourists coming to this particular spot from all over the world, over ribbons of oiled roads, and where men were flying through the air in air craft that traveled 100 miles an hour. Did he ever dream that there would ever be a city named Loving that would perpetuate his memory for all time? And sometimes I wonder what the wonderful country will be in fifty years hence. With the most wonderful climate on earth, rich soil, with prospects for gathering and storing water, where happy homes can be maintained, with schools equal to any, and the ever-advancing American stride—what will the Pecos Valley and Carlsbad in particular be in 1980?

Someone has said that he wished he could find words to convey to the people of today, the trueness, bravery, loyalty and honor of the old-time cowboys and their families. Words are not suitable, or will not convey any idea of these simple facts. I can only say, that like one who is watching his pal whom he has trusted all along breathe his last breath and depart into that country from whose bourne no traveler returns, they can only be saluted in silence.

COWBOY LORE

"For it's the land of frijoles and sin,
Where men ride fast and ponies are thin."
—From "On the Frisco River" Retold by M. Page

"Once and a half and a half all around. Treat them all
alike as you dance down.
Now rope the cow. Kill the calf. Swing that pretty girl
once and a half."
—From Cowboy Quadrille: "The Sally Goodin"
by James A. Burns

Range Campfire Scene in the Seven Rivers Area, New Mexico,
Unattributed, ca. 1890, NMHM/DCA #132452

The Cowboy with the White Hat

Submitted by Manuel Berg

All ye young ladies wherever you're at
Beware of the cowboy that wears a White Hat,
For today he will woo you and tomorrow will be
In Cheyenne or Denver like an Irishman's flea.
It's first in your parlor this young man will be
And then in Cheyenne this young dandy will see,
In Chicago's Art Gallery you'll find him in scorn,
Put out on the plains his White Hat he adorns,
Now a Lion White hat was not made to be beat,
But a Stetson white hat is this cowboy's conceit
As he sits in his saddle with his most princely air
You'd think his White Hat a most gorgeous affair;
With his great big sombrero with leggin's to match
Now all the young ladies think, "Here's a great catch."
But he dares you to try it
You never can do that;
He's surely no dude 'tho he wears a White Hat.
He reaches heart fate and for future cares not
So beware of the rider that wears a white hat.

From Mrs. J. S. Watson, 120 South Broadway, Albuquerque, New Mex.

This song was mainly sung by the young ladies around the Roswell and Three Rivers section, rather than the cowboys, during the 1890s. (Lion Hat, name of maker similar to Stetson.)

El Ciervo y La Oveja Siende Juez El Lobo

Submitted by Lorin W. Brown

Ante el Lobo una queja
El Ciervo presentó contra la Oveja,
Pretendia sin forma y sin testigo
Que le debia un celemin de trigo.
La Oveja, aunque inocente,
Viende en el tribunal tal Presidente
No contradije el hecho,
Y juzgo el Lobo como en un barbeche;
Se la mande pagar, fíjose el plazo,
Y la pobre salio de este embarazo.
Llegado el dia, ejecútola el Ciervo,
Pero como iba solo,
La respondio la Oveja, "Ve protervo
Que mi promesa la arranco tu fraude
Y del Juez exemigo la presencia,
De que nada te debo, en mi conciencia,
Voy tranquila y segura,
Solo hace ley la fuerza mientras dura."

Contributed by Sr. Pedro Vigil, 77 years of age, of Talpa, New Mexico.

The Sheep and the Deer With the Wolf As Judge

Translated by Lorin W. Brown

Before the Wolf a Sheep was brought
Charged by the deer, so trim and neat,
the evidence scant showed this a plot,
the charge, the accused owed him a peck of wheat,
The Sheep though innocent, tis said,
Looked on the judge with dread
and plead guilty to the charge as read.
The Judge forthwith issued a decree,
The Sheep must pay, he fixed the day,
Having agreed, the Sheep was freed.
The day assigned the deer appeared,
Alone he came, to collect he thought,
No Wolf being near the Sheep did sneer,
"You fraud, You know I nothing owe,
The fear of dire consequence
forced my plea, but now my innocence
Bids me not pay, be on your way;
Only while present does might hold sway."

The Good Samaritan by S. Omar Barker

by Genevieve Chapin

The Bible tells the story of the Good Samaritan
The hymn-books sing of "Bringin' in the Sheaves,"
Us cow-boys ain't religious, but we do the best we can
A-bringin' in of helpless baby beeves.
A late spring blizzard hits the range, an' in some far-off cove,
The cow-land stork, he makes delivery
Of a leggy bovine baby, which, as soon as he's arrove,
Begins to shiver like a shaken tree.
The raw wind whips him, sharp as knives, the cold up-humps his
    back,
He bawls. His ma, she does the best she knows,
But if some circlin' cowboy don't come ridin' on her track
Her little 'un will mighty soon be froze.
You pick th' little feller up. It ain't no easy trick
To hold him, while you mount yer spooky horse,
But yuh got t' git him up there, an' yuh got t' do it quick,
With that ol' cow snortin' round, an' gittin' cross.
Yuh make it to the saddle—an' yer job has jest begun;
You'd think that cow would foller, but she won't!
Now, t' drive a fightin' ma — now maybe sounds t' you like fun—
To us that has to do it, folks, it don't!
But finally, with achin' arms, yuh make it—if yuh can—
To shelter, both with calf an' bawlin' mother.
You've done yer noble durndest! You're a Good Samaritan—
So the Foreman sends yuh out t' git another!

On a ranch, near the little switch of Hudson, lives the writer of the poem,
Miss Sarah D. Ulmer.

Trail Dust by S. Omar Barker

by Genevieve Chapin

Each time has had its heroes—men whose blood ran warm and red,
And some are lusty still today, and some have long been dead.
But whether on the land or sea, in blizzards or in gales,
No braver lads have ever been those who drove the trails—
The trails from Texas to the North, whose hoofmarks now are gone—
With stampede to quell at night, and floods to swim at dawn.
Not days, but months, across lone plains they trailed the herd along,
These saddlemen whose danger-dust uprose mid laugh and song.
Oh, some were killed by rustler's lead, and some the blizzards froze,
And what some faced who did not die, the God of Courage knows!
The tracks of trekking herds, today they are but time-hidden scars,
But Oh, trail-dust has mingled with the timeless dust of stars!

On the Frisco River Retold by M. Page

from New Mexico Federal Writers' Project

The snow clung to the northern slope;
The Frisco coiled like a silver rope;
And hot on the scrub and the cactus gray
The level rays of the March sun lay.

From up the fire of the freighter's camp,
Unquenched by the chill of the valley damp,
The sweet dense smoke of the juniper wood
Rose up like joss to the great god Good.

A bald-faced steer, sides lank and thin,
Looked up from the mesquite with a yellow grin;
While on the arm of a stunted oak
A dingy buzzard the silence broke.

For it's the land of frijoles and sin,
Where men ride fast and ponies are thin.
Yet all who tarry within this land
Are held there tight by an iron hand.

Mañana, they say, they'll hit the trail
That leads from cactus to where the mail
Comes in each day and life throbs hard—
The land of the movies and the playing card.

But still they say while life rolls by,
And on the Frisco they'll surely die;
Their graves are deep 'neath boulders gray,
To keep the roving coyotes at bay.

Cowboy Quadrille: "The Sally Goodin"

Submitted by James A. Burns

Give honor to your pardner. Lady on your left. Join eight hands.
Circle west. Break. Swing on the corner. With your left hand.
Right your pardner.
Right and left grand. Promenade home.
All four gents face your pardner. Jig dance. Swing once more.
Leave her where you found her.
First couple out. Couple on right.
Break and dance the figure eight around that lady. Back and around that
    pretty little taw.
Dance six weeks in Arkansaw. Do Ladys Do Do.
Round eight when you get straight. Swing and promenade home.
Pull off your boots, smell your socks, get your pardner and rattle your
    Hocks.

Second couple out. Couple on your right. Face your pardner. Jig dance.
Swing and promenade home.
Same couple out. Break and swing Sally Goodin. And then your taw.
Then the girl with the lantern jaw. Then Sally Goodin. Then your taw.
    Then promenade with your Grandma.
Ring and twist. Come and go. Catch your pardner by the craw and swing
    her all over Arkansaw. Promenade home.
Rope your filly and watch her grin. Get your pardner and try it again.

Third couple out. Couple on your right. Face your pardner and jig all
    night.
Swing on the corner with your left hand. Right your pardner and right
    and left. Meet your pardner, turn right back you all gone wrong.
Once and a half and a half all around. Treat them all alike as you dance
    down.
Now rope the cow. Kill the calf. Swing that pretty girl once and a half.
And a half all around. Treat them all alike as you dance down. Get your
    pard and promenade around.

Fourth couple out, couple on your right. Break and all swing.

Swing on the corner like swinging on a gate. Ah your pardner. And promenade.

Four little sisters form a ring. Everybody swing a right hand swing.

Corner left. Pardner right. Work right and left. Meet your pardner and swing the Double L swing.

On the next four little sisters form a ring. Everybody swing the right hand swing.

Swing. Corner left. Pardner right. Work right and left.

Ladies to the center, gents take a walk. Skip that pardner.

Swing and leave her where you found her. Ladies to the center and gents take a walk.

Re-skip. Swing and promenade. For your last time.

Thank the ladies and kiss the fiddler.

Source of Information: Doughbelly Price, Eagle Nest, New Mexico.

Letter to James A. Burns, Accompanying the Cowboy Quadrille Calls by Doughbelly Price

from New Mexico Federal Writers' Project

In regards to the old time cowboy dances that has been danced in this country and in fact all the western countries there is some confusion.

It may seem silly to some of the up date boys and girls that the dance now days that the old timers did not know how to dance. But that is not the case at all.

The old time dance of Sally Goodin was one of the most difficult to dance as it took one ear listening to the caller. And the other one to get your mind made up as to what he was going to say next.

There was no Belly rubbing in those days. As is the case now that is all the dances consist of now. Is to see how close you can hold the girls.

You go to a dance now and you will not see no two dancing alike. Some doing the flea hop. Another doing the broken ankle. And still another couple not doing nothing but walking and giggling. And maybe too drunk to do that.

Then you went on to the dance floor to dance one of the old timers dance it give you a work out. In fact the name was mostly a kitchen sweat.

No symphony orchestra. (I think that is right.) Nothing but a fiddle. (No violins them days) and maybe a guitar. And caller. And you done what he said. Or you got the whole herd tangled up. And then some one would lay your ear down on your shoulder. And don't think that it was all drunkenness. If you had whiskey on your breath you might get turned down for a partner.

But back to the calling of the old time dances. I must say it is hard to put it down on paper. As the voice had to be raised and lowered to suit the music. And also had to be called to the music.

It was just as essential that a caller could call that way as it was to call. Not just sing it off. That was no good. But you had to call in time.

And all that comedy just had to come when they was swinging. And that was put in right on the dot.

There was plenty of men that knew what to say. But how to say them. And get them on time and get them right. Was another matter. And a good caller was in demand almost as a good fiddler. Almost the same comparison to some songs that you hear over the radio now and some of them squealing fillies that you hear.

Source of Information: Doughbelly Price.

At the Cowboy Dance Tonight a la Bill Knox

Submitted by Edith L. Crawford

Git yo' little sage hens ready; Trot 'em out upon the floor.
Line up there, you cusses! Steady! Lively now. One couple more.
Shorty, shed that Ol' sombrero! Broncho, douse that cigarette!
Stop your cussin', Casinero, Fore the ladies! Now all set!
S'lute yer ladies; all together! Ladies opposite the same;
Hit the lumber with your leather! Balance all, and swing your dame!
Bunch the heifers in the middle! Circle stags, an' do—ce—do—.
Pay attention to the fiddle! Swing her 'round an' off you go!
First four forward! Back to places! Second follow! Shuffle back!
Now you've got it down to cases! Swing 'em till their trotters crack!
Gents all right a heel an' toein'! Swing 'em, kiss 'em if you kin!
On to the next an' keep a—goin'! Till yo' hit yer pards again!
Gents to center; ladies 'round 'em! 'Round the circle double quick!
Grab an' kiss 'em while you've got them. Hold 'em to it if they kick!
Ladies, left hand to yer sonnies! Alaman' Grand right and left!
Balance all an' swing yer honey. Pick 'em up an' feel their heft!
Promenade like skeery cattle! Balance all, an' swing yer sweets!
Shake yer spurs an' make 'em rattle! Keno! Promenade to seats.

Retold from the *Capitan Progress*, Published at Capitan, New Mexico.

Cowboy Dances

Submitted by Edith L. Crawford

Miss Ward in the January Pearson's gives the following amusing description of her first Western dance.

"It was with many misgivings, in spite of my partner's assurance that he would pull me through, I took my place in the dance.

"'Honor your partners. Rights the same," So far I bowed as did they.

"'Balance you all,' With a plunge like a maddened steer, my pardner came toward me. I smothered a scream as I was seized and swung around like a bag of meal. Before I got my breath I was pushed out in answer to:

"'First lady out the right; Swing the man who stole the sheep, Now the one that hauled it home, Now the one that eat the meat, and now the one that gnawed the bone.'

"'Not being well acquainted with the private histories of the men in the set was a little disadvantage, but I was seized, swung, and passed on to the next until I finally arrived breathless at the starting point.

"'First gent swing your opposite pardner, Then your turtle dove, Again your opposite pardner, And now your own true love.'

"'I blushed in spite of myself as such public posing as my pardner's 'turtle dove' and 'own true love,' while his sweetheart over in the corner, transfixing me with a jealous glare, saw no humor in the situation.

"'Again the command: 'First couple out to the right, Cage the bird, Three hands round.' I found myself in the center of a circle former by my partner and the second couple, and then exchanged places with my pardner at the call:

"'Birdie, hop out and crow hop in, three hands around go it again. Allemane left, back to your pardner and grand right and left.

"'Come to your pardner once and a half, Yellow hammer right and jaybird left. Meet your pardner and all chaw hay, You know where and I don't care. Seat your pardner in the old arm chair.'

"By this time, feeling quite bruised and battered, I was ready for most any kind of a chair."

Retold from *Capitan Progress*, Published at Capitan, New Mexico.

A Cowboy Ball

Submitted by Frances Totty

Caller let no echo slumber
Fiddler sweatin' like a steer;
Hoof a poundin' at the lumber
Makin' noise the stars could hear.
Hug the gals up when we swing them
Raise 'em plum off their feet.
Balance all, ye saddle warmers!
Rag a little! Shake your feet!
On to next one, and repeat!
Balance to the next in waitin'
Promenade an' off you go!
Seat your pards and let 'em blow.

COWBOY TERMS

Basic Characters Used In Brands and Descriptive Terms Applied to Them.

Symbol	Term	Symbol	Term
—	Rail	O O	Double "O"
=	Two Rails	X	Walking X
≡	Stripes	H	Flying H
▭	Box	⌐	Lazy Seven
/	Slash	P	Tilted P
\	Slash	Q	Drag Nine
O	Circle Ring or Zero	A	A
⬭	Goose Egg	∧	Open A
⌒	Half Circle	A	Walking A
)	Quarter Circle	Ā	Flying A
#	Pig Pen	◇	Diamond
⊓	Bench	▷	Triangle
⊐	Half Box	∧	Rafter
∞	Two Links	⌣	Rocker

From the book, Hot Irons, by Oren Arnold and John P. Hale. The Mac-
Millan Company; New York, 1930.

**Glossary of Branding Terms, "Hot Irons," Oren Arnold and John P. Hale,
The MacMillan Company, New York, 1930 NMSRCA, NMFWP, WPA #161**

Contributions to the Language from the Spanish and Cowboy Slang

from New Mexico Federal Writers' Project

bronco: wild

caboodle: lot, aggregation

cienega: marsh

Chaparro: brush

crow bait: poor decrepit animal

cut for sale: examine the ground for signs—as tracks and droppings

dally: to wrap a rope around a saddle horn

dinero: money

duffle: personal effects

fandango: any dance or gay party

firewater: whiskey

frijoles: dried Mexican beans

grubstakes: provisions

hacienda: ranch

hear the owl hoot: have many and varied experiences

high lonesome: a big drunk

hombre: man

like the devil beating tanbark: fast and furious

llano: prairie or flat open plain

lobo: loafer wolf

mañana: tomorrow

marihuano: a narcotic

mesa: a flat topped hill

mescal: a drink made from mescal plant

mustang: a wild horse

olla: pot or jar

palo: tree

pastor: shepherd

peon: Mexican laborer

pinon: dwarf pines

Pinto: spotted horse or spotted bean

poor doe: lean tough venison; poor food

Pronto: quickly

Reach: to make a motion to draw a pistol

re: a cowboy who represents his brand at outside ranches

reata: rope

remuda: a bunch of saddle horses

rib-up: persuade

rustle: to steal

serape: a shawl

siesta: afternoon nap

sow bosom: salt pork

stamping ground: home range

swing a wide loop: lead a free life

tarantula juice: whiskey

vaquero: cowboy

vega: meadow, or stretch of flat country

war bag: sack or bag for personal belongings

wrangle: to herd horses

Cowland Glossary

from New Mexico Federal Writers' Project

Adios (ah-d'yóhs): Goodbye

Álamo (áh-le-mo): Cottonwood tree

Álamo Springs: Cottonwood Springs

Bedroll: Canvas-wrapped roll containing cowboy's bed clothes

Berrendo (ber-én-do): Antelope

Big loop: Lasso of a cattle thief

Bog his head: Said of a bucking horse which succeeds in getting his head down between his forelegs, allowing for more forceful bucking

Brand: Identifying sign burned on stock—sign of ownership

Brand artist: One who illegally alters a brand

Brand blotter: *See brand artist*

Bronco, bronc: Untamed or wild and unruly horse; not broken to saddle or harness; from the Span.: *bronco* (rough, ride)

Bronco peeler: Bronc buster

Buckboard: Four wheeled driving vehicle typical of the West

Bueno (buéh-no): All right; good

Bunk: Crude bed in cowboy's sleeping quarters

Bunk house: Building assigned to the cowboys for sleeping quarters

Burro: Donkey, original Spanish

Cabalgata (cab-bal-gáh-tah): Cavalcade

Cascabel (kas-kah-bel): A jingle or rattle

Chamiso (cha-mé-so): A desert shrub in New Mexico

Chaps: leather overalls or pants, protection from thorns, brush or the elements — from Span.: *chaparajos*

Chili (ché-le): hot green peppers

Choke the biscuit: Convulsive grip on saddle horn to avoid being thrown

Cholla (chó-ya): A kind of cactus

Chuck: Food

Chuck liner: To ride from ranch to ranch obtaining food in that manner

Chuck wagon: Kitchen on wheels; source of meals for cowboys when away from the home ranch

Cinchas: Strap which secures saddle to horse's back — from Span.: *cincha*

Conchas (kón-chas): Shells; a kind of ornament

Corral: Enclosure for stock —original Spanish

Corrida (cor-ré-dah): A race; a game

Cowboy's gait: Jog trot

Cow hand: Cowboy

Cowpuncher: *See cowhand*

Cowpunching: Taking care of cattle

Crop: Distinctive mark on a cattle's ear

Cussie (cus-se): Cook. From Span.: *cocinero*

Cut herd: To separate cattle, into groups or individual members

Cutting horse: Horse with particular aptness for separating individual animals from the herd

Dab it on: To make a cast with a lasso

Dale-gueltas (dah-lay-wél-tahs): Wrap rope on saddle horn

Dallie: *See dale-vueltas*

Diamond hitch: Knot used in securing packs on pack animals

Die-up: Wide spread death of cattle due to drought, a blizzard, etc.

Dogies (dóh-ghees, not dogees): Motherless calves

Drift: Concerted movement of stock on one direction

Dude: Eastern guest in the cattle country; usually a paying guest

Fan: While riding to strike bucking horses with hat

Fox-fire: static electricity that plays on the horns of cattle in an electrical storm

Gallery: Porch on ranch house

Gathering: A collection of cattle driven in from various parts of the range

Gift of gab: Loquacity

Gila (hé-la): A river in New Mexico

Go-easter: traveling bag

Grab leather: *See choke the biscuit*

Grama grass: wild grass; winter feed for grazing cattle

Hacienda (ah-see-én-dah): estate

Hackamore: A type of halter used in breaking horses; from Span.: *jáquima*

Haze: Ride close to an animal to steer it in the desired direction

High tail it: To depart in great haste

Hogging string: Short rope used to tie an animal's legs for branding, marking, etc.

Hombre (óm-breh): man

Honda (ón-dah): ring in a lariat

Hull: Slang for saddle

Iron: Implement used in affixing brand

Jáquima (há-ke-mah): Hackamore; a kind of halter

Javelinas (ha-va-lé-nahs): Wild cattle

Josh: To kid; make sport of

Las Brujas (las broó-has): The witches

Latch spring: Thong or string manipulating lock on door

Látigo (lá-te-go): Cinch strap

Lean in the collar: To put forth utmost effort

Line-back: Stock marked with distinctive dark line along back

Line camp: Camp established on the far boundaries of a ranch

Lobo (ló-bo): Wolf

Loco (ló-co): Crazy

Long-ropes: *See rustler*

Lope: Gait of a horse, short for gallop

Lose his head: *See bog his head*

Luminarias (loo-me-ná-re-ahs): Small bonfires

Maguey (Eng. Pron. mág-way): A desert plant

Maleta (ma-léh-tah): Saddle bag

Medicine talk: Deep discussion of ways and means

Mesa: (máy-sah): Tableland

Mesquite (usually pron. mes-keét): Shrub-like sagebrush

Milagro (me-láh-gro): miracle; wonder

Mill the herd: Induce circling motion to a herd of cattle

Morral (mor-rál): Nosebag; knapsack

Mott (motte): Clump of trees

Navaho: Southwestern tribe of Indians

Ojo del Indio (o-ho del Eén-de-o): Indian Spring

Ojo Sarco (o-ho sár-co): spring of two colors of water

On the prod: Angry enough to fight, looking for trouble

On your own: To be completely dependent on one's own efforts

Outfit: That which comprises a ranch and all that pertains to it

Outlaw: Wild horse or cow which uses every wile to remain free

Pack horse: Horse used for transporting supplies or camp equipment

Pack outfit: A train of pack horses and attendants

Palomino (pah-lo-mé-no): cream colored horse

Peón (peh-ón): laborer

Piled: To be thrown from a horse

Pilgrim: Newcomer to the West

Pinto (peén-toh): spotted, piebald

Playa (pláh-ya): sandy shore or beach

Pronto (prón-toh): Quick; right away

Puncher: *See cowpuncher*

Quirt: Short braided, leather whip used by horsemen, from Span.: *cuarta*

Ready-made: City bred

Remuda (re-moó-dah): Replacement horses

Rep: Agent for a ranch

Rincón (ren-kón): Corner

Roundup: Gathering of cattle from the range

Rustler: Individual with a penchant for other people's cattle

Sabe (sáh-be): To know or understand (slang)

Scalawag: Elusive steer

Shake hands with grandma: *See choke the biscuit*

Shaky horses: Wily, elusive and extremely tricky

Sidekick: Pal, comrade

Sierra Madre (se-er-ah má-dre): Mother Range

Siesta (se-és-ta): Afternoon nap

Sinkers: Biscuits

Sleepers: Calves secretly ear-marked by a would-be thief to forestall branding by rightful owner

Slow elk: Beef from steer belonging to someone else

Snake blood: Potential killer, said to have snake blood

Snubbing post: Firmly embedded post for securing lassoed stock

Soto (sotol) (so-toh): A yucca-like plant

Spin yarns: To indulge in narration truthful or otherwise

Spooky: ready to pitch, buck or run away on slightest provocation

Sugan quilt (soo-gan): Coarse blanket used by cowpunchers and sheepherders

Take a *pasear* (pah-see-yár): Short jaunt; aimless walk or ride

Tally: Count of livestock

Tarp: Short for tarpaulin

Tools: Eating implements, knife, fork and spoon

Top hand: First-rate cowboy and range hand

Trail along: To follow mother's guide or plans

Trail herd: Cattle driven from range to market

Turkshead: Turban-like knot used to secure loose ends of lasso

Uncock: Rid a horse of high spirits before settling down to day's work

Vámanos (váh-mo-nos): Let's go

Vaquero (vah-caré-o): Span.: for cowboy

Waddie: Cowboy

War bag: Buckskin bag or pouch containing cowboy's personal belongings

Waterings: Wells, springs or rivers where stock find water

Wrangler: Hand entrusted with care of horse herd, from Span.: *caballarango*

Glossary of Cowboy Terms Used in New Mexico (Condensed)

Compiled by T. F. Bledsoe
from New Mexico Federal Writers' Project
(Condensed by Ina Sizer Cassidy; Checked by Alice Corbin, Editor)

-A-

act up: To make trouble; to be presumptuous or forward

-B-

bad medicine: Anything deleterious

bad men: Men who put no value on human life, and who would kill at the slightest provocation

beef: To complain unnecessarily, or continually

bite the dust: To die

blab: To muzzle a calf in forcing him to become weaned. To tattle

blind trail: An indistinct trace left on trail by man or animal

blinkers: Eyes

blocker: A big loop

blow: To spend

bog down: To mire

bolt: To swallow whole. To run away

box canons, or canyons: Canons, or gorges with but one open end

brand: Registered mark of owner on livestock

bronc, bronco: An untamed horse

bronco-buster: A rider of broncos; a wild horse breaker. Also termed bronc-heeler, bronc-twister

broom tails, broomies: Range mares

buckaroo: Der. fr. Sp. *vaquero*, a cowboy

bucking strap: A loop on the saddle offering a convenient hand-hold during pitching

buffaloed: Frightened, confused

bulldogging: Method of throwing a steer, or cow by jumping from a horse's back, grabbing the horns and twisting the animal's neck

bunk: To sleep

busted, broke, gentled: Describing a wild horse that has been broken or tamed

-C-

center-fire: Saddle with one cinch

chaps: Short for *chaparejos*, leather trousers with the seat and crotch cut out

chuck: Food; daily ration

chuck-liners: A tolerated imposter and tramp who receives his food by following chuck wagons chuck wagon: The wagon used on a round-up to carry the food and cooking supplies; also hauled the punchers' bed rolls

chute (Fr. orig.): A narrow enclosure for driving livestock single file into cattle pens, or cattle cars, or for branding, de-horning, dipping, etc.

clean straw: Fresh bedsheets

clothes-line: Lasso; lariat; rope

cow-puncher (See puncher)

creasing: Shooting of a horse through top of the neck and touching but not injuring the cartilage, thus temporarily and completely stunning it

crinolina: Hoop-skirt. Circular spinning of a rope

cross-buck saddle: Usually contracted into "cross-buck." Type of pack-saddle

crossed the divide: Died

crow hop: To jump about with arched back and stiffened knees

cuff: To groom

cut: Cattle purposely separated from the main herd. Used also for sheep that have strayed from the main flock

cut loose: To abandon restraints; have a good time

cutting out: Segregating animals from the herd

-D-

dale vuelta: Fr. Sp. *dar la vuelta*, to give a turn or twist. Often used by cowboys when ordering someone to wrap a lasso around the horn of a saddle, a post, etc. From a command it has been adapted to a noun phrase, "he gave it a dally vuelta," "he took a dally."

dogie: A motherless calf, especially one that has lost its mother before being weaned, and has to subsist on what grass or weeds it can pick up

double-rigged, double rig: Saddle with two cinches

drift, drifting, drifted: General movement, or drift of cattle from one place to another for feed or water

dude-wrangler: Derisively applied by cowboys to a cowboy who "wrangles" guests at a dude ranch

dumped: Thrown, or bucked off a horse

-F-

fan it: To go quickly

fanning a horse: Slapping a horse with a sombrero to make him buck harder

faze: To influence; to have effect upon

file notches: To cut small notches (usually in the butt of a revolver)

first rattle out of the box: Meaning prompt action

flash: To produce suddenly; to exhibit; said of a concealed pistol suddenly produced, or a money roll

flea-bitten: Light colored horse with little specks of red or black showing in his coat

fly-by-night: A thief; dishonest, fraudulent

fool hen: Sage hen

forking: Mounting a horse

fouled: A trail trodden upon by an animal or person, and blotted out

fresh sign: recent marking, creating a "hot," or "fresh" trail

ganted: Gaunt

ganted up: Said of a horse after a hard ride without water; also applied to a cowboy when on short rations

gentling: Breaking a horse

getting the drop, pulling down: Getting the first aim, or shot at another person

gimlet: To cause saddle sores on a horse by heavy riding. Small, boring

go heeled: Armed

good medicine: Anything beneficial

Great Divide, the: Death

grub: Food

grub pi-i-ile; come and get it; fly at it; take it away: Call to meals

grub-stake: A sum of money or supplies advanced for an enterprise; i.e., for a share in the profits

gun, six-gun, six-shooter: terms for the revolver

hackamore: Der. fr. Sp. *jaquima*, halter

hand: Cowboy, ranch worker

head off: To turn a herd, or animal to stop it from going in the wrong direction

he country in pants: The range country

heifer-branded: A handkerchief tied on the arm of a man at a dance who volunteered to "dance lady fashion."

hell for leather: Rapidly

hen fruit: Eggs

his tail up: A horse anxious to go

hit the hay: To go to bed

hit the trail: Take to the road, or trail

hitch: Mistake

hog-tied: The legs, usually two hind and one front, of livestock fastened together after having been thrown by roping, tailing, or bulldogging

hoosegow: Der. fr. Sp. *juzgado*, jail, prison

horse-wrangler: Der. fr. Mex.-Sp. *caballerango*, one who watches over the *remuda* of horses and "wranglers," i.e. tends and gathers them for use

how: Greeting

howdedo: Commotion; exchange of pleasantries

hunt leather, pull leather, grab leather: To hold onto saddle horn, or straps when a horse bucks

it's high, low, jack and the game: From seven-up: an exclamation announcing successful accomplishment of any task jags: Sprees

jamboree: A dancing party; a drunken debauch; an active event such as a stampede, or pistol fight

jimcracks: Playthings; luxuries

-K-

keep cases: From faro; watch another person

-L-

lid: Hat; sombrero

light (alight): stranger; light: Invitation to dismount

lingo: Language; dialect

lit up: Drunk

locoed: Crazed; excited

lousy: Abounding, plentiful

-M-

make tracks: Start, leave

makin's: Cigarette papers and a bag of tobacco

man-killer: An insane or smart horse that plans and tries to kill men

maverick, sleeper: An unbranded animal

milling: Cattle moving in a circle

moocher: A sponger

mount: A group of saddle horses used by a cowboy for round-ups or trail work

mula blanca: (Sp. white mule), Illicit whiskey

mustangers: Those who capture mustangs

-N-

naturalize: To kill

neck-tie parties: Hangings

nester: A small farmer who came into the cattle country and fenced off a portion of the range for farming

norther: A tempest or northern blizzard; expression of Texas and eastern New Mexico

-O-

old sign: Old marking creating a "cold trail"

on the hoof: On foot

on the point: In position at the lead to direct cattle

on the prod: Angry; ready to fight

open range: Grazing lands open to anyone: unfenced

outlaw: A horse spoiled in breaking, or untameably wild

overplay his head: To show poor judgment

-P-

paint horse: A piebald, or mottled horse

pards: Partners

passed out, snuffed out, cashed in, passed: Died

paunch-ed-ing: To fuss around angrily or grumblingly

pitch in: To begin

pitching (See BUCK)

plain trail: Clearly visible sign (See SIGN)

plumb crazy: Entirely crazy

plumb petered out: Tired, exhausted

plunder: Cowboy's personal belongings other than the clothes he has on

pot: A shot from behind cover

pounding his ear: Sleeping

powwow: Indian consultation

prodding: Hurrying stock along

pull down: To level one's gun

puncher, or cow puncher: Der. fr. use of a metal-tipped prod for "punching" cows into chutes when loading them into cattle cars, and keeping them from jamming while in the cars

pull leather (See HUNT LEATHER)

pulled it off: Referring to the successful accomplishment of any task; also to a robbery

put his lights out: To kill him

put up a fight: To fight

-Q-

quirt: A flexible, woven leather whip

-R-

raking: To rowel a horse on the shoulder to make him buck harder

ranch-jumping: To file claim on a piece of uncoupled land, get control of the water, and then offer the property for sale at an enormous price

range country: The west where the cattle industry was paramount

range-raised: Horses bred and raised on the range

rattled: Crazy; excitedly confused

red eye: Whiskey

red-handed: Caught in the act of stealing, or with any incriminating evidence

renegades: Bad men; usually thieves in the cow country

ride heavy: To ride in such a way as to tire the mount, and cause saddle sores

ride him: To annoy, torment, tease

ride slick: To ride without securing a handhold on any part of the saddle

ride the chuckline: To follow from one chuck wagon to another

road agent: Stage robbers

road brand: A brand put on an animal about to be started on a long drive

rode to a finish: Said of a horse when ridden to exhaustion

rodeo: An exhibition of riding, roping, etc.

romp: To jump around; said of a bronco let loose to run around in the corral when first saddled

rope a heifer for life: To marry

rough-rider: A cowboy who can ride all types of horses

round-up: Gathering cattle, or horses on the range; held regularly in the spring, and again in either the late summer or early fall

round-up horse: Person in charge of the round-up

rukus: Noise; movement

rustle: To gather in; also to steal livestock; used also for the legitimate gathering or getting ready for things, as in the phrase, rustle the grub

rustlers: Cattle, or horse thieves

-S-

sashayed into (See CHASED INTO)

shinnery: Scrub oak

shod all around: Horses shod on each of their four feet

shooting up a town: Cowboys firing their revolvers freely, and with abandon after taking possession of a town while on a spree

show daylight: Space visible between man and saddle when a horse bucks

show the white feather: To become frightened and turn traitor

shove: To move a herd on a trail, or to another part of the range

shuck off: To remove; take off

single-rigged: Saddle with one cinch

skeered: Scared

skin one's self: to remove one's weapon

sky pilot: Preacher, minister

slam up: Excellent

slick car: Live stock with ears not cropped (See CROPPED)

slumgullion: A stew of meat and vegetables, like an Irish stew

snake: To drag by a rope from the saddle horn

snub: To tie up short to a post

snuff out: To kill

son of a gun: A stew made of heart, kidneys, and liver; the standard dish at a round-up

spilling: Throwing an animal in lassoing him; also, a bucking horse spills its rider when bucking him off

spilling the beans: revealing secret, or confidential information

spin, flip: presenting the revolver upside down with handle extended towards the other person

squatter: A person who moves onto private land owned in fee, in an attempt to acquire title by adverse possession

squaw hitch: A noose for lashing a pack singlehanded

squaw man: A white man married to an Indian

stake: Supplies, land, or capital furnished for ranching, prospecting, etc.

stampede: A wild rush of cattle, or horses due to fright

stock: Livestock

straight: Whiskey taken without diluting

straw: Bed

strays: Livestock belonging to a distant range

sulled: Sulked

summer range: The summer range for livestock is upon the higher benches, or on the upper levels of the hills

swing a wide loop: To tell a big tale

-T-

tailing: Pulling by the tail, employed in throwing or lifting fallen cattle

taps: Der. fr. Mex.-Sp. *tapaderas*, stirrup coverings

tarpoleon (tarpaulin), tarp: All canvases not specifically called either pack covers, or wagon sheets

tear: A spree

tenderfoot: A newcomer to the West

Texas long-horn: A breed of Texas cattle with long horns; often applied to Texas frontiersmen

three sheets to the wind: In a drunken state

throw: The act of wielding the lasso to catch an animal

throwing the bull: Telling exaggerated, or untrue stories

thumbing: Jabbing a horse's neck with the thumb to make him buck

to pecos: To shoot a man, and roll his body into the Pecos River

top hand: A first class cowboy

top horse: A first class horse

top rider: Best bronco-rider of an outfit

trail: To track; to keep on the tracks of an animal

trail boss: A foreman in charge of a herd that is being taken up the trail either to graze or to market

trail broken: Accustomed to the trail

trail herd: A herd of cattle that is to be taken by trail to market, or to a distant range

trail steer: Generally a steer that leads on a trail

-U-

Uncle Sam's children: Indians

-V-

vamoose the ranch, pull your freight, git: Commands to leave, get out

varmints: Any small obnoxious wild animal

-W-

waddy: A cow puncher

waltz into: To happen upon; to go. Also, to fight, or quarrel with another

war-paint: Full dress

war sacks: A sack that serves as the cowboy's traveling bag

wet: Stock stolen in Mexico, and smuggled across the Rio Grande, or vice versa

whoop: The characteristic yell of the cowboy; also to keep the cattle moving to avoid stampedes

wild and wooly: A typical bad man

winter: To keep cattle through the winter months

wolfer: A professional killer of wolves

woollies: Sheep

worked: Having cut animals out of a herd for branding, shipping, etc.

wouser: A mythical animal known to cowboy storytellers

wrangle (See HORSE WRANGLER)

wrangler (See HORSE WRANGLER)

wring: To twist an animal's tail

-Y-

young stuff: Young stock

Abbreviations Used

der.	derivation, derived
fr.	from
Mex.	Mexican
orig.	origin
Sp.	Spanish

Source of Information: Adams-Jenkins, Thelma, A Study of Cowboy Diction with a Glossary of Terms, a Thesis submitted for the Degree of Master of Arts in English, University of New Mexico, 1931; Rollins, Philip Ashton, The Cowboy, His Characteristics, His Equipment, and His Part in the Development of the West, Charles Scribner's Sons, New York; Thorp, N. Howard (Jack) Songs of the Cowboys, Boston and New York, Houghton, Mifflin Company, The Riverside Press, Cambridge, 1908 and 1921; Thorp, N. Howard (Jack), Mss. on Dogies; Personal knowledge of Ina Sizer Cassidy; Personal knowledge of Mrs. Alice Corbin Henderson; Webster's New International Dictionary, Second Edition, Unabridged, C. & C. Merriam Company, Springfield, Mass.; Funk & Wagnalls New Standard Dictionary of the English Language, Funk & Wagnalls Company, New York and London, 1913; Appleton's New English-Spanish and Spanish-English Dictionary, by Arturo Cuyas, Revised and Enlarged by Antonio Llano, D. Appleton-Century Company, New York, London, 1936; Introductory Essay: Contributions to Language, University of New Mexico, Albuquerque, Submitted by: Robert Young, Rewritten by: Tom Kromer.

Glossary of Range Terms

from New Mexico Federal Writers' Project

ALFORJA: saddle bag

ARROYO: watercourse or ravine; usually dry except after rains

APARETO: pack saddle and equipment

AUGUR: an argumentative discussion

BACK DOWN: to withdraw or retract

BEAT AROUND THE BUSH: to evade the issue

BED DOWN: to lie down for the night; said of a herd of cattle

BED GROUND: spot where a trail herd lies down for the night

BED ROLL: canvas-wrapped roll containing cowboy's bed clothes

BIG LOOP: lasso of a cattle thief

BLAB: a small thin board affixed to a calf's nose for the purpose of weaning it

BLAZE-FACED: an animal having a white face

BOG HIS HEAD: said of a bucking horse which succeeds in getting his head down between his forelegs, which allows more forceful bucking

BOOTHILL: a kind of burial ground; its inmates were flung into a grave with their boots on

BOX: the square enclosing a brand

BOX CANYON: a canyon with only one entrance

BOXSTALL: headstall, from the Spanish *bosal*

BRAND-BLOTTER: one who illegally alters a brand

BRANDING IRON: instrument for burning identifying marks (brands) into an animal's hide

BREAKS: many small rough canyons

BRONCO, BRONCHO: untamed or wild, unruly horse; not broken to saddle or harness; from the Spanish *bronco*, rough, rude

BRONCHO BUSTER: See buckaroo

BRONCHO PEELER See buckaroo

BRONCO TWISTER See buckaroo

BROOMIES, BROOMTAILS: wild range horses

BUCKAROO: cowboy, range hand; corruption of Spanish *vaquero* for cowboy

BUFFALO: to overawe, to bewilder

BUFFALOED: mental confusion; from the frantic circular movement of these animals when frightened or excited

BULLDOGGING: to throw a steer by seizing its horns and twisting its neck

CACHE: a hidden store of supplies or valuables

CALIFORNIA-RIG, CENTER-FIRE, CENTER-RIG: terms for a saddle equipped with only one cinch

CALL HIS JAWBONE: live on credit

CASH IN: to profit in a deal or transaction; to convert into cash

CASH IN CHIPS: to die

CAVVYYARD, CAVVY, CAYUSE: bunch of saddle horses for the use of the cowboys; from Spanish *caballada*

CHAPARRAL: dense, thorny brush

CHAPS: leather overalls or semi-pants worn for protection from thorns, brush, and the elements; from the Spanish *chaparajos*.

CHOKE THE BISCUIT: convulsive grip on the saddle horn to avoid being thrown

CHOUSE: to hurry cattle or horses

CHUCK: food

CHUCK WAGON: kitchen on wheels; source of meals for the cowboys when away from the horse ranch

CINCH: saddle which secures saddle to horse's back; from the Spanish *cincha*

COMB: to search a certain locality thoroughly for cattle hiding in the brush

CONCHAS: metal adornments, usually of silver, flat or concave in shape; used on saddle, bridles, belts and spurs

COOKEY: range land cook

COPPER: to meet strategy with strategy

CORRAL: enclosure for penning stock; built of poles or boards

COW POKE: cowboy

COW PUNCHER: cowboy

COWS: in the vernacular of the West, means mixed cattle, both male and female

COWWADDY: cowboy

CREASE: temporary stunning of wild horses to facilitate capture by shooting them at just the right spot on the neck to produce the desired result

CROSS THE DIVIDE: to die

CUTTING PONY: a mount with particular aptness for separating individual animals from the herd

CUT TRAIL: stringing out of a trail held for inspection by trail cutter

DALED, DALE VUELTED, DALLIED: to give a turn of the lariat on the saddle horn to secure it after a successful throw; from the Spanish *dar la vuelta*

DIAMOND HITCH: a diamond-shaped knot used in securing packs on pack animals

DOBE DOLLAR: Mexican dollars (pesos)

DOGIE: motherless calf; derived from Spanish *dogal*, to tie by the neck

DOHUNNY: objects, small in size, novel in construction, of no particular use

DOUBLE-BARRELED, DOUBLE-FIRE, DOUBLE-RIG, DOUBLE-RIGGED: terms for saddle equipped with two cinches

DRAG: the last and slowest animals of a trail herd

DRAW: act of drawing six-shooter for use

DRIFT: the concerted movement of cattle in one direction ahead of a storm or in search of food or water

DRIFT FENCE: fence erected to keep cattle from drifting

DUST A COW: throw a handful of dust into a charging cow's eyes to avoid being gored

DUST THE TRAIL: to travel a trail

EAR-MARK: to cut ears of cattle for identification

EATING TOOLS: knife, fork and spoon

FALL ROUND-UP: for the purpose of "cutting out" (separating from the herd) cattle for the market; also "beef round-up"

FANDANGO: a dance (original Spanish)

FANNING: rapid firing system of shooting a six-shooter

FAT IN THE FIRE: irretrievable blunder

FEEL LIKE CHAWIN': trailmen's term for hunger

FELTED: See dallied

FLAME THROWER: cowboy term for gun or six-shooter

FLASH RIDER: one who gentles unbroken horse for so much a head

FORK: to ride a horse

FREEZE ONTO IT: to hold fast

FUZZIES: wild range horses

GET DOWN TO CASES: to get to the essentials of a matter

GHOST CORD: an illicit attachment used by the unethical with the *jáquima*

GIFT OF GAB: loquacity, a good talker

GO TO THE BRIDGE WITH: a trustworthy friend

GOT: to succeed in killing your adversary in a gunfight

GRAB LEATHER: to hold onto any part of the saddle while riding a pitching horse

GREASER: term of contempt for Mexicans

GRINGO: term of contempt for those, with exception of Indians, who did not speak Spanish

GRUBSTAKE: food and supplies furnished a prospector for an interest in any mineral discovery

HACKAMORE: a halter with loop over horse's nose; used in breaking horses; from Spanish *jáquima*

HAIR-BRANDING: temporary brand made by burning the hair only; often called "road brand,"
it is applied when cattle are to be driven some distance and then sold

HAIRPIN: to ride a horse, more specifically, a bucking bronco

HAIR-TRIGGER: a gun trigger made extremely sensitive by filing, altering the spring, etc.; hasty-tempered

HALF-BREED BIT: type of bridle bit

HATRACK: an exceedingly bony animal of the bovine species

HAZE: to steer an animal in the desired direction by riding close to it

HAZER: a cowboy who assists in breaking a horse

HEAP: a large number, a great many

HEELING: roping a calf by the hind legs

HE'S SOLD HIS SADDLE: one who is financially or morally insolvent

HIGH-TAIL IT: to hurry, to cover ground quickly

HONDA: small loop at the end of lasso used to form the necessary noose

HOORAW: derision

HORNING IN: to interfere in matters that do not concern one

HORSE SENSE: instinctive practical common sense

HULL: cowboy term for saddle

HUMP YOURSELF: to make haste, work diligently

HUNG UP: to be thrown from a horse and catch a foot in the stirrups

HUNKY-DORY: quite to one's content; comfortable, pleasant

HUSTLE: to proceed or carry out some duty or errand with dispatch

HYMN: song sung to cattle, however racy or blasphemous, for its quieting effect

INJUN BROKE HORSE: a horse broken for mounting on either side

JAMBOREE: any exciting event

JÁQUIMA: See hackamore

JAWBONE: credit

JERKY: sun-dried meat

JUMP: to come up on someone suddenly; to flush

JUMP A LOT OF DUST: a big round-up; great haste

KACK: cowboy term for saddle

KAYAKS: pack-saddle bags

KEEP CASES ON: to observe another's actions and analyze them

LARIAT: lasso

LASSO: a rope used to catch stock; made of buffalo hide or rawhide in early days; now commonly of hemp forty to seventy feet in length; Spanish *lazo*

LATIGO: cinch strap (original Spanish)

LAZY: letter of a brand . . . executed in a reclining position

LEAD STEER: steer which guides a trail herd, keeping the lead throughout the drive

LEG UP: assistance in mounting; friendly aid

LIGHT A SHUCK: depart for an unknown destination, usually in secret haste

LINE CAMP: a camp established on the far boundaries of a ranch

LINE RIDER: a cowboy who guards ranch boundaries, turning back stray stock and repairing fences

LINGO: language, dialect; a humorous or contemptuous designation of foreign language

LLANO: a plain (original Spanish)

LOCO: crazy (original Spanish)

LOCOED: said of stock crazed from feeding on one of several toxic plants, such as loco weed

LONGHORN: Spanish cattle brought into Texas from Mexico; distinguished by their long horns

LONG HORSE: a horse capable of covering great distances at great speed

LONG SWEETNIN': molasses

MAÑANA: tomorrow (original Spanish)

MAVERICK: an animal without brand or ear-mark; name derived from Sam Maverick, a Texan, who left most of his cattle unbranded

MESA: table-land; from Spanish for table

MESQUITE: a bush common to the Southwest; Mexican–American Spanish origin, deriving mainly from the Aztec

MILLING: the circling of a herd of cattle, induced or otherwise, within a limited space

MORRAL: nosebag (original Spanish)

MOSEY ALONG: to travel along with no set speed

MOSEY-HEAD: a steer or cow which hides out in the brush in the daytime, ventures out to water and to graze only at night

MOUNTAIN CANARY: nickname for burro

MUSTANG: horses directly descended from Spanish *mesteños* brought by the Conquistadores

NESTER: a homesteader

NIGHT HAWK: cowboy who stands guard over the herd at night during the roundup

NOONIN': halt for midday meal

NORTHER: a blizzard coming out of the north

OLD MAN: generic term for the owner of a cattle outfit

ON THE HOOF: buy or deal for live animals

ON THE PECK: See on the Prod

ON THE PROD: angry enough to fight; looking for trouble

ON YOUR OWN: to be completely dependent on one's own efforts

OUTLAW: a wild horse or cow that uses every wile to remain free

OUTRIDING: ridings beyond the ranch and range boundaries in search of strays

PAINT: a piebald horse (from the Spanish *pinto*)

PAINTER: panther, mountain lion, cougar

PALAVER: a discussion of ways and means

PAY DIRT: gold bearing sand

PEG HORSE, PEG PONY, PEGGER: a cutting pony with marked ability to change his course as abruptly as that of the cow or calf he is pursuing

PIGGIN' STRING: short rope used to tie a calf's legs to facilitate branding, castrating or the injection of shots for blackleg

PILE: to be thrown by a horse

PILE ON YOUR HORSE: to mount

PILGRIM: newcomer to the West

PLUNDER: a cowboy's personal belongings or baggage

POUR THE LEATHER: to use quirt or whip on a horse or a team

PRONTO: quick, fast, and sudden (original Spanish)

PULL YOUR FREIGHT: command to leave the vicinity; usually backed by threats

PUNCH CATTLE: the care of cattle throughout the year's round of duties

PUNCHER: cowboy

QUIRT: short braided whip for use in the saddle (from Spanish *cuarta*)

RAMRODDING THE OUTFIT: bossing the range or ranch

RANCH: the physical components of a cattle raising outfit; land, buildings, fences, etc.

RANNY: cowboy or range hand

READY-MADE MAN: one dressed in store clothes; city bred

REMONTA, REMONTHA: See remuda

REMUDA: the bunch of saddle horses from which are chosen those to be used for the
   day; a relay of remounts (from the Spanish *remudar*, to change or replace)

RIDE DRAG: ride with the rearmost members of a trail herd while on the move

RIDER: cowboy

RIDE THE CHUCKLINE: practice of unemployed hands of riding from one ranch to
   another securing their meals in that manner while seeking employment

RIDING SIGN: act of following tracks made by either man or beast

RIM-FIRE: term for saddle equipped with two cinches

RING BIT: a certain type of bridle bit

ROAD AGENT: highwayman

ROAD BRAND: a special and temporary brand applied to all cattle composing a trail
   herd

RODEO: roundup gathering of the cattle of one particular ranch or vicinity for the
   purpose of banding, ear-marking, etc. (original Spanish)

ROLL HIS TAIL: the action a steer's tail assumes when he is about to take off in panic-
   stricken flight

ROMAL: continuation of one bridle rein to form a flexible whip or quirt

RUNNING IRON: a type of branding which may be used like a pencil to produce
   required brand

RUN MEAT: a buffalo hunt

RUSTLER: individual with a penchant for appropriating other people's cattle

SALTY: a decided character. Forthright, full of personality

SASHAY: to ride or walk casually toward a definite goal; exuberant pantomime

SCRATCHING: cowboy term for using spurs

SET BRAND: branding iron fashioned into a solid block of type, affixing entire brand

SHAKE HANDS WITH GRANDMA: See grab leather

SHINNERY: a dense growth of shin oak

SHIN OAK: any of several species of oak of low growth

SHOOTING IRON: weapon, six-shooter or rifle

SHUCK YOUR SHOOTING IRON: to disarm

SINKERS: biscuits

SINGING TO THE CATTLE: practice of the cowboys while on the trail of singing to the cattle at night, to reassure and quiet them

SINGLE BARRELED, SINGLE-FIRE, SINGLE-RIG: terms for saddle equipped with only one cinch

SKY PILOT: preacher, minister

SLEEPER CALF: a calf that has been ear-marked surreptitiously by a would-be thief to forestall branding by its rightful owner with a view of doing so himself

SLICK EAR: an unbranded colt

SLICKER: raincoat

SLOW ELK: beef from a steer belonging to someone else

SOD-BUSTER: a homesteader; one who plows

SPADE BIT: type of bit for bridle

SPILLED: to be thrown by a horse

SPOOKY: ready to pitch, buck or run away on the slightest provocation; said of a horse or steer

SPRING ROUNDUP: often called the calf roundup, since calves are largely dealt with

STAMPEDE: headlong, panic-stricken flight; from the Spanish *estampida*

STRAYS: stock that has wandered beyond the confines of the home range

STRIKE OUT: to depart precipitately for other regions

STRIKEOVER: re-designing of a brand

STRING: the mounts allotted to one particular rider; saddle horses belonging to an individual ranch or person

SWALLOW HIS HEAD: See bog his head

SWING A BIG LOOP: said of a rustler, the large loop of his lasso falling over the neck of an animal not belonging to him—inadvertently, as it were

TAIL: to throw an animal by seizing its tail, inducing it to lose its balance by a sudden jerk or pull on that member

TAKE A PASEAR: to take a walk or aimless ride; *pasear* is an original Spanish infinitive used as a noun

TALLEY STRING: string with knots tied in it, used to facilitate the counting of stock

TALLY MAN: cowboy entrusted with the counting of a heard of stock

TANK: earthen dam for the retention of water for stock

TAPS: wedge-shaped leather coverings for front and sides of stirrups (from Spanish *tapaderos*)

TARP: square of canvas, outer covering for a bedroll; contraction of tarpaulin

TENDERFOOT: newcomer to the West

THE MAKIN'S: tobacco and cigarette paper

THEODORE: a cord, part of the bosal; from the Spanish *fiador*

THE OLD LADY, THE OLD WOMAN: cook for a cow outfit

TO BUILD A CIGARETTE OR A SMOKE: to roll a cigarette

TO DAB IT ON: to lasso

TO DEVIL: tease or play harmless jokes on another

TO GO INTO A HUDDLE: a conference to determine a course of action

TO HAVE SNAKE BLOOD: incorrigibly bad; wild; a killer

TOP-HAND: first rate cowboy and range hand

TO RAISE: to catch first sight of an object or an individual

TO SNAKE: to drag something at the end of a lasso

TOTE: to carry

TRAIL CUTTER: accredited agent of local ranchman; he has the privilege of inspecting and identifying possible stray animals from his outfit within the herd being driven

TRAIL HERD: cattle driven for long distance from range to market

TRIMMING THE HERD: removal of strays and realignment of the trail herd

TURKSHEAD: an ornamental, turban-like knot at the end of a lariat

UNCOCK A HORSE: to let a horse get rid of his high morning spirits by pitching and bucking before settling down to the sober work of the day

VAMOOSE: get going; from the Spanish *vamos*

VENT BRAND from the Spanish *venta* meaning sale, a facsimile of the seller's brand affixed to the purchased animal's hide

VIGILANTE: frontier citizen organized to control lawlessness; original Spanish for watchman or guard

VUELTED: See dallied

WAR BAG: buckskin bag or pouch in which personal articles are carried

WET STOCK: stock stolen in Mexico, driven across the river and sold north of the Rio Grande

WHITE-FACES: Hereford cattle

WRANGLER: herder in charge of the remuda or horse herd; from the Spanish *caballerango*

ZACATON: bunch grass

Bibliography [for Glossary of Range Terms]

Rollins, Philip Ashton; *The Cowboy*; Charles Scribner's Sons; New York, 1930, Simpson, Charles; *El Rodeo*; John Lane; London, 1940, New Mexico WPA Writers' Project MS, *Cowland*, 1940, New Mexico WPA Writers' Project; *New Mexico, A Guide to the Colorful State*; Hastings House; New York, 1940, *Webster's New International Dictionary*, 2nd Ed. unabridged; 1937.

Kenneth Fordyce
Raton, New Mexico

March, 1939
2000 words
PLACE NAMES

PLACE NAMES
RANCHES OLD AND NEW
COLFAX COUNTY

Allen Ranch   T 31 N R 23 g   In the Maxwell Land Grant.
    An old ranch located two miles south of Raton.

Armstrong Ranch   T 31 N R 21 E   In the Maxwell Land Grant.
    A Dude Ranch located twenty miles up the Canadian Red river
    from Raton.

Baldwin Ranch   T 31 N R 24 E   In the Maxwell Land Grant.
    First known as the Cook ranch; then the Baldwin ranch, but in
    later years the Van Buskirk ranch. It is four and one-half miles
    east of Raton on the lower Sugarite river.

Bartomino Ranch   T 31 N R 23 E   In the Maxwell Land Grant.
    The headquarters of this ranch are at the old site of Blossburg,
    five miles up Dillon Canyon from Raton.

Belford Ranch   T 30 N R 24 E   In the Maxwell Land Grant.
    Seven miles south and three miles east of Raton.

Berry Place   T 31 E R 25 E   In the Maxwell Land Grant.
    The Berry Place is located on Johnson Mesa, twenty miles east
    of Raton.

Brackett Ranches   First T 29 N R 20 E   In the Maxwell Land Grant.
    Located on the Upper Vermejo River above Dawson.
                   Second T 27 N R 21 E   In the Maxwell Land Grant.
    Located on the Vermejo River seven miles west of Maxwell.

Brunelli Ranch   T 32 N R 23 E   In the Maxwell Land Grant.

    Located fourteen miles up Dillon Canyon from Raton, near the
    Colorado line.

Carey Ranch   T 30 N R 23 E   In the Maxwell Land Grant.
    Located four and one-half miles south of Raton on the Canadian
    Red river.

Chase Ranch   T 27 N R 19 E   In the Maxwell Land Grant.
    Located four miles north of Cimarron on the Ponil river. The
    originator of this ranch is Mr. M. M. Chase, who came from
    Iowa in 1873.

Chico Ranch   T 25 N R 24 E
    Located fifteen miles east of Springer on the Chico creek.

Chico Springs Ranch   T 26 N R 25 E
    Located seventeen miles east of Maxwell on Holkeo creek.

Clouthier Ranch   T 25 N R 22 E   In the Maxwell Land Grant.
    Three miles west of Springer on Urracca creek.

Clutton Ranch   T 26 N R 19 E   In the Maxwell Land Grant.
    Located three miles southwest of Cimarron on the Cimarroncita
    river.

Cook Ranch   T 31 N R 24 E   In the Maxwell Land Grant.
    Four miles east of Raton on the lower Sugarite River. Later
    called the Baldwin Ranch, then the Van Buskirk Ranch.

Crow Creek Ranch   T 28 N R 25 E   In the Maxwell Land Grant.
    Eight miles northwest of Maxwell on Curtis creek. One time the
    home of Rev. O. P. McMains, prominent in the Land Grant War.

Cunningham Ranch   T 23 N R 21 E   In the Maxwell Land Grant.
    Nine miles south of Springer on Ocate creek.

Curtiss Ranch   T 30 N R 21 E   In the Maxwell Land Grant.
    Located on Cow creek, in the mountains, fourteen miles west of
    Otero.

Dane Ranch   T 28 N R 20 E   In the Maxwell Land Grant.
    Located on the Vermejo river near Dawson, a coal town.

Dawson Ranch   T 28 N R 25 E   In the Maxwell Land Grant.
    Located on the Vermejo river at the site where Dawson town is
    now. The originator was Mr. J. B. Dawson, a first settler. (See
    "J. B. Dawson" on file.)

Delano & Dwyer Ranch   T 29 N R 24 E   In the Maxwell Land Grant.
    Eight miles east and eight miles south of Raton, near Green
    mountain.

Doggett Ranch   T 29 N R 24 E   In the Maxwell Land Grant.
    Nine miles south and four miles east of Raton on the Una de Gato
    creek.

Doherty Ranch   T 31 N R 27 E   In the Maxwell Land Grant.
    Located six miles west of Folsom at the eastern boundary of
    Colfax County.

Dorsey Ranch   T 26 N R 26 E   In the Maxwell Land Grant.

Owned by U. S. Senator Stephen A. Dorsey. It was headquarters for
many other smaller ranches under other names but owned by Senator
Dorsey. It was located twenty miles east and three miles south of
Maxwell on Holkeo creek. (See - "Society in Territorial Days" or
"The Dorseys" on file.)

Dyer Ranch   T 27 N   R 21 E   In the Maxwell Land Grant.
    Located six miles west of Maxwell on the Vermejo river.

Finley Ranch   T 31 N   R 24 E
    Located eight miles northeast of Raton in Yankee canyon.

Floyd Ranch   T 31 N   R 25 E
    Located on Johnson Mesa, twenty miles east of Raton.

Gillespie Ranch   T 29 N   R 24 E
    Sixteen miles east of Springer.

Gol Ranch   T 32 N   R 17 E   In the Maxwell Land Grant.
    Located in the northwest corner of the county.

Graiz Ranch   T 31 N   R 17 E
    Located at Trinchera Pass near Folsom.

Hack Ranch   T 30 N   R 27 E
    Located at the east end of Johnson Mesa, thirty miles east of
    Raton.

Hadley Ranch   T 29 N   R 24 E
    Located on the north slopes of Tenaja and Eagle Trail mountains.

Hereford Ranch   T 29 N   R 24 E
    Located on the north slopes of Tenaja and Eagle Trail mountains.

Himstead Ranch   T 30 N   R 24 E
    Located seven miles southeast of Raton on the lower Sugarite
    Creek.

Howarth Ranch   T 30 N   R 24 E   In the Maxwell Land Grant.
    Located nine miles southeast of Raton.

Ingersoll Ranch   T 26 N   R 26 E
    Located seven miles east and four miles south of Maxwell on
    Holkeo Creek. One time owned by Mr. Robert Ingersoll, prominent
    attorney and reputed atheist. (See - "The Dorseys" on file)

Jack Ranch   T 31 N   R 27 E
    Located five miles west of Folsom.

Johnson Ranch   T 30 N R 26 E
    Located in Johnson Park, six miles north of the T-O Ranch which
    is on U. S. Highway No. 64-87 and sixteen miles east of Raton.
    This ranch was originally owned by Mr. Lige Johnson.

Jones, Ellis Ranch   T 31 N R 24 E   In the Maxwell Land Grant.
    Located four miles east of Raton on the lower Sugarite River.

Kelcher Ranch   T 31 N R 27 E
    Located at Trinchera Pass near Folsom.

King, John Ranch   T 29 N R 27 E
    Located five miles west of Capulin on U. S. Highways Nos. 64-87.

Knox Ranch   T 31 N R 24 E
    Located seven miles from Raton up Yankee canyon.

Lacy Ranch   T 28 N R 20 E   In the Maxwell Land Grant.
    Located on the Vermejo River near Dawson coal town.

Lee Ranches   (1)   T 28 N R 24 E
    Located between Tenaja and Eagle Tail mountains on the southern
    slopes.
                   (2)   T 29 N R 20 E   In the Maxwell Land Grant.
    Located on the upper Vermejo river.

Littrell Ranch   T 26 N R 19 E   In the Maxwell Land Grant.
    Located two miles northeast of Cimarron on the Ponil.

Mackey Ranch   T 31 N R 26 E
    Located on Johnson Mesa.

Marcy Ranch   T 27 N R 27 E
    Located thirty-one miles east of Maxwell. Owned at one time by
    Mr. Russell Marcy, of Marcy & McCuistion Institute fame
    (Raton).)See - Article on dedication of Institute on file
    called: "July 4, 1884 in Raton.")

Maxwell Home Ranch   T 27 N R 21 E   In the Maxwell Land Grant.
    At one time owned by Mr. Lucien B. Maxwell (See "The Maxwell
    House at Cimarron" on file). Tis ranch was located ten miles west
    of Maxwell on the Vermejo river.

McCarn Ranch   T 31 N R 24 E   In the Maxwell Land Grant.
    Located two miles east of Raton on the lower Sugarite river.

McCuistion Ranch   T 26 N R 27 E

Located thirty miles east of Maxwell. At one time owned by Mr. O.
W. McCuistion. (See article on dedication of Marcy & McCuistion
Institute in Raton on file called "July 4, 1884 in Raton.")

McCuistion Ranch   T 30 N R 27 E
     Located two miles west of Mt. Capulin.

McMurdo Ranch   T 29 N R 23 E   In the Maxwell Land Grant.
     Located eleven miles south of Raton on the Canadian Red River.

Nairn, Jack Ranch   T 26 N R 19 E   In the Maxwell Land Grant.
     This ranch is more like a country home than a ranch. It is
     located next to the Philmont ranch between Rayado and Cimarron.

Owens Ranch   T 30 N R 27 E
     Located at the east end of Johnson Mesa.

Peck Ranch   T 25 N R 27 E
     Located thirty miles east of Springer on Holkeo Creek.

Philmont Ranch   T 26 N R 19 E   In the Maxwell Land Grant.
     Located four miles east of Cimarron. Owned by Mr. Waite Phillips,
     millionaire-sportsman of Tulsa, Oklahoma. This is more of an
     estate than a ranch. It has an airport, race track, magnificent
     home with guest house and is a village all by itself.

Popejoy, Ernest Ranch   T 30 N R 27 E
     Located in Johnson Park, north of the T-O Ranch. It is about
     twenty miles east of Raton. It was first known as the Johnson
     ranch.

Porter Ranch   T 26 N R 20 E   In the Maxwell Land Grant.
     Located seventeen miles northwest of Springer on the Cimarron
     river.

Rock Ranch   T 24 N R 23 E
     Located about a mile from Taylor Springs.

Roger Ranch   T 28 N R 25 E
     Located seven miles east of Tenaja mountain.

Sandusky Ranch   T 31 N R 24 E
     Four miles east of Raton on the lower Sugarite river is the
     location.

Shackleford Ranch   T 31 N R 25 E
     Located in Yankee Canyon ten miles northeast of Raton.

Shaw Ranch   T 30 N R 25 E
    Located seven miles east of Raton.

Shotwell Ranch   T 32 N R 19 E   In the Maxwell Land Grant.
    Located three miles from the Colorado line on the Canadian Red
    River.

Shoup Ranch   T 27 N R 21 E   In the Maxwell Land Grant.
    Located eight miles west of Maxwell on the Vermejo River.

Simons' Ranches (Ed and Tom) T 31 N R 26 E
    Located on Johnson Mesa.

Smith Ranch   T 32 N R 22 E   In the Maxwell Land Grant.
    Located three miles north of Brilliant and twelve miles up Dillon
    Canyon from Raton.

Springer Ranch   T 26 N R 20 E   In the Maxwell Land Grant.
    Fifteen miles northwest of Springer on the Cimarron River.

Springer Ranch #2   T 27 N R 19 E   In the Maxwell Land Grant.
    Located three miles north of Cimarron on the Ponil.

Sproule Ranch   T 31 N R 24 E   In the Maxwell Land Grant.
    Located five miles east of Raton on the lower Sugarite River.

Stockton Ranches (Clarence and Claude) T 30 N R 23 E
    Located six miles south of Raton of either side of U.S. Highway
    No. 85 and on the banks of the Canadian Red River.

Temple Ranch   T 26 N R 26 E
    Located four miles south and twenty-two miles east of Maxwell (at
    Chico).

Tinsley Ranch   T 28 N R 24 E
    Located between Eagle Tail and Tenaja mountains on the south
    slopes.

T-O Ranch   T 30 N R 26 E
    Originally called the Meloche ranch, since it was started by Mr.
    Antime J. Meloche. (See "Antime Joseph Meloche" on the file). It
    is located sixteen miles east of Raton on the Una de Gato creek
    and on U. S. Highways Nos. 64-87. The T-O is now owned by Mr. A.
    G. Thomson.

Towndrow Ranch   T 31 N R 27 E
    Located on Johnson Mesa.

Troy Ranch   T 28 N R 25 E

Located five miles east of Tenaja mountain.

True Ranch   T 30 N R 24 E
     Located seven miles southeast of Raton.

Twitty Ranch   T 31 N R 20 E   In the Maxwell Land Grant.
     Located on the Canadian red River near the Colorado line.

Vallejo Ranch   T 25 N R 20 E   In the Maxwell Land Grant.
     Located near Miami, between Cimarron and Springer. This is a Polo
     Ranch, a dude ranch (so-called); and a very high class vacation
     center.

Van Buskirk Ranch   T 31 N R 24 E   In the Maxwell Land Grant.
     This was formerly the Cook Ranch, then the Baldwin Ranch, and
     finally the Van Buskirk Ranch. It is located five miles east of
     Raton on the lower Sugarite River.

Whistler Ranches (Clarence and Ralph) T 30 N R 24 E
     Located on the lower Sugarite River eight miles east of Raton on
     U. S. Highways Nos. 64 and 87.

White Ranch   T 28 N R 23 E   In the Maxwell Land Grant.
     Located seventeen miles South of Raton on the slopes of the Eagle
     Tail mountain.

Winters Ranch   T 31 N R 24 E   In the Maxwell Land Grant.
     Located four or five miles east of Raton on the lower Sugarite
     River.

Wolfe Ranch   T 32 N R 20 E   In the Maxwell Land Grant.
     Located on the Canadian red River, near the Colorado line.

Wrigley Ranch   T 29 N R 23 E   In the Maxwell Land Grant.
     Located nine miles south of Raton on the Canadian red River.

W-S Ranch   T 26 N R 19 E   In the Maxwell Land Grant.
     Located on the outskirts of Cimarron. This ranch is owned by Mr.
     Brownlow Wilson, Englishman, writer, and stockman. The brand and
     name came from the original owner of the ranch, Mr. William
     Slaughter.

Locations and information from Maxwell Land Grant Map 1889.

Source of Information: Names and locations for these ranches recorded for the purpose of preserving names of 1st settlers and ranch locations. Following information was secured from Maxwell land grant and it would be almost impossible to get further data. Maxwell land grant map compiled from original Plats in Surveyor Gen's (?) office in Santa Fe, a private survey of M. L. G. Co, 1889.

WORKS PROGRESS ADMINISTRATION
SANTA FE, NEW MEXICO
FEDERAL WRITERS' PROJECT
INA SIZER CASSIDY
STATE DIRECTOR
#9 RENEHAN BUILDING

FRED G. HEALY
STATE ADMINISTRATOR

June 20, 1938

Mr. N.H. Thorp
Box 27
Alameda, New Mexico

Dear Jack:

Please send me the following information as soon
as possible:

(1) What was the local slang name for whiskey
among the early time residents of Silver City? *red eye* *Rot gut*

(2) What did the cowboys of Silver City of that
period call money? *Dough*

(3) What were the dance hall girls and the ladies of *sage hens*
easy virtue at that time called, that is, what *bats*
was the popular name among the cowboys and miners? "
Their shacks were called "dead falls."

(4) How should the statement be made that the cowboys
came into town on a Saturday night for instance,
for a hilarious time? I can't see that it would
be proper to say that they "loped into town on a
caballo." *a "bunch" of the W boys rode*

into town & eased up to the bar

(5) Was the term "cayuse" used much in New Mexico for
horse? *yes — horses were sometimes*
called "sticks,"

(6) Was there any difference in these terms as used
by the cowman and the miner or were the terms the
same?

Very truly yours,

F.G. Healy
Administrator

By: *Ina Sizer Cassidy*
INA SIZER CASSIDY
STATE DIRECTOR WRITERS' PROJECT

ISC:w

Letter to Mr. N. H. Thorp from F. G. Healy, June 23, 1930, NMSRCA,
NMFWP, WPA #161

List of Photographs

Courtesy of the Palace of the Governors Photo Archives (NMHM/DCA)

List of New Mexico Federal Writers' Project Documents

WPA—Works Progress Administration
NMFWP—New Mexico Federal Writers' Project
NMSRCA—New Mexico State Records Center and Archives

A Cowboy Ball, Submitted by Frances Totty, July 2, 1937, NMFWP, WPA #167, NMSRCA

A Chuck-Wagon Supper, N. Howard Thorp, November 4, 1937, NMFWP, WPA #118, NMSRCA

A Day on the Round Up, W. M. Emery, August 7, 1936, NMFWP, WPA #118, NMSRCA

Along the Rio Grande, N. Howard Thorp, November 10, 1936, NMFWP, WPA #118, NMSRCA

An All But Forgotten Cattle Trail by Albert W. Thompson, New Mexico Federal Writers' Project, February 9, 1937, The Cattleman, Volume XXIII, No. 9, NMFWP, WPA #114, NMSRCA

An Unusual Log House, Kenneth Fordyce, The American Guide, August 22, 1938, NMFWP, WPA #115a, NMSRCA

As It Happened in Curry County, New Mexico Writers' Project, no date, NMFWP, WPA #192, NMSRCA

At the Cowboy Dance Tonight, a la Bill Knox, Submitted by Edith L. Crawford, no date, NMFWP, WPA #162, NMSRCA

Aztlan (New Mexico) Outlaws, N. Howard Thorp, January 6, 1938, NMFWP, WPA #88a, NMSRCA

Basílico Garduño, New Mexico Sheepherder, Lorin W. Brown, no date, NMFWP, WPA #106, NMSRCA

Billy the Kid Story, Edith L. Crawford, June 20, 1938, NMFWP, WPA #212, NMSRCA

Brands, Edith L. Crawford, June 16, 1939, NMFWP, WPA #115b, NMSRCA

"Burned Out" by Apaches, Joyce Hunter, February 1, 1937, NMFWP, WPA #199, NMSRCA

Cattle and Sheep Grazing, Report of the Governor of New Mexico, Made to the Secretary of the Interior for the Year 1879 by Lew Wallace, New Mexico Federal Writers' Project, NMFWP, WPA #103b, NMSRCA

Cattle and Sheep Industry and Early Day Ranch Life, Georgia B. Redfield, July 5, 1939, WPA #118, NMSRCA

Cattle, Horses and Men, J. H. Culley, no date, NMFWP, WPA #112, NMSRCA

Cattle Industry in Lincoln County, New Mexico, Edith L. Crawford, June 23, 1939, NMFWP, WPA #209, NMSRCA

Cattle Industry of Otero County, F. M. Casey, July 29, 1939, NMFWP, WPA #104b, NMSRCA

Cattle Shipping and Trading Posts in the Early Days, Georgia B. Redfield, July 31, 1939, NMFWP, WPA #104b, NMSRCA

Chisum-Hagerman Ranch, Redfield and Cooke, July 20, 1936, NMFWP, WPA #115a, NMSRCA

Comanche Indians on Chisum Cattle-Trail by Georgia B. Redfield, January 28, 1937, NMFWP, WPA #114, NMSRCA

Condensed Version of "The Story of Early Clayton, New Mexico" by A. W. Thompson, D. D. Sharp, May 21, 1938, NMFWP, WPA #238, NMSRCA

Contributions to the Language from the Spanish and Cowboy Slang, New Mexico Federal Writers' Project, no date, NMFWP, WPA #161, NMSRCA

Cowboy Dances, Submitted by Edith L. Crawford, July 12, 1937, NMFWP, WPA #162, NMSRCA

Cowboy Hardships, Mrs. Belle Kilgore, July 3, 1937, NMFWP, WPA #118, NMSRCA

Cowboy Quadrille: "The Sally Goodin," Submitted by James A. Burns, January 30, 1937, NMFWP, WPA #162, NMSRCA

Cowboys and Early-Day Cow Camps, Georgia B. Redfield, August 7, 1939, NMFWP, WPA #115a, NMSRCA

Cow Camp Entertainments, W. M. Emery, July 6, 1937, NMFWP, WPA #118, NMSRCA

Cowland Glossary, New Mexico Federal Writers' Project, no date, NMFWP, WPA #161, NMSRCA

Customs and Conditions of Early Ranch Life (Lea County), Mrs. Benton Mosley, December 7, 1936, NMFWP, WPA #118, NMSRCA

De Baca County History: Billy the Kid at Fort Sumner, J. Vernon Smithson, May 19, 1936, NMFWP, WPA #212, NMSRCA

"De Baca County" (Excerpt), J. Vernon Smithson, no date, NMFWP, WPA #194, NMSRCA

Delivered at Fort Defiance Before August 15, 1869 by Command of Major General Getty, New Mexico Federal Writers' Project, no date, WPA #92a, NMSRCA

Description of a Ranch: G.O.S. Ranch, Mrs. Mildred Jordan, October 5, 1936, NMFWP, WPA #115b, NMSRCA

Drift Fences: History of Cattle and Sheep Industry in Chaves County, New Mexico, Georgia B. Redfield, July 10, 1939, NMFWP, WPA #104b, NMSRCA

Early Character Isom Like, Pioneer by Colonel Jack Potter, Carrie L. Hodges, no date, NMFWP, WPA #154, NMSRCA

Early Days of a Cowboy on the Pecos, James F. Hinkle, September 4, 1940, NMFWP, WPA #104a, NMSRCA

Editorial, "Parties and Reservation," *Santa Fe Weekly Gazette*—May 20, 1865 from New Mexico Federal Writers' Project, NMFWP, WPA #90, NMSRCA

El Ciervo y la Oveja Siende Juez El Lobo, (The Sheep and the Deer with the Wolf as Judge), Contributed by Sr. Pedro Vigil, Translated by Lorin W. Brown, September 23, 1938, NMFWP, WPA #152, NMSRCA

Farmington (Excerpt), R. T. F. Simpson, no date, NMFWP, WPA #226, NMSRCA

Folklore and Folkways: A Horse's Love for His Home, W. M. Emery, February 12, 1937, NMFWP, WPA #153, NMSRCA

Fried Snakes, N. Howard Thorp, September 3, 1937, NMFWP, WPA #164, NMSRCA

From Hackett's "Historical Documents," Lorin Brown, no date, NMFWP, WPA #117, NMSRCA

Glossary of Branding Terms, "Hot Irons," Oren Arnold and John P. Hale, The MacMillan Company, New York, 1930 NMSRC, NMFWP, WPA #161

Glossary of Cowboy Terms Used in New Mexico (Condensed), Compiled by T. F. Bledsoe, Condensed by Ina Sizer Cassidy, Checked by Alice Corbin, editor, June 10, 1937, NMFWP, WPA #161, NMSRCA

Glossary of Range Terms, New Mexico Federal Writers' Project, no date, NMFWP, WPA #161, NMSRCA

Governor's Report to the Secretary of the Interior, 1885 by Edmund C. Ross, New Mexico Federal Writers' Project, no date, NMFWP, WPA #103b, NMSRCA

Governor's Report to the Secretary of the Interior, 1890: Gradual Change in Cattle Raising Methods by Governor L. Bradford Prince, New Mexico Federal Writers' Project, no date, NMFWP, WPA #103b, NMSRCA

Governor's Report to the Secretary of the Interior, 1897 by Miguel A. Otero, New Mexico Federal Writers' Project, no date, NMFWP, WPA #103b, NMSRCA

Hellroaring Mesa, Clay W. Vaden, April 22, 1936, NMFWP, WPA #184, NMSRCA

Heroines of Pioneer Days (Excerpt), Clay W. Vaden, no date, NMFWP, WPA #183, NMSRCA

Historic Ranch House on the Gila, Clay W. Vaden, March 30, 1936, NMFWP, WPA #115b, NMSRCA

History of Cattle in the Southwest, American Guide, Kenneth Fordyce, June 27, 1939, NMFWP, WPA #104b, NMSRCA

History of Portales Springs, Vernon Smithson, March 22, 1937, NMFWP, WPA #221, NMSRCA

History of San Juan County, Janet Smith, March 10, 1936, NMFWP, WPA #225, NMSRCA

History of Sheep Industry in Chaves County, Georgia B. Redfield, June 8, 1939, NMFWP, WPA #202, NMSRCA

Indian Story, Edith L. Crawford, March 7, 1933, NMFWP, WPA #189, NMSRCA

Introduction (Excerpt), Allen A. Carter, January 27, 1937, NMFWP, WPA #202, NMSRCA

John Hittson, Cattle King by Edgar C. McMechen, New Mexico Federal Writers' Project, The Colorado Magazine, Volume XI, September 1934, Number 5, "Cattle Trails of New Mexico and Trade," NMFWP, WPA #112, NMSRCA

Killing the Lobo Wolf, Colonel Jack Potter, no date, NMFWP, WPA #137, NMSRCA

Kit Carson Ranch, James A. Burns, June 6, 1936, NMFWP, WPA #190a, NMSRCA

Lea County and Contiguous Plains: The Role of the Horse on the Southern Plains (Excerpt), Mrs. Benton Mosley, no date, NMFWP, WPA #208, NMSRCA

"Lead Steers" of the Trail Days by Jack Potter, Mrs. Belle Kilgore, May 14, 1937, NMFWP, WPA #154, NMSRCA

Letter to James A. Burns, Accompanying the Cowboy Quadrille Calls by Doughbelly Price, New Mexico Writers' Project, January 30, 1937, NMFWP, WPA #162, NMSRCA

Letter to Mr. N. H. Thorp, F. G. Healy, June 23, 1930, NMSRCA, NMFWP, WPA #161, NMSRCA

Llano Estacado, W. M. Jones, no date, NMFWP, WPA #97, NMSRCA

Mavericks, Reyes Martinez, December 23, 193-, NMFWP, WPA #233, NMSRCA

Maxwell Ranch, Thorp and Breit, April 17, 1936, NMFWP, WPA #115b, NMSRCA

Maxwell's Ranch: The "Closest Call" of Maxwell's Life by Colonel Henry Inman, Helen Speaker, May 19, 1939, NMFWP, WPA #115a, NMSRCA

Melrose (Excerpt), Dad DeGraftenreid, Mrs. Ida G. Boyles, no date, NMFWP, WPA #192, NMSRCA

Memoirs of Early Days in New Mexico: On the Trail to New Mexico in 1869 (Excerpt), Manville Chapman, April 12, 1930, NMFWP, WPA #188, NMSRCA

Mexican Version, Dogies, Dogal, N. Howard (Jack) Thorp, American Guide, December 16, 1936, NMFWP, WPA #161, NMSRCA

Note on the *Partido* System, Lorin W. Brown, no date, NMFWP, WPA #109a, NMSRCA

Ojo de Nuestra Señora Ranch Owned by Mariano Sabino Otero, N. Howard Thorp, February 23, 1936, NMFWP, WPA #115b, NMSRCA

Old Cow Outfits near Gallup, *Gallup Gazette*, March 14, 1940, New Mexico Federal Writers' Project, NMFWP, WPA #115a, NMSRCA

Old State Line Fence: From *Evening News-Journal*, Clovis, New Mexico, Mrs. Belle Kilgore, July 3, 1937, NMFWP, WPA #191, NMSRCA

Old Time Ranchmen of the Pecos Valley, N. Howard Thorp, September 30, 1937, NMFWP, WPA #115a, NMSRCA

Old Trails Crossing the Pecos, Georgia B. Redfield, April 4, 1939, NMFWP, WPA #112, NMSRCA

On the Frisco River Retold by M. Page, New Mexico Federal Writers' Project, no date, NMFWP, WPA #143, NMSRCA

Peon, Vaquero, Ranchero and Caballero, Bright Lynn, May 18, 1939, NMFWP, WPA #170, NMSRCA

"Pinon Country," Haniel Long, page 81, no date, NMFWP, WPA #117, NMSRCA

Pioneer: "A Hard Trail into New Mexico," American Guide, Kenneth Fordyce, February 12, 1937, NMFWP, WPA #112, NMSRCA

Pioneer: "A Remarkable White Steer," American Guide, Kenneth Fordyce, February 19,1937, NMFWP, WPA #189, NMSRCA

Pioneer: "Hunting on First Street," American Guide, Kenneth Fordyce, March 5, 1937, NMFWP, WPA #188, NMSRCA

Pioneer: "No Labor Trouble" and "Rest," American Guide, Kenneth Fordyce, March 5, 1937, NMFWP, WPA#188, NMSRCA

Pioneer: "Overnight in the Open," American Guide, Kenneth Fordyce, March 5, 1937, NMFWP, WPA #188, NMSRCA

Pioneer Stories: The Collins Family, Betty Reich, July 2, 1936, NMFWP, WPA #213, NMSRCA

Place Names: Bell Ranch, San Miguel Co., Bright Lynn, October 29, 1938, NMFWP, WPA #227, NMSRCA

Place Names, Ranches Old and New, Colfax County, Submitted by Kenneth Fordyce, March, 1939, NMFWP, WPA #115a, NMSRCA

Rough sketches compiled by Pauline Briscoe, Excerpted from "Grazing" by B. W. Kenney, NMFWP, WPA #109a, NMSRCA

Retold from the Probate Files of Lincoln County, New Mexico, Edith L. Crawford, January 10, 193?, NMFWP, WPA #212, NMSRCA

Santa Fe Weekly Gazette, March 18, 1865, New Mexico Federal Writers' Project, NMFWP, WPA #92a, NMSRCA

Santa Fe Weekly Gazette, August 12, 1865, News Notice, New Mexico Federal Writers' Project, NMFWP, WPA #92a, NMSRCA

Santa Fe Weekly Gazette: Comancheros, Important Military Orders, March 6, 1869, New Mexico Federal Writers' Project, no date, NMFWP, WPA #92a, NMSRCA

Seven HL Ranch (Excerpt), Georgia B. Redfield, July 24, 1939, NMFWP, WPA #115b, NMSRCA

Some First Herds of Cattle Brought to the Pecos Valley in Chaves County, New Mexico, Georgia B. Redfield, July 14, 1939, NMFWP, WPA #104a, NMSRCA

Some Tales from the Past: Rustlers and Romance, B. W. K., from American Guide Series Over the Turquoise Trail, Compiled by The Workers of the Federal Writers' Project of the Works Progress Administration of New Mexico, no date, NMFWP, WPA #163, NMSRCA

Stories of Old Timers by Tom Gray, Carrie L. Hodges, November 21, 1936, NMFWP, WPA #239, NMSRCA

Tales of Old Timers: The Staked Plains by Colonel Jack Potter, Carrie L. Hodges, August 14, 1936, NMFWP, WPA #154, NMSRCA

"Tall Tales": Strawberry Roan's Rival, W. M. Emery, January 4, 1937, NMFWP, WPA #104a, NMSRCA

The Battle at the Box S., L. Raines, August 3, 1936, NMFWP, WPA #115a, NMSRCA

The Cowboy with the White Hat, Submitted by Manuel Berg, March 22, 1937, NMFWP, WPA #167, NMSRCA

The Good Samaritan by S. Omar Barker, Genevieve Chapin, from *Villages: Quay County*, no date, NMFWP, WPA #219, NMSRCA

The Goodnight Cattle Trail, Georgia B. Redfield, November 20, 1936, NMFWP, WPA #116, NMSRCA

The Grant County Herald, June 2, 1877: "Wholesale Slaughter of Cattle by Indians," New Mexico Federal Writers' Project, no date, NMFWP, WPA #104b, NMSRCA

The Indian Fight at Loving by Noel L. Johnson, Collected by W. E. Wheeler, March 28, 1936, NMFWP, WPA #90, NMSRCA

The Last Great Roundup of the Llano Estacado, Vernon Smithson, July 17, 1937, NMFWP, WPA #97, NMSRCA

The Mustangs of New Mexico, N. Howard Thorp, July 30, 1937, NMFWP, WPA #111, NMSRCA

The New Mexican, Santa Fe, New Mexico, November 10, 1865, New Mexico Federal Writers' Project, no date, NMFWP, WPA #92a, NMSRCA

The Old Bar W Ranch, Lincoln County, New Mexico, Howard N. Thorp, February 17, 1936, NMFWP, WPA #115a, NMSRCA

The Old Barber House: Former Residence of New Mexico's Cattle Queen, W. L. Patterson, August 17, 1936, NMFWP, WPA #218, NMSRCA

The Old R. M. Gilbert Ranch, Now the W. C. Marable Ranch, Katherine Ragsdale, June 6, 1936, NMFWP, WPA #115a, NMSRCA

The Prairie Fire of 1906 As Told by Clyde Stanfield, New Mexico Federal Writers' Project, November 2, 1936, NMFWP, WPA #191, NMSRCA

The Raiders, Ernest Prescott Morey, September 1, 1938, NMFWP, WPA #203, NMSRCA

"The Snowstorm of 1889," Carrie L. Hodges, December 5, 1936, NMFWP, WPA #118, NMSRCA

The Spanish Vaquero and His Influence on the Language of the Range and Roundup, from History of Grazing, Section II B (3), Lorin W. Brown, no date, NMFWP, WPA #109a, NMSRCA

The Staked Plains' Stories (Excerpts), *Evening News-Journal*, Clovis, New Mexico, June 1, 1936, Mrs. Belle Kilgore, April 3, 1937, NMFWP, WPA #153, NMSRCA

The Stampede, W. M. Emery, April 12, 1937, NMFWP, WPA #115b, NMSRCA

The W. S. Cemetery, H. P. Collier, July 30, 1936, NMFWP, WPA #182, NMSRCA

Trail Dust by S. Omar Barker, Genevieve Chapin, from *Villages: Quay County*, no date, NMFWP, WPA #219, NMSRCA

Uncle Jimmie: Cowboys' Cruel Prank, Joyce Hunter, July 6, 1937, NMFWP, WPA #118, NMSRCA

William F. Sumpter, W. M. Emery, December 23, 1936, NMFWP, WPA #239, NMSRCA

Names Index

www.ingramcontent.com/pod-product-compliance
Lightning Source LLC
Chambersburg PA
CBHW020820270326
41928CB00006B/386